The expression "Son of Man," used in the Gospels almost exclusively by Jesus, has been the object of intensive study since the Protestant Reformation, yet scholars have come to no agreement on its origin or meaning. Research in this area has been described as "a veritable mine field" and "a can of worms." Because of the scope and complexity of the literature, no comprehensive survey of the subject has been written in the twentieth century. Delbert Burkett's book fills this need. It provides a comprehensive historical overview of the debate from the patristic period to 1996, evaluates the various theories, and summarizes the present state of the question. Burkett concludes that despite nineteen centuries of "Son of Man" study there is no consensus concerning the meaning or origin of the expression; the debate is therefore a prime example of the limits of New Testament scholarship.

DELBERT BURKETT is Associate Professor of New Testament and Christian Origins in the Department of Philosophy and Religious Studies at Louisiana State University. He is the author of one previous book – *The Son of the Man in the Gospel of John* – and he has published articles in *New Testament Studies* and *Novum Testamentum*.

SOCIETY FOR NEW TESTAMENT STUDIES

MONOGRAPH SERIES

General editor: Richard Bauckham

107

THE SON OF MAN DEBATE

The Son of Man Debate

A History and Evaluation

DELBERT BURKETT

Louisiana State University

CAMBRIDGE
UNIVERSITY PRESS

PUBLISHED BY THE PRESS SYNDICATE OF THE UNIVERSITY OF CAMBRIDGE
The Pitt Building, Trumpington Street, Cambridge, United Kingdom

CAMBRIDGE UNIVERSITY PRESS
The Edinburgh Building, Cambridge CB2 2RU, UK
http://www.cup.cam.ac.uk
40 West 20th Street, New York NY 10011–4211, USA   http://www.
cup.org
10 Stamford Road, Oakleigh, Melbourne 3166, Australia

© Cambridge University Press 1999

First published 1999

Printed in the United Kingdom at the University Press, Cambridge

Typeset in Times 10/12 pt   [CE]

A catalogue record for this book is available from the British Library

Library of Congress cataloguing in publication data

Burkett, Delbert Royce.
The Son of Man debate: a history and evaluation / Delbert Burkett.
   p.   cm. – (Society for New Testament Studies. Monograph series; 107)
Includes bibliographical references and indexes.
ISBN 0 521 66306 7 (hb)
1. Son of Man – History of doctrines.   I. Title.   II. Series: Monograph series (Society for New Testament Studies); 107.
BT232.B87   1999
232′.1–dc21   99–19515   CIP

ISBN 0 521 66306 7 hardback

This book is dedicated to my parents, Joe and Lorene Burkett, who have unfailingly supported me wherever my intellectual pilgrimage has taken me.

CONTENTS

PREFACE

I could not have completed the history of research in the present work without the assistance of several persons and institutions. I wish especially to thank Sarah Nixon and her assistants in the Interlibrary Loan office at Appalachian State University. I have lost track of the number of books and articles that they obtained for me. I owe thanks also to the Southern Regional Education Board for a research travel grant that enabled me to visit the rare book collections at several major libraries. My appreciation goes to those libraries as well: the Library of Congress, the Folger Shakespeare Library, the John K. Mullen Denver Memorial Library of Catholic University of America, the Krauth Memorial Library of Lutheran Theological Seminary, the Van Pelt Library of the University of Pennsylvania, the Library Company of Philadelphia, the Burke Library of Union Theological Seminary, the New York Public Library, and the Divinity Library of Duke University. Finally I wish to thank Louisiana State University for a Summer Research Stipend that gave me the time to complete this book.

Chapter 8, a slightly modified form of "The Nontitular Son of Man: A History and Critique," *NTS* 40 (1994) 504–21, has been used with permission.

ABBREVIATIONS

ABD	*Anchor Bible Dictionary*. Ed. D. N. Freedman. New York: Doubleday, 1992
ANF	The Ante-Nicene Fathers
ASTI	*Annual of the Swedish Theological Institute*
ATR	*Anglican Theological Review*
AusBR	*Australian Biblical Review*
BETL	Bibliotheca ephemeridum theologicarum lovaniensium
BETS	*Bulletin of the Evangelical Theological Society* (= *JETS*)
BJRL	*Bulletin of the John Rylands University Library of Manchester*
BK	*Bibel und Kirche*
BLit	*Bibel und Liturgie*
BR	*Biblical Research*
BSac	*Bibliotheca sacra*
BT	*The Bible Translator*
BTB	*Biblical Theology Bulletin*
BWANT	Beiträge zur Wissenschaft vom Alten und Neuen Testament
BZ	*Biblische Zeitschrift*
BZAW	Beihefte zur Zeitschrift für die alttestamentliche Wissenschaft
CBQ	*Catholic Biblical Quarterly*
CCL	Corpus Christianorum, series Latina
CJT	*Canadian Journal of Theology*
CSEL	Corpus scriptorum ecclesiasticorum Latinorum
CUOS	Columbia University Oriental Studies
CurTM	*Currents in Theology and Mission*
ETL	*Ephemerides theologicae lovanienses*
ETR	*Etudes théologiques et religieuses*
EvQ	*Evangelical Quarterly*
EvT	*Evangelische Theologie*

ExpT	*Expository Times*
HBT	*Horizons in Biblical Theology*
HNT	Handbuch zum Neuen Testament
HTR	*Harvard Theological Review*
IBS	*Irish Biblical Studies*
ICC	International Critical Commentary
ITQ	*Irish Theological Quarterly*
JBL	*Journal of Biblical Literature*
JETS	*Journal of the Evangelical Theological Society*
JJS	*Journal of Jewish Studies*
JPT	*Jahrbücher für protestantische Theologie*
JR	*Journal of Religion*
JSJ	*Journal for the Study of Judaism in the Persian, Hellenistic and Roman Period*
JSNT	*Journal for the Study of the New Testament*
JSNTSS	Journal for the Study of the New Testament, Supplement Series
JTS	*Journal of Theological Studies*
LumVie	*Lumière et vie*
LXX	Septuagint
MGWJ	*Monatsschrift für Geschichte und Wissenschaft des Judentums*
MPG	Migne, *Patrologiae cursus completus*, series Graeca
MPL	Migne, *Patrologiae cursus completus*, series Latina
MT	Masoretic text
NovT	*Novum testamentum*
n.s.	new series
NTL	New Testament Library
NTS	*New Testament Studies*
NTT	*Nederlands Theologisch Tijdschrift*
PM	*Protestantische Monatshefte*
RB	*Revue biblique*
RelSRev	*Religious Studies Review*
ResQ	*Restoration Quarterly*
RevAug	*Revue augustinienne*
RevExp	*Review and Expositor*
RGG	*Die Religion in Geschichte und Gegenwart*
RTL	*Revue théologique de Louvain*
SBLMS	Society of Biblical Literature Monograph Series
SBT	Studies in Biblical Theology
ScEc	*Sciences ecclésiastiques*

SE	*Studia evangelica*
SJT	*Scottish Journal of Theology*
SNTSMS	Society for New Testament Studies Monograph Series
ST	*Studia theologica*
TBei	*Theologische Beiträge*
TDNT	*Theological Dictionary of the New Testament*
ThBü	Theologische Bücherei
ThT	*Theologisch Tijdschrift*
TRev	*Theologische Revue*
TRu	*Theologische Rundschau*
TSK	*Theologische Studien und Kritiken*
TU	Texte und Untersuchungen
TWNT	*Theologisches Wörterbuch zum Neuen Testament*
TZ	*Theologische Zeitschrift*
USQR	*Union Seminary Quarterly Review*
VT	*Vetus testamentum*
WMANT	Wissenschaftliche Monographien zum Alten und Neuen Testament
WTJ	*Westminster Theological Journal*
WUNT	Wissenschaftliche Untersuchungen zum Neuen Testament
ZDMG	*Zeitschrift der deutschen morgenländischen Gesellschaft*
ZNW	*Zeitschrift für die neutestamentliche Wissenschaft*
ZTK	*Zeitschrift für Theologie und Kirche*
ZWT	*Zeitschrift für wissenschaftliche Theologie*

INTRODUCTION

The Greek expression ὁ υἱὸς τοῦ ἀνθρώπου, usually translated "the Son of Man," plays a key role in the christology of all four canonical Gospels. While it appears in about fifty different sayings in the New Testament, all but one of these occur in the Gospels. There the expression almost always occurs on the lips of Jesus. Since Jesus always speaks of the Son of Man in the third person, one could infer that he is referring to someone other than himself. In most of the sayings, however, it is clear that Jesus uses the phrase to refer to himself.

This expression has been a central issue in New Testament studies since the beginning of modern scholarship. Because it is used almost exclusively by Jesus, many scholars have seen it as a key to Jesus' own self-consciousness. In the nineteenth century, for example, H. J. Holtzmann affirmed,

> Nothing can be more certain than that he himself chose it as the most apt . . . to designate what was typical of his personal nature, what was characteristic of his appearance and calling. Therein is contained the entire importance of the name. (H. Holtzmann 1865: 213)

Today scholarship can no longer take for granted that Jesus actually used this expression in the way the Gospels describe. We know now that the Gospels often attribute to Jesus ideas and sayings that actually originated at a later time, in the life of the early Christian church. Even if Jesus did not use the expression, however, it remains important for understanding the origins of christology. Its frequent occurrence in the Gospel tradition shows that it represented an important strand of thought in the early Christian community. If it does not tell us about Jesus himself, it does tell us what the earliest Christians believed about him.

But what exactly does it tell us? That is the problem. The Gospels never explain the phrase, and though it has been the object of intensive study since the Protestant Reformation, scholars have come to no agreement on even the most basic questions concerning it. What does it mean? Where does it come from? To whom does it refer? Is it a title or not? Does it tell us something about Jesus or about the faith of the early church?

Occasionally, scholars have thought that the problem was solved. In 1906, for example, Albert Schweitzer asserted,

> Broadly speaking . . . the Son-of-Man problem is both historically solvable and has been solved.
>
> (Schweitzer [1906] 1968: 283)

The history of scholarship since Schweitzer has not vindicated his confidence. Scholars now ask whether the problem is in fact solvable.[1] Research in this area has been described as "a veritable mine field" (Boring 1982: 239). How far scholarship has come from Schweitzer's view is illustrated by Reginald Fuller's assessment of the current state of the question:

> The problem of the Son of Man is a can of worms. No one can write anything about it which will command general assent or provide a definitive solution.   (Fuller 1990: 721)

The failure of scholarship to provide a definitive solution to the problem does not stem from lack of effort. Scholars have proposed widely divergent theories to account for the expression, in the process creating a vast literature on the subject. As W. D. Davies remarks,

> Study of the mysterious synoptic title, "the Son of man," has become a specialized field of its own wherein scholarly discord reigns supreme . . . the ever-mushrooming literature on the Son of man offers a host of conflicting and sometimes confusing claims and counter claims.
>
> (Davies and Allison 1988–91: 2.43)

Because of the scope and complexity of the literature, most writers on the subject survey only the most recent works or discuss only a few aspects of the problem. The need now exists for a comprehensive historical overview of the debate with an evaluation of the

---

[1] Higgins 1969; Schweizer 1975: 103. For a reply to Higgins, see Hooker 1979.

current state of the matter. This is the need that I propose to fill in this study.

Previous surveys of research

Early surveys of opinion on the "Son of Man" problem appeared in commentaries, usually at Matthew 8.20, where the term first occurs in the New Testament (e.g. Wolf 1725; Köcher 1766). At the beginning of the nineteenth century, Wessel Scholten wrote the first major monograph devoted to the topic and gave a comprehensive survey of views from the patristic period to his own time (Scholten 1809: 141–209). At the end of the nineteenth century, Heinrich Appel could still write a comprehensive survey of this sort in twenty-seven pages (Appel 1896: 1–27). After that time, as the scholarship on the subject proliferated, scholars began to limit their surveys to the most recently published works. One exception was Mogens Müller, who wrote extensive excursuses on important aspects of the debate (M. Müller 1984a). Still, no comprehensive survey of the subject has been written in the twentieth century.[2]

As the twentieth century comes to a close, the time seems appropriate to remedy that lack. The present study sketches the main lines of the debate from the patristic period to 1996. It thus supplies a guide to the complex issues and developments that have led to the current impasse.

Overview of the debate

A brief overview of the "Son of Man" debate may help the reader to keep in perspective the more detailed chapters that follow.

The earliest interpretations of the expression ὁ υἱὸς τοῦ ἀνθρώπου were based on the Greek form of the phrase and took "son" in a literal, genealogical sense (Chapter 1). Both patristic authors and Gnostics understood the phrase to identify Jesus as the son of some particular parent, such as Mary, Adam, or the Gnostic god Anthropos. This type of interpretation prevailed through the Middle Ages.

With the flourishing of Semitic studies after the Reformation, interpreters sought to identify the Semitic phrase that underlay the

---

[2] Surveys of research on "Son of Man" from 1725 to the present are listed in the appendix.

Greek expression ὁ υἱὸς τοῦ ἀνθρώπου. They began to base their interpretations on the Semitic idioms *bar enash*, *ben adam*, or *hahu gabra*. New interpretations arose, three of which would become widespread: (1) "Son of Man" as an expression of Jesus' humanity (without reference to a parent); (2) "Son of Man" as a messianic title derived from Daniel 7.13; (3) "son of man" as a nontitular idiom by which a man could refer to himself. Other interpretations that gained less popularity included the derivation of "Son of Man" from Ezekiel or the Psalms.

In the sixteenth and seventeenth centuries, the interpretation of "Son of Man" as an expression of Jesus' humanity predominated (Chapter 2). Interpreters usually saw an element of lowliness in the expression and sometimes contrasted the lowly humanity of this expression with Jesus' divinity.

In the eighteenth and nineteenth centuries, more and more scholars began to support the Danielic/messianic theory, until it became the dominant interpretation by the end of this period (Chapter 3). Often, however, interpreters saw a human element in the expression as well, supposing that it emphasized the humanity of the Messiah. A new perspective on the Son of Man's humanity emphasized its superior or ideal quality rather than its lowliness. Typical interpretations of this period included "Son of Man" as the lowly human, the ideal human, the Messiah, the lowly human Messiah, and the ideal human Messiah.

In 1733 the explorer James Bruce found three Ethiopic manuscripts of 1 Enoch in Abyssinia, and translations became available in the 1820s and 1830s. In the Similitudes of 1 Enoch, scholars discovered a "son of man" that seemed to be a pre-existent heavenly being. They began to assume that Jesus took over pre-Christian apocalyptic ideas about this heavenly son of man. The human messianic Son of Man thus gave way to the heavenly messianic Son of Man (Chapter 3). This interpretation grew in popularity through the last half of the nineteenth century and predominated in the first six decades of the twentieth.

During the same period, new questions came to the fore. To whom did the expression refer: Jesus, someone other than Jesus, or some corporate entity that included Jesus (Chapter 4)? How many of the sayings went back to Jesus himself: all, some, or none (Chapter 5)? Scholars also explored a variety of other theories besides the messianic theory (Chapter 6).

The apocalyptic/messianic interpretation based on 1 Enoch came under attack at the end of the nineteenth century and again in the last four decades of the twentieth. Various factors joined to cast in doubt the view that the title "Son of Man" or a unified Son of Man concept existed in pre-Christian Judaism (Chapter 7). At the same time, the interpretation of "son of man" as a nontitular idiom by which a man could refer to himself in the third person gained in popularity. Many scholars began to believe that Jesus used some such idiom to refer to himself and that the church subsequently misunderstood it as a messianic title derived from Daniel 7.13 (Chapter 8). Other scholars tried to revive the idea that a unified "Son of Man" concept existed in pre-Christian Judaism (Chapter 9).

At the end of the twentieth century, two interpretations predominate: the apocalyptic/messianic (in several variations) and the idiomatic/nontitular (also in several variations). Several other interpretations, however, can still be found in the literature. Progress has been made in a number of areas, and a measure of agreement has been reached on some issues (Chapter 10). Yet nineteen centuries of "Son of Man" study have led to no consensus concerning the meaning or origin of the expression. The Son of Man debate thus serves as a prime illustration of the limits of New Testament scholarship.

1

GENEALOGICAL INTERPRETATIONS

The earliest interpreters of ὁ υἱὸς τοῦ ἀνθρώπου took υἱός ("son") in a literal genealogical sense: for them it identified Jesus as the son of some particular parent. On the one hand, Gnostics interpreted the phrase as "the son of Anthropos (ἀνθρώπου)," Anthropos being a Gnostic god. On the other hand, early orthodox writers interpreted the phrase as "the son of the human," identifying "the human" as Mary or Adam. After the Reformation, a few interpreters identified "the human" as Joseph.

The son of Anthropos

In certain Gnostic sects, such as the Ophites and Valentinians, "Anthropos" ("Man") was the name of an "aeon" or god.[1] This designation apparently developed from speculation on Genesis 1.26: if "man" is made in the image of God, then God must in some sense be a primal "Man."[2] In various Gnostic writings, a second god emanated from this first Man. This second god is identified as Christ and designated "son of Man" (υἱὸς ἀνθρώπου), i.e. son of the god Anthropos. Some texts even refer to a third aeon called "son of son of Man":

> The first aeon, then, is that of Immortal Man. The second aeon is that of Son of Man, who is called "First Begetter" ... The third is that of son of Son of Man, who is called "Savior." (*Eugnostos the Blessed* III, 85.9–14; V, 13.12–13; J. M. Robinson 1990: 236)

Thus the Gnostics took "son" in a genealogical sense, identifying "Man" as a god rather than a human being.

---

[1] On the Gnostic usage, see Schenke 1962; Borsch 1970: 58–121; Colpe [1969] 1972: 474–76.

[2] Schenke 1962: 64–93; Borsch 1970: 117–19.

The son of the human

While the Gnostic interpretation emphasized Christ's divine sonship, the orthodox interpretation emphasized his descent from a human parent. Patristic authors viewed "son of man" as a reference to Jesus' humanity. They related the phrase to the orthodox doctrine of Christ's two natures. Whereas "Son of God" referred to Jesus' divine nature, "son of man" referred to the human nature that he assumed in the incarnation. This contrast appears for the first time in Ignatius (d. c. 108):

> you come together in one faith and in Jesus Christ, who was of the line of David according to the flesh, the son of man and Son of God (τῷ υἱῷ ἀνθρώπου καὶ υἱῷ θεοῦ).
>
> (*Ephesians* 20.2)

The same contrast appears frequently in other patristic authors and has recurred down to modern times.[3]

When patristic interpreters sought to explain "son of (the) man" more explicitly, they took "son" in a genealogical sense and "the man" or "the human" as a reference to a particular person. Jesus was thus "the son of the human," with "the human" referring to either the Virgin Mary or Adam. Justin first posed these two alternatives in his *Dialogue with Trypho* (c. 135):

> He called himself "son of a human" (υἱὸν ἀνθρώπου), then, either because of his birth through a virgin (who was, as I said, of the line of David and Jacob and Isaac and Abraham) or because Adam[4] himself was the father of these who have been enumerated, these from whom Mary derives her descent.
>
> (*Dialogue with Trypho* 100; MPG 6.709)

Isidore of Pelusium (d. c. 450) stated the same two alternatives,[5] while Gregory of Nazianzus (d. 389) accepted both: "It seems to me he is called . . . son of a human (υἱὸς ἀνθρώπου) both because of

[3] E.g. Tertullian, *Adv. Prax.* 2 (MPL 2.179); Irenaeus, *Adv. Haer.* 3.19.1; Bede, *In Lucae evangelium expositio* at Luke 9.22 (CCL 120.202); Theophylactus 1631: 342 at Luke 6.5; Baeck 1937.
[4] The Greek text here has "Abraham," but this is generally emended to "Adam," since otherwise Abraham is said to be the father of himself.
[5] "Son of a human (υἱὸς ἀνθρώπου) – either of Adam or of the virgin, her from whom he received the flesh" (Isidore of Pelusium, *Catena* at Matt. 16.13; quoted by Appel 1896: 2).

Adam and because of the virgin, those from whom he came – from him as from a forefather, from her as from a mother" (*Oratio* 30; MPG 36.132).

The son of Mary

Most patristic authors preferred the interpretation "son of Mary," recognizing that *anthropos* ("human") can refer to woman as well as man. As Irenaeus stated,

> So he, the Son of God our Lord, being the Word of the Father, is also son of a human (υἱὸς ἀνθρώπου), because he had his human generation from Mary – who descended from humans and who was herself a human (ἄνθρωπος) – thus becoming the son of a human (υἱὸς ἀνθρώπου).
>
> (*Adv. Haer.* 3.19.3)

Tertullian set out this position with the logic of a lawyer:

> nor can he be constituted the son of a human (*filium hominis*), unless he be born from a human, either father or mother . . . Since he is from a divine Father, he is certainly not from a human one. If he is not from a human father, it follows that he must be from a human mother.[6]

The same interpretation appears frequently in the patristic period and through the Middle Ages.[7] In accord with this interpretation, some of the Bible translations of the Middle Ages rendered the phrase as "son of the Virgin" (N. Schmidt 1903: 4715).

The interpretation "son of Mary" continued into the Reformation period, for example in the work of Martin Luther ([1530–32] 1959: 14, 129, 161–62). Erasmus (d. 1536) was apparently the first to argue against it. He maintained that in the expression "the son of the man," "the man" must be Adam. The reference cannot be to

---

[6] Tertullian, *Adv. Marc.* 4.10 (MPL 2.407). Cf. *De carne Christi* 5 (MPL 2.806–807).

[7] Ammonius Saccas, Catena on John 1.51 (J. Reuss 1966: 211, fragment 55); Gregory of Nyssa, *Contra Eunomium* 1 (MPG 45.341D); Ambrose, *Ennarratio in Psalmum* 39 (MPL 14.1115D); Jerome, *Breviarium in Psalmos* on Ps. 8.4 (5) (MPL 26.888a); Augustine, *Sermo ad populum* 121.5 on John 1.14 (MPL 38.680); Cyril of Alexandria, in *Acta concilii Epheseni* (quoted by Scholten 1809: 147 and by Appel 1896: 2); Euthymius Zigabenus (c. 1100), *Evangelii secundum Matthaeum ennarratio*, on Matt. 8.20 (MPG 129.293).

Mary since the article is masculine: τοῦ ἀνθρώπου, not τῆς ἀνθρώπου.[8]

Though noting Erasmus' objection, some commentators of the seventeenth century continued to interpret the phrase as "the son of Mary."[9] Several lexicons of the eighteenth century gave the same definition.[10] Already dying out at the end of the eighteenth century, this interpretation practically disappeared in the nineteenth. It resurfaced in the twentieth century in the works of Clemens Henze and a few Catholic authors who followed him (Henze 1956: 73).

The son of Adam

While most patristic authors favored "son of Mary" over "son of Adam," Athanasius opted for the latter. He equated "son of a man" with the "second Adam" of Paul:

> For the Logos, crafter of the universe, appeared as son of a man (υἱὸς ἀνθρώπου), not becoming some different (type of man), but a second Adam . . . So if on earth he became "son of a man" (though begotten not from the seed of a man but from the Holy Spirit), the meaning will be "son of one who is the first-formed, i.e. Adam."
>
> (*Contra Apollinarium* 1.8; MPG 26.1105–1108)

Calvin likewise adopted the interpretation "son of Adam" (Calvin [1559] 1960: 1.477).

While patristic authors generally ignored the articles in the New Testament expression, Erasmus emphasized them. He argued that in "the son of the man," the second article indicates a particular man, Adam. Likewise, the first article points to a particular son of Adam: that exceptional son, the restorer of the human race.[11]

Following Erasmus, many interpreters stressed the first article: Jesus was not simply *a* son of Adam, but *the* son of Adam κατ᾽

[8] Erasmus 1705: at Matt. 8.20; 11.26 (11.19); 16.13; John 1.1. This argument from the article appears also in Pseudo-Justin (before 1583, cited by Scholten 1809: 155–56) and reappears in the commentary of Cornelius à Lapide ([1638] 1891–96: 1.338–40 at Matt. 8.20).
[9] Drusius 1612: at Matt. 8.20; 11.19; Del Rio 1614: pt. 1, 479–83; Mariana 1619: 927 at Matt. 8.20; 932 at Matt. 16.13.
[10] Rechenberg 1714: 605–606 s.v. *filius hominis*; Stock 1725: s.v. ἄνθρωπος, υἱός; J. Schwartz 1736: s.v. ἄνθρωπος, υἱός (cited by Scholten 1809: 150, 165); Schleusner [1792] 1824: 1.168–69 s.v. ἄνθρωπος, 2.909–10 s.v. υἱός.
[11] Erasmus (d. 1536) 1705: at Matt. 8.20; 11.26 (11.19); 16.13; John 1.1.

ἐξοχήν (*par excellence*), the second Adam mentioned by Paul (1 Cor. 15.22, 45–49).[12] Most inferred that the phrase identified Jesus with some particular son of Adam already mentioned in the Old Testament. They found this son of Adam especially in "the seed of the woman" who would crush the serpent's head (Gen. 3.15). They further identified this seed with the seed of Abraham (Gen. 12.7, 13.15), the seed promised to David (1 Sam. 7.12), the son predicted by Isaiah (Isa. 9.6), the human form seen by Ezekiel (Ezek. 1.26), and the "one like a son of man" seen by Daniel (Dan. 7.13). The "son of Adam" was thus the seed or son promised throughout the scriptures.[13] This line of interpretation continued through the nineteenth and early twentieth centuries.[14]

In the late twentieth century, the ancient patristic interpretation lived on. According to Olaf Moe, Jesus called himself "Son of the human" instead of "Son of Adam" directly, because he was thinking not only of the man Adam, but of the human being described in Genesis 1.27, created as man and woman (Moe 1960: 124). Like Erasmus, Cortés and Gatti stress the articles: "Jesus is the Son *par excellence* of the Man *par excellence*, namely *the* Son of Adam . . . *the* Descendant of Adam" (Cortés and Gatti 1968: 472).

Similarly, Ragnar Leivestad suggested that Paul's expression "the second, the last Adam" gives the proper interpretation of Jesus' self-designation. Jesus designated himself *ben adam* in contrast to *ben David* in order to indicate that his messiahship extended to humanity, not just Israel (Leivestad 1968: 102–103; 1971/72: 267). Later, Leivestad withdrew this suggestion, terming it "wishful thinking" (1982: 251).

Fritz Neugebauer (1974/75), John Bowman (1989), and Robert Funk (1996: 89–94) have also advocated the interpretation "Son of Adam." Bowman suggests that Jesus may have called himself "Son of Adam" in order to identify himself as the Messiah, since in Jewish thought the spirit of Adam would be in the Messiah. Funk

---

[12] E.g. Heinsius [1639] 1640: 34 at Matt. 8.20.
[13] Lightfoot 1675: at Matt. 16.13; Gaillard 1684 (summarized by Köcher 1766: 191 and Scholten 1809: 202–203); Lampe 1724–26 (quoted by Scholten 1809: 204–205); Bengel [1742] 1893: 1.171–72 at Matt. 16.13; Lange 1743: 2.31 at Matt. 8.20; 2.32 at Matt. 9.6; 2.41 at Matt. 12.6; Elsner 1767–69: at Matt. 12.8; Michaelis [1773–90] 1790–92: 1.111 at Matt. 8.20; Morus 1796: at John 12.34 (summarized by Scholten 1809: 200).
[14] Cremer [1867] 1895: 559–60 s.v. υἱός; Gess 1870: 182–94; Wörner 1882: 39–51; Grau 1887: 178–218; Bard [1908] ²1915; Gottsched 1908: 22–24; Badham 1911.

even uses "son of Adam" to translate Daniel 7.13, where the Aramaic expression is not *adam* but *enash.*

The son of Joseph

With the Reformation, a new genealogical interpretation appeared. According to Pseudo-Justin (before 1583), when Jesus called himself "the son of the man," he meant "the son of Joseph." He identified himself as such not because Joseph was his true father, but because Joseph as his guardian was called his father (cited by Scholten 1809: 155–56).

Christoph August Heumann (1740) gave a more complex theory relating the phrase to Joseph. In Heumann's view, Jesus' enemies contemptuously referred to his low social standing by calling him "son of the man" in the sense "son of the plebeian."[15] By "the plebeian" they referred to Joseph, whom they did not consider worthy of naming. Jesus picked up their expression, using it as if to say "He whom you call *the son of the man* and despise because of the humility of his person."

While these interpreters retained the idea of Jesus' virgin birth, E. I. C. Walter (1791) took "son of the man" to mean that Jesus actually was the son of Joseph, a view previously held by certain Jewish writers.[16]

Evaluation

These genealogical interpretations have been justly criticized. If the expression meant "son of the human," indicating descent from Mary or Joseph, why would Jesus so frequently emphasize that he was born of a human being when none of his hearers had any doubt of this (Scholten 1809: 149)? If the phrase meant "son of Adam," it would have to indicate some special son of Adam to distinguish this son from all the rest. But such a particular son cannot be found in Genesis 3.15, which refers not to the seed of Adam but to the seed of woman. Furthermore, the New Testament never refers to Genesis 3.15 (Beyschlag 1894: 1.60–62).

---

[15] Heumann 1740 (summarized by Köcher 1766: 191 and Scholten 1809: 157–58). This interpretation presupposes that *adam* in Hebrew refers to a man of the lower classes, an erroneous idea that will be discussed in Chapter 2.

[16] Walter 1791 (summarized by Scholten 1809: 158–60). Jewish authors cited by Münster 1537: 70.

Genealogical interpretations proceed from the Greek form of the expression, which very naturally yields a genealogical sense. The earliest interpreters, who spoke Greek as their native language, unanimously saw in the Greek phrase a filial relation between a son and a parent. What these interpreters did not recognize was the possibility that a Semitic expression underlay the Greek. As we shall see, it was this recognition more than anything else that caused the genealogical interpretation to fall out of favor.

2

THE HUMAN SON OF MAN

Patristic and medieval authors based their interpretation of ὁ υἱὸς τοῦ ἀνθρώπου on the Greek (or Latin) form of the expression. With the flourishing of Semitic studies after the Reformation, scholars recognized that Jesus would have spoken Aramaic or Hebrew rather than Greek. They searched behind the Greek expression for the underlying Semitic original. Lying close at hand they found the Hebrew idiom *ben adam* (Aramaic *bar enash* or *bar enasha*). Taking a step that has determined the course of "Son of Man" research ever since, they assumed that this idiom underlay the Greek expression.

As patristic authors recognized, the natural sense of the Greek expression is "son of the man" or "son of the human." It would express a filial relationship between Jesus and a specific parent. The Semitic *ben adam* or *bar enasha*, on the other hand, translates literally as "son of man." In this idiom, "son of" designates an individual as a member of a group, and "man" specifies the group to which he belongs. The idiom therefore simply means "man." With this recognition, scholars began to assume that the New Testament phrase expressed Jesus' humanity without referring to a parent.

As a designation for Jesus' humanity, the expression "the Son of Man" might emphasize that which he had in common with humanity, either human nature *per se* or human nature in its lowliness and weakness. On the other hand, the definite article before the phrase might point to Jesus as the Son of Man *par excellence*, emphasizing that which set him apart as an extraordinary human being. These different possibilities gave rise to three varieties of interpretation: the Son of Man as the simply human, the lowly human, or the superior (ideal) human.

The simply human Son of Man

Taking "Son of Man" as equivalent to "man," the Swiss Reformer Ulrich Zwingli (1531) understood it to refer to Jesus' true manhood, that which he had in common with all men:

> "Son of Man" is a circumlocution for "man," but this circumlocution explains the property of the thing. For it wishes to indicate that he is true man in all things (except sin) and similar to us.[1]

Like Zwingli, a number of other scholars in the sixteenth and seventeenth centuries took "Son of Man" as a Hebrew idiom for "man" and saw it as an expression of Jesus' human nature.[2] Later authors took this view as well.[3]

The lowly human Son of Man

Interpreters who took "Son of Man" as a Semitic idiom for "man" often found an element of lowliness and humility associated with it, since the idiom often appears in Old Testament passages where the lowliness of humanity stands in contrast to the majesty of God. This idea of the lowly Son of Man appears already in the work of Martin Bucer (or Butzer), one of the first to interpret "Son of Man" in light of the Hebrew idiom (1527):

> [Jesus] repeatedly calls himself "son of man," in the quite frequent fashion of Scripture, and generally when he lowers himself and proclaims his humility.[4]

Different varieties of the lowly Son of Man appeared, depending on the type of lowliness associated with the term: lowliness of nature, lowliness of social standing, or lowliness in contrast to some higher concept.

---

[1] Zwingli 1531 at either Matt. 9.5 (so Scholten 1809: 172) or Matt. 8.20 (so Appel 1896: 4).

[2] Châteillon 1551: at Matt. 8.12, 20; Zegers 1553: at Matt. 12.8; Wild 1559: at Matt. 8.20; Piscator 1613: 92, 99, 129; Glass 1623: 671 (Lib. III, Tract I) s.v. בנים; E. Schmid 1658: 674 at John 5.27; Hackspan 1664: 3.50–52; Olearius [1699] 1721: 92 (par. 11) on Luke 17.24.

[3] Tholuck [1857] 1860: 93–94; Friedrich Philippi 1868: 411–18; Schenkel 1872; Alexander 1900: 307–17; J. A. Robinson 1906: 60–66; Sanford 1923.

[4] Bucer 1527: at Matt. 8.20 or 9.6 (cited by Scholten 1809: 172).

Lowliness of nature: the weak, miserable man

For some interpreters, "Son of Man" implied participation not merely in human nature *per se*, but in human nature seen as lowly, weak, and miserable. Heinrich Bullinger wrote:

> For thus it signifies that he is true and consubstantial with us, true man born of man according to the flesh. Further, it expresses beautifully the misery of human nature. Since he would share in this with us, it was necessary that he have all human miseries, with the exception of sin, in common with us. (Bullinger 1542: 85 at Matt. 8.20)

For Benedict Aretius, since Jesus was the Son of Man *par excellence*, it followed that he was the unhappiest and most miserable of men (Aretius 1577: at Matt. 8.20; 16.13). Likewise for Cornelius Jansen (d. 1638), Son of Man was an expression of human misery (C. Jansen 1639: at Matt. 8.20; 16.13), and Henry Hammond interpreted the expression as a reference to the weakness of Jesus' human state (Hammond 1639: 3.96, 109–10). J. L. von Wolzogen explained that the Hebrew expression for man often designates "the fragility and infirmity of human nature, and of the miserable state of men." Jesus therefore used this expression "to signify his humble and miserable state in this world" (Wolzogen, after 1656: 1.260). According to Jakob Alting also, Jesus called himself "Son of Man" to show that he was not ashamed of his lowly human condition.[5] In the nineteenth century, Karl Friedrich Nösgen argued that the phrase expressed the essential quality of man as it is emphasized in Old Testament passages: i.e. lowliness and frailty, with a destiny to suffer (Nösgen 1869: 1–115; 1891: 154–63).

Lowliness of class: man of the lower classes

For other interpreters, the title "Son of Man" implied not lowliness of nature but lowliness of social class. This view goes back to an interpretation of Psalm 49.3 by the rabbi David Kimchi, who saw a distinction here between *bene adam* (as men of lower class) and *bene ish* (as men of higher class). Sebastian Münster used this interpretation to explain Jesus' self-designation (assumed to be *ben adam*):

---

[5] Alting 1685–87: 18 at John 6.62 (cited by Scholten 1809: 203–204).

> Christ calls himself "son of man" in the manner of
> Scripture, which calls the man born of the lowest class
> "son of man." Thus Christ was made in the likeness of
> men, that is, as if one of the common people of men.
>
> (Münster 1537: 70)

Other authors followed Münster,[6] the most influential of whom
was Hugo Grotius (1641).[7] After Grotius, the same view appeared
frequently down to the end of the eighteenth century.[8] It was
criticized by the Hebraist Johann David Michaelis, who called it "a
shameful error" that shows "a manifest ignorance of Oriental
languages" (1792: 1.20–21). Michaelis points out that it is based on
an argument from a particular passage (Ps. 49.3) to a universal
application that is not supported by any other occurrence of the
phrase. For example, God calls Ezekiel *ben adam*, though Ezekiel is
one of the priestly aristocracy. After Michaelis, the interpretation
of "Son of Man" as a man of lower class rarely appears.[9]

Lowliness by contrast

Many who adopted the new idiomatic interpretation of "Son of
Man" as "man" continued to contrast the phrase with "Son of
God." For these interpreters, it expressed Jesus' lowly human
nature, assumed at the incarnation, in contrast to his divine
nature.[10]

For others, the phrase contrasted Jesus' lowliness not with divine
nature but with Jewish expectations of a glorious Messiah. This
idea appears as early as 1718 in the commentary on Matthew by

---

[6] Vatablus (d. 1547) 1660; Musculus 1544: 225 at Matt. 8.20 (#2, 3 under *Quid ex
responsione Christi*); Matt. 16.13 (under *Sed redeamus ad Christum*); Matt. 26.64;
Stephanus 1553: at Matt. 8.20 (cited by Scholten 1809: 162–63); Marlorat 1561: 54
at Matt. 8.20; Lucas 1606: 1.21 at Matt. 8.20.

[7] Grotius [1641] 1972: 2.1.97 at Matt. 8.20. Cf. at Matt. 12.8; 12.32; 16.13; Mark
2.28; John 5.27.

[8] Dowman 1645: vol. 2 at Matt. 8.20, John 3.13, John 5.27; Tirinus 1645: 2.94;
Poussines (d. c. 1650) 1713: 75–83 (par. XXXII); Walaeus 1653: 83–84 (= Grotius);
Vorst 1665: ch. 13, par. 2; Calovius [1676] 1719: 1.254 (= Grotius); Schöttgen 1717:
s.v. ἄνθρωπος, υἱός; Less 1776; G. Campbell 1789: 1.234–38; Vogt 1790: 1.150–51.

[9] An exception is Schenkel [1864] 1869: 77–78, 367–69.

[10] Schlichting (d. 1564) after 1656: 1.21, 27–28, 43; C. Jansen 1576: at John 1.52;
5.27; Maldonado [1596–97] 1888: 274–76; Calixtus 1624: book 2, ch. 5, p. 105;
Menochio 1630: 2.13, 14; Novarini 1642: 117; Baxter 1685: at Matt. 12.32; John
5.27; Le Clerc [1699] 1701: 54, 106, 253; A. Clarke [1810–17] 1836: 5.109–10; Kipp
1904; Cavalier 1923; Bleibtreu 1926.

Beausobre and Lenfant (at Matt. 8.20). Over a century later, the prominent scholar Ferdinand Christian Baur made the most widely noticed statement of this view:

> In contrast to a Messiah appearing with earthly power and glory to set up a kingdom of earthly faith and worldly rule, he wished only to be a man, in the simple, unassuming sense belonging to the concept of a human subject as such; man in the most authentic and broadest sense as one who holds nothing remote from himself and deems nothing foreign to himself which in a human existence belongs to the lot of a human life, be it even the least and lowliest thing . . . man finally too as one who considered it his most special calling to undergo all suffering and sacrifices which are not to be separated from his destiny.
>
> (Baur 1860: 280–81; cf. 1864: 81)

Similar views were expressed by C. B. E. Uloth (1862) and B. D. Eerdmans (1894).

The superior human Son of Man

While some saw the Son of Man as a lowly human, others saw him as a superior human. The latter interpretation emphasized the first article in the phrase: *the* Son of Man (= *the* Man), which thus pointed to Jesus' uniqueness, as the man different from all others. Variations on this theme included the pre-eminent man, the ideal man, and the man who is the goal of human history.

The pre-eminent man

Jean Hardouin (1741) proposed that "the Son of Man" meant "the firstborn of men," in the sense of rank rather than birth order. Just as "*the* Son of God" with the article means "the firstborn among many brothers" (Rom. 8.29) and "*the* son of the king" with the article means the firstborn son, so "*the* Son of Man" with the article should be understood as "the pre-eminent one, and therefore the firstborn of other sons of men, and therefore even by that name the one ruling over all others" (Hardouin 1741: at John 1.51). Gabriel Mosche (1788–90: 1.583) similarly interpreted "the Son of Man" as "the most eminent man, the noblest, most excellent man, the man without equal."

The ideal man

In the nineteenth century, the pre-eminent man developed into the ideal man. Scholars of that century often traced the beginning of this conception to Friedrich Schleiermacher, though Schleiermacher only indicates that the term suggests a difference between Christ and other men:

> For He could not have given Himself [the name Son of Man] if He had not been conscious of sharing completely in the same human nature as others; but it would have been meaningless to claim it specially for Himself, if He had not had a reason for doing so which others could not adduce – if, that is, the name had not had a pregnant meaning, which was meant to indicate a difference between Him and all others.   (Schleiermacher [1821–22] 1928: 422)

The earliest to use the actual phrase "ideal man" in this connection may have been Augustus Tholuck, who interpreted "Son of Man" as a messianic designation, but also found in it a second meaning:

> In addition, however, the Redeemer also appears to have chosen this expression to indicate by it that he was the true ideal man, who represented humanity in its original purity.
> (Tholuck 1827: 62)

Some followed Tholuck in understanding "Son of Man" as a combination of ideal man and Messiah (see Chapter 3). Others understood the term to mean the ideal man without messianic connotations. For example, Isaak August Dorner felt that the phrase referred to Jesus' human nature as "true and perfect man." By it Jesus intimates "that He corresponds more perfectly than the others to the concept of man, that He is man of a nobler extraction, the pure Son of man" (Dorner [1839] 1861–63: 1.54, 55).

Others likewise felt that "the Son of Man" designated "the idea, the archetype [*Urbild*], the representative of humanity" (Lutz [1847] 1861: 291); "the normative and model man . . . the ideal of humanity" (E. Reuss [1852] 1860: 1.230); "the sole right, authentic man who corresponds to the idea" (Ebrard [1851–52] 1862–63: 2.15); "the normal man, the perfect representative of the race" (Godet [1871] 1875: 268); "the representative of the whole race . . . in whom all the potential powers of humanity were gathered . . . in whom the complete conception of manhood was absolutely attained . . . who gathers up into Himself all humanity, and becomes the source of a higher life to the race" (Westcott 1908: 1.76–77).

The goal of human history

Another variation on the superior Son of Man identified him as the goal of human history. Like the interpretation "Son of Adam," this interpretation identified "Son of Man" with Paul's "second Adam." The Son of Man was "the goal of the history of humanity" (Luthardt [1852–53] 1876–78: 1.330); "the goal toward which looks the whole salvation history guided by God" (Thomasius [1853] 1857: 2.15); "the one at whom the history of the Adamic race aimed; who formed its conclusion in contrast to the one who began it" (Hofmann 1886: 47; cf. 1857–60: 1.420–23, 2.1.77–82); "who realized in principle its ideal destiny as redeemed" (Bartlet 1892: 436); "that member of the human race in whom the history of the race comes to its conclusion" (Zahn 1903: 353).

The human Son of Man in the twentieth century

The human Son of Man declined in popularity after the nineteenth century. In the twentieth century, this interpretation recurred occasionally in the form of either the lowly human Son of Man or the superior human Son of Man.

The lowly human interpretation found support from Schalom Ben-Chorin (1967: 132–35), who asserted that Jesus used the expression in the sense "man per se," as "the man exemplary in his insignificance." Other interpreters have seen in "Son of Man" successive stages of lowliness and exaltation. Wilfrid Stott, describing "Son of Man" as "a title of abasement," finds two contrasting conceptions in the use of the phrase: "the insignificant frailty and weakness of man and the final state of man triumphant, crowned and having 'the dominion'" (Stott 1972: 281). Likewise, John Bowker (1977) suggests that Jesus combined two main senses of the phrase "son of man" in the Old Testament, speaking of himself as a weak mortal man subject to death (Psalms and Job) but one who would nevertheless be vindicated by God (Daniel 7).

The superior human interpretation survives among scholars who see the Son of Man as an ideal, representative, or exemplary figure. As ideal man, he is both ideal servant and ideal king (Stephenson 1917/18). He is "the representative man," "man at his best," "the true ideal not only of Israel but of humanity" (Dougall and Emmet 1922: 277, 278, 279); the "archetype or pattern of perfect human nature" (Davis 1961: 39–40); the model for all humanity (Elliott 1970); "a representative and exemplary figure," "the representative of the righteous man," and the one "who calls men to follow his example and share his destiny" (Pamment 1983: 127); "'*the* human being,' the Man *par excellence*, the focal point of the human race in its relation to God" (J. Ross 1991: 197).

Evaluation

Ultimately the interpretation of "Son of Man" as an expression of Jesus' humanity failed because it made the title superfluous: Jesus had no need to emphasize his simple humanity, since it would have been apparent to all. As Beyschlag pointed out, "Jesus could not possibly have felt any need of again and again assuring his contemporaries of his true human nature, which none of them could doubt" (Beyschlag 1894: 1.61). The idea that Jesus emphasized his human nature in contrast to his divine nature is anachronistic, since it presupposes the orthodox dogma of Christ's two natures, concepts that "belong to the theology of the fifth century, and not to the biblical mode of thinking or speaking" (Beyschlag 1894: 1.61). Furthermore, as James Stalker emphasized,

> the statements made about "the Son of man" are anything but characteristic predicates of humanity . . . things are predicated about "the Son of man," which are the reverse of simply human.   (Stalker 1899: 47–48)

For instance, it does not belong to the characteristic peculiarity of human nature to forgive sins, as in Matthew 9.6 (Usteri 1886: 9), or to come on the clouds of heaven.

Bernhard Weiss raised similar arguments against the concept of the "lowly" human Son of Man:

> For the genuine humanity of the man who stood before them, and therefore, also the weakness that belonged to His human nature as such, and the fact that it was subject to suffering and death . . . these were points as to which they had no doubt; and neither the homelessness (Matt. viii.20) nor the suffering which is claimed for the Son of Man in Mark viii.31 belongs to the common fate of man.
>   (B. Weiss [1868] 1893: 1.74)

The "lowly human" perspective also ran aground on the fact that "majesty and glorification are predicated of the Son of Man just as emphatically as lowliness and suffering" (Beyschlag 1894: 1.61). The specific interpretation of "Son of Man" as a man of the lower classes finds no support in Hebrew or Aramaic usage, as Michaelis pointed out.

The concept of "Son of Man" as the superior man – the pre-eminent man or ideal man or goal of human history – was likewise rejected for failing to interpret the phrase in its historical context. As Wellhausen wrote, "[Jesus] was no Greek philosopher and no modern humanist, nor did he speak to philosophers and humanists" (Wellhausen 1899: 6.200–201). Specifically with respect to the "ideal man" interpretation, Beyschlag noted that "the great majority of passages do not suggest it, and the idea itself contains an element of abstract theology which seems out of place in the mind of Jesus" (Beyschlag 1894: 1.61).

Looking back on these interpretations, one is struck by the wide range of nuances that have been imported into the same phrase – from miserable lowliness to ideal perfection. The phrase "son of man" has been a blank slate on which scholars have written their own conceptions of humanity. This fact more than any other criticism tells against these interpretations.

3

THE APOCALYPTIC/MESSIANIC SON OF MAN

Chapters 1 and 2 focused on theories which derive the significance of "Son of Man" from the expression itself, either in its Greek form or its presumed Semitic original. A second type of theory finds the significance of the expression in its use in some particular passage of scripture or other literature. In the history of debate on the subject, no proposal has gained wider acceptance than that which derives the expression from apocalyptic literature, especially Daniel 7.13. In this passage "one like a son of man (*bar enash*)" comes to the Ancient of Days on the clouds of heaven to receive sovereignty, glory, and a kingdom. Since the Son of Man in the Gospels is also depicted as coming with the clouds (Mark 13.26; 14.62), many scholars have inferred that Daniel 7.13 is the source of the Gospel expression.

Two Jewish apocalypses in the tradition of Daniel – 1 Enoch and 4 Ezra – have likewise been cited as possible sources for the Gospel Son of Man. In the Similitudes (or Parables) of 1 Enoch (chapters 37–71), Enoch sees a human figure in heaven who is identified as "the son of man to whom belongs righteousness" (1 Enoch 46.3). He is "the Elect One," concealed with God before creation, anointed by God's Spirit with wisdom, and appointed to sit on God's throne to judge the wicked. Similarly, in 4 Ezra 13, Ezra has a dream in which he sees the figure of a man come up out of the sea and fly with the clouds of heaven. In the interpretation of the dream, God identifies him as "my Son," who will destroy the wicked and gather Israel.

Since 4 Ezra, generally dated to the end of the first century CE, would have had no direct influence on the New Testament, it has played less of a role in the debate than Daniel and 1 Enoch. Consequently the following discussion will focus on Daniel 7.13 and the Similitudes of Enoch.

The Danielic son of man

The "one like a son of man" in Daniel has been variously interpreted as the Messiah, an angel, or a symbol for the people of God.[1] Though the vision itself identifies the figure with "the people of the saints of the Most High" (Dan. 7.27; cf. 7.18, 22), Jewish interpreters close to the time of Jesus identified the figure as the Messiah. Thus whether the Danielic figure originally represented the Messiah or not, numerous scholars have believed that the expression "Son of Man" in the Gospels refers to this figure understood in a messianic sense.

In the early period of Christianity, a few church fathers already associated Jesus with Daniel 7.13. Tertullian, for example, assumed that Jesus drew his self-designation as "Son of Man" from the prophecy in Daniel:

> What now, if Christ be described in Daniel by this very title of "Son of man?" Is not this enough to prove that He is the Christ of prophecy? For if He gives Himself that appellation which was provided in the prophecy for the Christ of the Creator, He undoubtedly offers Himself to be understood as Him to whom (the appellation) was assigned by the prophet.[2]

Interpreters of the period often identified the figure in Daniel as the pre-existent Logos or Christ. They assumed that he was called "son of man" (i.e. human being) even before the incarnation in a prophetic or proleptic sense, "because of his ultimate incarnation."[3]

The triumph of Daniel 7.13

In the Reformation period, Martin Chemnitz (d. 1586) also appealed to Daniel 7.13 as the source of the Gospel expression: "There is no doubt, however, that the appellation was borrowed from the 7th chapter of Daniel, verse 13, where the Prophet thus

---

[1] For surveys of the history of interpretation of Daniel 7.13, see P. Casey 1979; M. Müller 1984a: 33–65; Caragounis 1986: 35–48.

[2] Tertullian, *Adv. Marc.* 4.10 (ANF 3.359); cf. *De carne Christi* 15 (ANF 3.534).

[3] Eusebius, *Hist. Eccl.* 1.2.26. Cf. Epiphanius in *Adv. Haer.* 2.1, haer. 57.8 (MPG 41.1008); Theodoret (cited by Scholten 1809: 170); Calvin [1561] 1948: at Dan. 7.13.

describes the person of the Messiah" (Chemnitz 1600: 2.150 at John 3.13). He goes on to say that from this passage the people called the expected Messiah "Son of Man," and from the same passage Christ adapted the title to himself.[4]

In the seventeenth and eighteenth centuries, a number of authors accepted the Danielic/messianic interpretation.[5] Not until the nineteenth century, however, did it become predominant. Near the beginning of that century, Wessel Scholten adopted it in the first major monograph on "Son of Man":

> The appellation ὁ υἱὸς τοῦ ἀνθρώπου, as often as it was employed by Jesus, indicates *that certain man* who in human form was exhibited to Daniel in a symbolic vision (Dan. 7.13), and, moreover, that King, appointed by God, who would rule humanely over men, the same who was indicated by the name *Messiah*.   (Scholten 1809: 67)

Friedrich Lücke also adopted the Danielic explanation in his commentary on John ([1820] 1840–43: 1.459–65). After Scholten and Lücke, scholars increasingly began to look to Daniel 7.13 as the primary Old Testament root of the New Testament "Son of Man."

Not all scholars welcomed the Danielic interpretation. Friedrich Schleiermacher, for one, thought such a derivation from Daniel 7.13 "a peculiar notion" (Schleiermacher [1821–22] 1928: 422 n. 5). Likewise, C. H. Weisse labeled the derivation of the concept from Daniel 7.13 as an attempt to assassinate the originality of Jesus (Weisse 1856: 104). By the end of the nineteenth century, however, H. J. Holtzmann could write,

> The derivation of the term from Dan. 7.13 (already attempted by expositors of the Reformation period, such as Chemnitz) may today be regarded as an almost universally recognized and secured result of the discussions of our theme that otherwise diverge in so many ways.
> (H. Holtzmann [1897] 1911: 1.314 n. 5)

---

[4] In summarizing the reasons for Jesus' use of the title, however, Chemnitz includes three other explanations of it along with the Danielic/messianic.

[5] E.g. Cameron 1632: 137–38; Leigh 1650: 22, 148; Bynaeus 1691–98: 1.71–76; Whitby [1703] 1808: 1.103 at Matt. 12.8; Eichhorn 1791: 45; 1795; Stolz 1796–1802: 1.106; Herder [1796] 1880: 189–90, 242–43; K. Schmidt 1798; Donker Curtius 1799: 92–93, 185.

The human messianic Son of Man

Among interpreters who derived "Son of Man" from Daniel 7.13, some took the title as a practical equivalent for "Messiah" with no further connotations.[6] As Willibald Beyschlag expressed this view, "Messiah might just as well be substituted for Son of Man" (Beyschlag 1894: 1.63). Others were loath to relinquish the older view that the title referred to Jesus' human nature. Hence they simply combined the two interpretations. As John Cameron wrote, "the appellation 'Son of Man' both signifies the office of Christ and at the same time includes his human nature" (Cameron 1632: 137–38). A similar perspective appears in numerous writers of the nineteenth and early twentieth centuries.[7]

Many authors with this view went a step further in emphasizing one pole or another of the Messiah's human nature: its lowliness or its ideal character. The view of the Son of Man as a lowly human Messiah has had numerous adherents.[8] One influential exponent was W. M. L. De Wette:

> We must . . . presume that Jesus called himself the Son of Man because he represents the Messiah . . . in his human, unprepossessing individuality, exactly as Daniel too wishes to designate the human form of the same and as Ezekiel (of whom Jesus also perhaps took consideration) represents himself in comparison with God as son of man, i.e. as weak mortal. (De Wette [1836] 1845: 103)

[6] Whitby [1703] 1808: at Matt. 12.8; K. Schmidt 1798; Donker Curtius 1799: 92–93, 185; Cölln 1836: 2.16; Strauss [1835–36] 1860: 293–301; Renan [1863] 1936: 122; B. Weiss [1868] 1893: 1.73–78; Beyschlag [1891–92] 1894: 1.56–67; Krop 1897: 91–102, 118–32; Stevens 1899: 41–53; 1901: 81–94; Harnack [1907] 1908: 239 n. 1; Loisy 1907: 1.243; Tillmann 1907a; Montefiore [1909] 1927: 1.76–77; Dewick 1912: 153–63.

[7] Küttner 1780: 17, 29, 119; H. Meyer 1832: 82–83; [1876] 1884: 183–85; Gass 1839: 81–150; Alford [1849–61] 1874: at Matt. 8.20; Arnoldi 1856: 210–11; A. Bruce [1889] 1909: 166–78; Stalker 1899: 75–76; C. Schmid [1853] 1870: 107–15; Milligan 1902; Schlatter 1921: 165–69; Joüon 1930.

[8] Chemnitz 1600: 2.150; Leigh 1650: 22, 148; Cappel 1657: at Matt. 8.20; John 5.27; Cellarius [1680] 1700: 588–92; Bynaeus 1691: 1.71–76; Gill 1744: 1.67; Mac-Knight [1756] 1950: 476; Schöttgen 1765: 60 s.v. ἄνθρωπος; Rosenmüller [1777] 1815: 181–83; Eichhorn 1791: 45; Stolz 1796–1802: 2.106; Herder [1796] 1880: 189–90, 242–43; Scholten 1809: 67–68; Ewald 1828: at Rev. 1.13; De Wette [1836] 1845: 102–103; Stier [1843–48] 1855–58: 1.355; Hengstenberg 1858: 3.82–92; Hilgenfeld 1863; Keim [1867–72] 1876–83: 3.79–92; Hausrath [1868–] 1878–80: 2.230–31; Holsten 1868: 179–96; 1891; Wendt [1886–90] 1892: 2.142; Sanday 1891: 29–32; Derambure 1908–1909; Denney 1909: 286–98; Vosté 1949.

Almost as frequently, interpreters have combined the ideas of Messiah and superior or ideal man.[9] This interpretation of Son of Man as the ideal human Messiah was popularized especially by Augustus Neander. While affirming that the title alluded to the Messiah described in Daniel 7.13, Neander thought that Jesus had a more important reason for using it:

> He called himself the "Son of Man" because he had appeared as a man; because he belonged to mankind; because he had done such great things even for *human* nature (Matt ix.8); because he was to glorify that nature; because he himself was the realized ideal [*Urbild*] of humanity.   (Neander [1837] 1888: 99)

Ultimately the human messianic Son of Man fell prey to an objection similar to that raised against the human Son of Man: Jesus had no need to emphasize the humanity of the Messiah, since the Jews had no other thought than that the Messiah would be the human Son of David. Beyschlag directed this objection specifically against the lowly human Messiah:

> Then we must ask, who at that time needed to be assured of the human nature of the Messiah? Or if the lowliness of this human nature is to consist in its creaturely weakness, whether there is any other kind of man than weak, creaturely? Jesus would in this way have again and again assured people of what was self-evident to everyone.
>   (Beyschlag 1894: 1.61–62 n. 3)

Likewise the ideal human Messiah faced the same objection as the ideal man: it failed to interpret the phrase in its historical context, introducing concepts from nineteenth-century humanism.

The Enochic Son of Man

After Daniel, 1 Enoch stands as the apocalyptic writing most frequently named as the source of the title "Son of Man." This

[9] Messiah as "the pre-eminent man": Mercken 1722 (cited by Scholten 1809: 205); Storr 1793: 201; Kühnöl [1807] 1823: 231. Messiah as the ideal man: Tholuck 1827: 61–62; Olshausen [1830] 1858: 1.217–21, 377, 442, 455; Hase [1829] 1860: 136; [1876] 1891: 514; Böhme 1839: 84–92; Baumgarten-Crusius 1843–45: 1.77; Wittichen 1868: 61–62, 66–69, 97–98, 137–58; 1876: 111, 140–41, 338–39; Mangold 1877; Brückner 1886; V. Stanton 1886: 237–50; Schnedermann 1893–95: 1.206–209; MacRory 1915; Harrison 1951.

apocalypse is quoted in the New Testament book of Jude (verses 14–15) and called "scripture" in Barnabas 16.5. Later patristic authors referred to it, but from the fourth century on it fell into disrepute (Charles [1893] 1912: lxxxi–xcv). From the eighth century on, it was known only from citations in patristic authors and a fragment in the *Chronographia* of Georgius Syncellus. That situation continued until 1773, when the explorer James Bruce found three Ethiopic manuscripts of it in Abyssinia (J. Bruce [1790] 1813: 2.412–17). The work first became generally available to modern scholars through its translation into English by Richard Laurence (1821). Heinrich Ewald (1828) was one of the first to use the book as background for the New Testament expression "Son of Man."

Debate on the relevance of 1 Enoch for the Son of Man problem has focused on two primary issues: whether the Enochic Son of Man is human or superhuman and whether the Similitudes, that part of 1 Enoch in which the Son of Man appears, precedes the Christian era or not.

The heavenly Messiah

In his translation of 1 Enoch, Laurence pointed out two passages (1 Enoch 48.3–5; 61.8–13) which he believed described the Messiah, or "Son of Man," as a pre-existent divine being (Laurence 1821: xl–xliii). Soon scholars began to interpret not only the figure in 1 Enoch but also the figure in Daniel 7.13 as a heavenly Messiah.[10] Thus the view arose that Jesus used "Son of Man" to identify himself as the Messiah of apocalyptic literature, understood as a pre-existent, heavenly being. This view ultimately replaced the concept of the Son of Man as a purely human Messiah.

This conception of the Son of Man as a heavenly Messiah found its classic expression in the work of Heinrich Ewald ([1855] 1883: 103–21, 230–33). According to Ewald, after the end of the Davidic dynasty, the Jewish messianic hope was "celestialized." The Messiah was now conceived as a heavenly being, eternally existing in heaven. Such a concept appears in Daniel 7.13, from which the pre-Christian author of 1 Enoch borrowed the name "son of man," turning the phrase into a title for the Messiah. Very soon the book of Enoch was avidly read by certain sections of the people, so that

---

[10] Gfrörer 1838: 2nd Abtheil, 293–94; Lücke [1820] 1840–43: 1.459–65; Hitzig 1843: 133.

the idea of the celestial Messiah became more and more prevalent. Jesus took the name "Son of Man" from Daniel, where it refers to this heavenly Messiah. "When he applied this name to himself, no attentive and instructed reader of the Old Testament could mistake the exalted meaning which must attach to it" (Ewald [1855] 1883: 231).

After Ewald, more and more interpreters began to adopt the view that "Son of Man" as Jesus used it referred to a superhuman, celestial, apocalyptic Messiah.[11] At the turn of the century the superhuman messianic interpretation found several influential advocates, including W. Baldensperger ([1888] 1892), Johannes Weiss ([1892] 1971), R. H. Charles ([1893] 1912), Wilhelm Bousset (1903: 32–33, 57–59), and Albert Schweitzer ([1906] 1968: 267–87). Charles, for example, affirmed that "the Apocalyptic Messiah" of 1 Enoch stands in contrast to the Davidic Messiah of the prophets:

> The Son of Man as portrayed in the Parables is a super-natural being and not a mere man. He is not even conceived as being of human descent . . . This title, with its supernatural attributes of superhuman glory, of universal dominion and supreme judicial powers, was adopted by our Lord.   (Charles [1893] 1912: 307)

Consistent with this view was Charles' translation of chapter 71 of 1 Enoch. In this chapter of the Similitudes, where Enoch himself is apparently identified as the Son of Man, Charles emended the text, eliminating any such identification.

This concept of the Son of Man as a heavenly being received a further boost from scholars who traced the apocalyptic Son of Man to an earlier superhuman figure in non-Jewish religions.[12] Scholars derived the apocalyptic Son of Man from such varied sources as Babylonian myths about Adapa or Ea-Oannes,[13] Iranian (Persian) myths about a Primal Man,[14] and Canaanite myths concerning the

---

[11] Beyschlag 1866: 9–34; [1885–86] 1901–1902: 1.246–55; Keerl 1866: 212–30; Oehler [1854–68] 1883: 2.1479–84; Anger 1873: 81, 84; Keil 1877: 224–28; Hermann Schmidt 1889.

[12] For a historical survey of this view see M. Müller 1984a: 46–63.

[13] A. Jeremias 1899; Hommel 1899/1900; Winckler 1905: 3.2.297–301; H. Jansen 1939.

[14] Bousset 1907: 196–97, 219; 1926: 262–68; Clemen 1909: 116–22; Reitzenstein 1921: 115–23; Creed 1925; von Gall 1926; Kraeling 1927; Mowinckel [1951] 1954: 346–450, esp. 420–37; Riesenfeld 1954: 84.

transfer of power from one deity to another.[15] Though many scholars did not accept these derivations,[16] the suggestions illustrate the degree to which the apocalyptic Son of Man had come to be regarded as a superhuman being.

The idea that "Son of Man" meant a pre-existent heavenly Messiah became the prevailing view through the first six decades of the twentieth century. For some scholars, such a view implied that Jesus used the term of himself with a consciousness of his own divinity or pre-existence in heaven.[17]

Other scholars attacked this view. Paul Billerbeck asserted that "pre-Talmudic Judaism knows nothing of a pre-existent Messiah" (Billerbeck 1905: 150). He argued that in the Similitudes of Enoch, the Messiah or Son of Man has ideal pre-existence in the thought world or world plan of God. He is chosen by God before the world's creation and his identity is kept a secret, but he does not have real pre-existence. He is a human being who has been taken to heaven to dwell and appointed to execute judgment. Rudolf Otto ([1934] 1943: 214–17) and Matthew Black (1948/49a: 14) agreed that the son of man in 1 Enoch has only ideal pre-existence, while T. W. Manson (1950: 126) similarly emphasized the human nature of the Danielic son of man.

Despite these reservations, the superhuman interpretation of the apocalyptic Son of Man prevailed. As Ethelbert Stauffer expressed this view, "'Son of Man' is just about the most pretentious piece of self-description that any man in the ancient East could possibly have used" (Stauffer [1941] 1955: 108).

Date of the Similitudes

The first translators of 1 Enoch dated the book as a whole to the pre-Christian period.[18] It was thus possible to assume that 1 Enoch influenced the Son of Man idea in the New Testament. That view was questioned by de Sacy (1822: 593–94), who saw evidence of a

[15] Emerton 1958; Morgenstern 1960; 1961; Colpe [1969] 1972: 415–19.

[16] E. A. Graham (1931) reviewed the documentary evidence for the Primal Man and concluded that such speculations had no influence on Daniel 7, 1 Enoch, or the New Testament Son of Man. M.-J. Lagrange (1931: 242–58) and William Manson (1943: 7–11, 174–90) also criticized the Iranian Primal Man theory.

[17] Kühl 1907: 65–87; Feine 1910: 48–69; Roslaniec 1920; Headlam 1923: 297–306; A. Ross 1934; Cruvellier 1955: 50; Hammerton-Kelly 1973: 100; Ladd 1974: 145–58, esp. 155.

[18] Laurence 1821: xxvii–xxviii; A. Hoffmann 1833–38.

Christian hand in the book,[19]and by Lücke, who at first concluded
that the book as a whole came from a Christian author.[20]

After Lücke ([1832] 1852: 142) distinguished the Similitudes as an
independent unit within the book, scholars generally accepted the
pre-Christian origin of 1 Enoch, while differing on the date of the
Similitudes. Most accepted a pre-Christian date for the Similitudes
as well.[21] Others maintained that they were a Christian work[22] or
that they contained Christian interpolations.[23] Those who saw a
Christian influence generally felt that the Enochic Son of Man was
derived from the New Testament figure rather than vice versa.

At the end of the nineteenth century, two influential scholars
supported a pre-Christian date for the Similitudes. W. Baldensperger claimed that "the pre-Christian authorship of the Similitudes stands beyond doubt," calling the opposing view
"antiquated" (Baldensperger [1888] 1892: 14; cf. 13). The Similitudes, he said, bear little trace of a Christian character, and no
Christian would identify Enoch with the Son of Man, as appears to
be the case in chapter 71. He emphasized that "the body of ideas in
this writing is presupposed in the documents of the New Testament" (Baldensperger [1888] 1892: 13). R. H. Charles agreed,
dating the Similitudes to the years 94–79 BCE (Charles [1893]
1912: 67, 72–73). Since Charles' work became the standard reference on 1 Enoch for most of the twentieth century, it had a major
influence in establishing a pre-Christian date for the Similitudes as
the prevailing view.[24]

The view of Baldensperger and Charles received further impetus
from the influential works of Johannes Weiss and Albert
Schweitzer. Weiss acknowledged his debt to Baldensperger in
accepting the view that "For Jesus, the proper form in which the
figure of the Messiah was to be thought of was the Son of man of

[19] As did Dorner [1839] 1861–63: 1.152.
[20] Lücke [1832] 1852: 89–144. So also Hofmann 1852; [1853] 1857–60: 1.420–23;
Weisse 1856: 214–24; Ferdinand Philippi 1868.
[21] Lücke [1832] 1852: 142; Ewald 1854; [1855] 1883: 113–14 n. 3; Dillmann 1853:
xxiii–xxiv, 156–57, 160; Köstlin 1858; Weizsäcker 1864: 427–28; Langen 1866: 64;
Sieffert 1867: 27–29; Wittichen 1868: 63 n. 1; Anger 1873: 83; H. Meyer [1876] 1884:
183; Schodde 1882; Wieseler 1882.
[22] Hilgenfeld 1857: 150–84; Colani 1864: 23; Vernes 1874: 187 n. 1; Tideman
1875; Oehler [1854–68] 1883: 2.1482; V. Stanton 1886: 63.
[23] Drummond 1877: 17–73; Stalker 1899: 68.
[24] Reservations about an early date for the Similitudes continued to be expressed
by Hilgenfeld (1888; 1892), Dalman ([1898] 1902: 243), and Drummond (1901:
542–44).

Daniel and *Enoch*" (J. Weiss [1892] 1971: 116). Schweitzer, in turn, supported Weiss, hailing his solution of the Son of Man question as "the only possible one" (Schweitzer [1906] 1968: 282).

After Schweitzer, most scholars took for granted the pre-Christian origin of the Parables.[25] Some, such as Charles (1892/3; [1893] 1912), Otto ([1934] 1943), and Sjöberg (1955), gave more credit to 1 Enoch than to Daniel for shaping Jesus' self-consciousness as the Son of Man. Generally, scholarship seemed content with a pre-Christian date for the entirety of 1 Enoch. That settled opinion for the most part remained undisturbed until the discoveries at Qumran raised the whole issue anew, as described below in Chapter 7.

Disputed issues

While the interpretation of "Son of Man" as an apocalyptic title prevailed until the 1960s, two important issues concerning the title remained in dispute: (1) to whom did the title refer? and (2) which Son of Man sayings (if any) were authentic sayings of Jesus? The positions taken on these questions will be discussed in the next two chapters.

[25] In disagreement, Messel (1922: 4ff.), Lagrange (1931: 243–44), and J. Y. Campbell (1947: 145–48) maintained the Christian origin of the Son of Man passages in the Similitudes, while Glasson ([1945] 1963), Dodd (1953: 241–43), and Fuller (1954: 98) suspected a Christian provenance for the Similitudes as a whole.

4

THE QUESTION OF REFERENCE

If Jesus used the expression "Son of Man," to whom did he refer? The question arises from the fact that in all the Son of Man sayings, Jesus speaks of the Son of Man in the third person, as if referring to someone else, though in most cases the context makes clear that he is speaking of himself. This oddity has given rise to five main interpretations that seek to account for it. (1) Jesus habitually referred to himself in the third person with a title. (2) Jesus referred to himself not with a title, but with an Aramaic idiom by which one could refer to oneself in the third person. Later the church misinterpreted the idiom as a messianic title. (3) Jesus referred not solely to himself, but to a collective or corporate entity which included himself. Later the church misinterpreted the collective reference as a reference to Jesus alone. (4) Jesus referred not to himself, but to another messianic figure distinct from himself. Later the church applied the messianic title to Jesus. (5) Jesus did not speak about himself in the third person, but the early church did. References to the Son of Man in the third person reflect the language of the church speaking about Jesus.

Son of Man as a titular self-designation

The Evangelists leave the impression that Jesus regularly spoke about himself in the third person with a christological title, "the Son of Man." This portrayal was never questioned or explained by interpreters in the pre-critical period. Even now, many accept it as historically accurate without explaining it. Those who have tried to explain such a self-referring title have interpreted it as cryptic, idiomatic, proleptic, or borrowed.

A cryptic self-designation

Some interpreters see the title as intentionally cryptic, used by Jesus to conceal his self-consciousness. They relate this usage to the "messianic secret": Jesus thought of himself as the messianic Son of Man, but since he did not wish to identify himself openly as such, he used the third-person language to conceal his identity (e.g. Schnackenburg 1959: 116). This explanation, however, depends on the historicity of the messianic secret and presupposes that pre-Christian Judaism expected a messianic figure called "the Son of Man," two hypotheses that numerous scholars today would question.

An idiomatic self-designation

Other interpreters have sought to justify the self-referring title as idiomatic, citing parallels from other literature. A. Díez Macho (1981; 1982), for example, calls attention to the use of the third personal pronoun for the first in the Targums. Occasionally, a name in the third person replaces the first personal pronoun. For instance, in Targum Pseudo-Jonathan at Exodus 12.17, Yahweh speaks of himself in the third person, saying, "on this very day *Yahweh* [MT "I"] freed your hosts from the land of Egypt" (Díez Macho 1982: 196). This usage, however, probably arose in translation as the Targumist shifted from Yahweh's first-person perspective in the MT to his own perspective in speaking about Yahweh. From this usage in translation, no conclusions can be drawn concerning the normal spoken language.

A proleptic self-designation

Other scholars see the title as proleptic. They theorize that Jesus used the third-person language to refer not to himself in his present earthly role, but to what he would become in the future, namely the Son of Man. Johannes Weiss ([1892] 1971) apparently introduced this idea. According to Weiss, Jesus preached the kingdom of God as something still completely in the future. Jesus believed not that he already was the Son of Man but that he would *become* the messianic Son of Man of Daniel and Enoch in the future kingdom. Jesus' use of "Son of Man" was thus more a claim for the future than an actual self-designation in his ministry.

Rudolf Otto expressed the same idea. Basing his theory on 1 Enoch, Otto saw Enoch as a prophet who proclaimed the future Son of Man, then was exalted to become the one whom he had proclaimed. Jesus' consciousness of mission clothed itself in these apocalyptic ideas: he knew himself as "the one destined to be the Son of Man" (Otto [1934] 1943: 213). In his ministry, "he worked proleptically with the powers of the Son of Man," but he did not teach that he was already the Son of Man (Otto [1934] 1943: 219). Several scholars followed Weiss and Otto.[1]

Against this position, Morna Hooker stated a decisive objection:

> There is nothing in the Marcan sayings to suggest that Jesus believed that he was destined to "become" Son of man; the "future" sayings all refer to "coming," not "becoming," and none of the other sayings contains a hint that Jesus regards himself as acting only as the Son of man *designatus*.   (Hooker 1967: 188)[2]

A borrowed self-designation

Still other interpreters suggested that Jesus borrowed the expression, taking over a scornful epithet directed against him by his opponents. In the view of Christoph August Heumann (1740), Jesus' enemies called him "the son of the man" in the sense "the son of the plebeian,"[3] and Jesus picked up this third-person expression to refer to himself.

According to David Smith (1906/1907), when John the Baptist announced that Jesus was the Son of God, the multitude responded, "This is no Son of God; he is a *son of man*." Jesus picked up this scornful nickname and used it as a title of lowliness to indicate that his messianic glory was not what they expected: not earthly majesty but the glory of sacrifice.

Similarly, John Pairman Brown (1977: 370–75), taking "son of man" to mean "this fellow" or "this man," saw it as a name given to Jesus by opponents or outsiders. Jesus took up literally what was said about him by others.

---

[1] Mowinckel [1951] 1954: 447–48, 450; Percy 1953: 238–59; Fuller 1954: 103 (Fuller later abandoned this position: Fuller 1965: 122–23); J. Jeremias 1971: 265, 275–76; Higgins 1964: 199–200, 202.

[2] See also the review of Otto by Bultmann (1937).

[3] See Chapter 2 for a discussion of the erroneous view that *adam* in Hebrew refers to a man of the lower classes.

In these three interpretations, the third-person reference originated on the lips of Jesus' opponents, who would naturally speak
about Jesus in the third person. Jesus then took over the title to
speak of himself. All three theories face the objection that the
Gospels never represent Jesus' opponents as using the expression.

Son of man as a nontitular idiom

Since it would be odd to refer to oneself continually with a title,
many scholars have favored the view that Jesus used the expression
"son of man" not as a title, but as some type of Aramaic idiom by
which one could refer to oneself in the third person. Since we will
survey these theories in Chapter 8, we will not discuss them here.

Son of Man as a corporate entity

From a third perspective, Jesus used the title "Son of Man" to refer
not solely to himself, but to a collective or corporate entity, of
which he himself was the head. This interpretation is generally
based on Daniel 7.13, where the "one like a son of man" is a
symbolic figure representing the "saints of the Most High," i.e. the
kingdom or people of God. Some scholars have supposed that
Jesus used the term "Son of Man" in this same symbolic corporate
sense. He naturally referred to this entity in the third person,
though he himself was included in it.

The collective interpretation of "Son of Man" appears, perhaps
for the first time, in the comments of Simon Episcopius (d. 1643) on
Matthew 8.20:

> And so by "Son of Man" Christ here designates not only
> himself, but also all those who were in his service or who
> were ever going to be his disciples; as if it said "The Son of
> Man along with his own," in the manner of the customary
> diction of Holy Scripture, in which the whole kingdom is
> sometimes designated by the name of the king and leader
> alone: as is seen expressly at Daniel 7.13, to which passage
> the Saviour seems to have referred here when he names
> himself Son of Man.   (Episcopius 1650: at Matt. 8.20)

Over two hundred years later, a similar interpretation appeared
in the work of Sytse Hoekstra (1866): Jesus interpreted "son of
man" in Daniel 7.13 not as the Messiah but as a new community of

the saints. This original interpretation was lost in the Gospels, where the expression was applied to Jesus himself.

J. Estlin Carpenter and Albert Réville followed in the same tradition of interpretation, while imparting distinctive nuances to it. For Carpenter, the Son of Man was not a person, but the kingdom of God, understood as "a great moral crisis, in which the divine forces of Love and Truth will be displayed among men" (Carpenter 1890: 248, 387–88). Réville found the collective sense in three sayings (Mark 2.10; 2.28; Matt. 25.31), in which the Son of Man is "humanity conceived in its ideal perfection" (Réville 1897: 2.194).

Most scholars who followed the collective interpretation derived "Son of Man" from Daniel 7.13.[4] According to William Sanday, however, Jesus also had in mind Psalm 8. There he found a collective idea in the term "Son of Man" and regarded himself as the representative of this collective humanity (Sanday 1908: 129). Subsequently, Nils Messel (1922) argued for a corporate interpretation of "son of man" in the Similitudes of Enoch.

The work of T. W. Manson became better known than that of his predecessors, and the corporate interpretation is usually associated with his name (T. Manson [1931] 1935; 1950; 1953). For Manson, the Son of Man is "an ideal figure and stands for the manifestation of the Kingdom of God on earth in a people wholly devoted to their heavenly King" (T. Manson 1935: 227). The term becomes a designation of Jesus alone when his mission to create the Son of Man, the kingdom of God's people, succeeds neither among the people nor among his disciples. Then "he stands alone, embodying in his own person the perfect human response to the regal claims of God" (T. Manson 1935: 228).

After Manson, numerous other scholars adopted the corporate interpretation to one degree or another.[5] Theodore W. Jennings, for example, finds that in the Gospel sayings as a whole the term "the son of man" designates not an individual, but "the new humanity which corresponds to the new creation, the reign of God" (Jennings 1990: 241). This new humanity consists of all who are called to liberate the earth, including John the Baptist, Jesus,

[4] Drummond 1901; Larsen 1902; A. Cadoux 1920; Micklem 1929: 217–18.
[5] C. Cadoux 1943: 90–103; Rowley [1944] 1963: 136–37; Bulcock 1945; W. Wilson 1946; Taylor 1946/47; 1953: 25–35; Black 1948/49b; Cullmann [1957] 1963: 156; Perrin 1963: 90–100; Jay 1965: 32–43; Gaston 1970: 393–95, 408–409; Kellner 1985; Jennings 1990; Moule 1952: 90; 1974: 415; 1977: 20–22; 1995.

and his disciples. C. F. D. Moule, similarly, affirms that Jesus drew the expression from Daniel 7 and used it in a corporate sense as a symbol for himself and his followers as "the people of the saints of the Most High" (Moule 1952; 1974; 1977; 1995).

The weakness of this interpretation is that none of the Son of Man sayings require it, while most demand a reference to Jesus alone. It can only be adopted, therefore, on the assumption that most or all of the sayings have been modified to reflect a more individual reference.

Son of Man as a Messiah other than Jesus

While it would be unnatural to refer to oneself continually in the third person, it would be quite normal to refer to someone else in this way. Some scholars, therefore, have supposed that Jesus distinguished between himself and another individual whom he proclaimed as the coming Son of Man. D. F. Strauss was apparently the first to draw this conclusion (Strauss [1835–36] 1860: 293–301). Noticing that in some sayings Jesus seemed to refer to someone else, while in others he clearly referred to himself, Strauss supposed two stages in Jesus' thought. At first he thought of himself as a forerunner, announcing another as the messianic Son of Man. Only later did he begin to conceive of himself as the Son of Man.[6]

Julius Wellhausen found the same distinction as Strauss (Wellhausen [1905] 1911: 95–96). He explained it, however, not as two stages in Jesus' own thought, but as a difference between the thought of Jesus and the thought of the church. Jesus referred to another figure as the coming Son of Man. Subsequently, however, the early church identified Jesus himself as the Son of Man. Wellhausen found the earlier authentic usage particularly in Mark 8.38 and 13.26. Other scholars of the day likewise saw a distinction between Jesus and the Son of Man in one or another of these passages.[7]

Later Rudolf Bultmann became the most influential proponent of this view. Like Wellhausen, he posited two stages of tradition. The earlier tradition goes back to Jesus, who spoke of another individual as the coming Son of Man. The later tradition arose in

---

[6] In this same tradition stand B. W. Bacon (1922) and David Flusser (1968: 103).
[7] Völter 1907; Foakes Jackson and Lake 1920: 1.377–78.

the early church, which identified Jesus himself as the Son of Man.[8] Numerous scholars followed Bultmann,[9] including H. E. Tödt ([1959] 1965), who wrote the most significant monograph representing this position. Until the late 1960s this reconstruction was one of the most widely accepted solutions of the problem.

The objections traditionally raised against this position are summarized by I. H. Marshall:

> there is no evidence that Jesus expected the coming of some Messianic figure other than himself . . . The evidence that he was really speaking about somebody else rests solely on the alleged distinction found in Luke 12:8f. (*cf.* Mk. 8:38), Mark 14:62 and Matthew 19:28. None of these texts demands to be interpreted in this way, and it is clear that the early church did not think that they referred to somebody else, nor did it find them sufficiently ambiguous to need reformulation . . . The defenders of this view have the utmost difficulty in explaining how Jesus visualized the relationship between himself and this shadowy figure.
>
> (Marshall [1976] 1990: 73)

In addition, this theory has suffered two other serious blows. First, it was based primarily on Mark 8.38 (= Luke 12.8–9 in Q), which Wellhausen and Bultmann took as a genuine saying of Jesus in which he distinguished himself from the Son of Man. Since Bultmann, however, other scholars have argued that this saying is a construction of the early church. Ernst Käsemann took this position because the saying has the character of prophecies uttered by Palestinian Christian prophets (Käsemann [1954] 1964: 43–44; [1954/55] 1969: 77). Philipp Vielhauer developed a further argument against the authenticity of the saying: it reflects a situation that existed in the early church but not in the lifetime of Jesus, namely pressure on Christians to deny their confession of faith in Jesus (Vielhauer 1957: 68–71; 1963: 141–47). Many scholars today, therefore, take the position that the saying is a formulation of the post-Easter church.[10] If the saying is a construction of the church,

---

[8] Bultmann [1921] 1968: 112, 122, 128, 150–52; [1948–53] 1951–55: 1.28–31.

[9] Sharman 1944: 80–83; Bornkamm [1956] 1960: 228–31; R. Casey 1958; Knox 1958: 94–95; Enslin 1961: 137–48; Hahn [1963] 1969: 23–28; Fuller 1965: 121–25; Formesyn 1966: 19–23; Haufe 1966: 140; Balz 1967: 120–25; Jüngel 1967: 215–62; H. Braun 1969: 55–58; Guy 1970.

[10] Kümmel (1975: 211 n. 6) lists Teeple, Haenchen, Perrin, Conzelmann, Gaston, Edwards, Lührmann, P. Hoffmann, Schulz, Seitz, Lohse. Numerous others could be

then its supposed distinction between Jesus and the Son of Man is illusory, since the church would never have designated anyone but Jesus as the Son of Man.

The second problem with the Wellhausen/Bultmann theory is its supposition that Jesus pointed to a Son of Man whose coming was generally expected in the Judaism of his day. Since the late 1960s, many scholars have come to believe that no such expectation existed in pre-Christian Judaism (see Chapter 7). If it did not, Jesus could not have referred to such a figure.

Son of Man as language of the church

The four theories reviewed above share the assumption that Jesus himself used the expression "Son of Man" in some sense. With this assumption they try to explain why Jesus would have referred to the Son of Man in the third person. Other scholars have tried to explain the sayings as primarily creations of the church. In explaining how such sayings of the church came to be attributed to Jesus, Bultmann emphasized the role of Christian prophets (Bultmann [1921] 1968: 127–28). These often spoke in the first person in the name of the risen Lord, and eventually sayings spoken by the risen Jesus through prophets came to be regarded as prophecies of the earthly Jesus. Several scholars have explained the Son of Man sayings from this perspective.[11] However, while this view would explain why "Son of Man" appears primarily in words attributed to Jesus, it would not explain the exclusively third-person speech in most of the sayings (Schweizer 1975: 102). We would expect the risen Jesus no less than the earthly Jesus to speak of himself in the first person (as in Rev. 1–3), not the third.

Third-person speech referring to Jesus would be most natural if someone other than Jesus were speaking not *as* him but *about* him. The simplest explanation of the third-person language is therefore that it represents the language of the church speaking about Jesus. The church would naturally refer to Jesus in the third person.

A few previous scholars have pointed toward this solution of the

mentioned: e.g. Lindeskog 1968: 160; A. Collins 1987: 402. Jacobson is representative: Q/Luke 12.8–9 presupposes "a trial before Jewish elders (?) in which the addressees are told to renounce Jesus, or at least to admit that they are followers of Jesus" (Jacobson 1992: 188).
[11] Käsemann 1969: 82–107, 108–37; Vielhauer 1957: 60, 70; 1963: 171–73; Boring 1982: 239–50.

problem. For William Wrede, the peculiar third-person use of "the Son of Man" indicated that Jesus himself did not use the phrase:

> The most important, even if not the only, argument for the assumption that Jesus did not use this self-designation still appears to me to be the impossibility of imagining in reality a manner of speaking such as that which the Evangelists expect of him. A king can no doubt say once, "the King wills it," and by that mean himself; a constant mode of expression of such a kind, however, would be an absurdity, in the East as well as among us . . . It is merely our early habituation to the words of the Evangelists that allows us to pass over it so easily.   (Wrede 1904: 359)

While Wrede saw the third-person references as evidence that the sayings were not genuine words of Jesus, he offered no explanation for the usage. A few years later, Bousset adopted the same view and suggested an explanation:

> One can indeed also point out a priori that this oft-repeated speech of Jesus about himself in the third person evokes the impression of a certain unnaturalness, if it is taken seriously as historical, but that on the other hand the riddle is immediately solved if we may here recognize in general a stylized form of the community's language and that in particular the oft-recurring formula ἦλθεν ὁ υἱὸς τοῦ ἀνθρώπου from the outset creates the impression of a specifically hieratic stylizing.   (Bousset [1913] 1970: 36)

What Bousset recognized was the simple fact that while we do not normally speak about ourselves in the third person, other people do so refer to us. If Jesus spoke normally, he no more spoke about himself in the third person than anyone else. The early church, however, did refer to him in the third person. The third-person references to Jesus as the Son of Man may thus reflect the language of the church speaking about Jesus, not Jesus' language about himself.

The Son of Man tradition has preserved one clear example of this natural third-person usage. In Acts 7.56 Stephen refers to the Son of Man:

> Behold I see the heavens opened and the Son of Man standing at the right hand of God.

Here the third-person language about the Son of Man is natural in the mouth of an early Christian evangelist speaking about Jesus. If Bousset is correct, this saying preserves the original context in which third-person language about the Son of Man arose: the early Palestinian church speaking about Jesus.

It is possible that if more non-Gospel material from early Palestinian Christianity had survived, we would see more examples of the type of Son of Man saying represented by Acts 7.56. However, most of the material that we have from Palestinian Christianity occurs in the Gospels. In that context, the Son of Man sayings have been attributed to Jesus himself. This attribution produces the impression that Jesus spoke about himself in the third person.

An analogous phenomenon occurs in third-person references to "the Son" or "the Son of God" on the lips of Jesus. Son of Man researchers have generally overlooked the fact that the Jesus of the Gospels refers to himself with other christological titles besides "Son of Man." He speaks of himself in the third person as "the Son"[12] as well as "the Son of God."[13] Such third-person language occurs, for example, in John 3.16–18:

> For God so loved the world that he gave his only *Son*, so that everyone who believes in *him* should not perish but have eternal life. For God sent *the Son* into the world not to judge the world, but so that the world might be saved through *him*. He who believes in *him* is not judged; but he who does not believe has already been judged, because he has not believed in the name of the only *Son of God*.

This passage, attributed to Jesus, consistently refers to him in the third person as "the Son," "the Son of God," or simply as "him." Such language attributed to Jesus in speaking about himself differs in no respect from the third-person language attributed to John the Baptist in speaking about Jesus:

> The Father loves *the Son* and has put everything in *his* hand. He who believes in *the Son* has eternal life. He who disbelieves *the Son* shall not see life.　　(John 3.35–36)

---

[12] Mark 13.32 (Matt. 24.36); Luke 10.22 (Matt. 11.27); John 3.16, 17; 5.19, 20, 21, 22, 23, 26; 6.40; 8.36; 14.13; 17.1.

[13] John 3.18; 5.25; 11.4.

No critical Johannine scholar today believes that these words were actually spoken by the historical Jesus or the historical John. They represent the christology of the Johannine community. Language of the community speaking about Jesus has been retrojected onto the lips of John the Baptist and Jesus. These examples may provide a basis for understanding the similar third-person references to the Son of Man in the Gospels: the church retrojected its own language about Jesus as the Son of Man onto the lips of Jesus himself. Since this issue is related to the question of the authenticity of Son of Man sayings, we will return to it at the end of the following chapter.

5

THE QUESTION OF AUTHENTICITY

A second disputed issue, beyond the question of reference, is the question of which sayings actually represent the words of Jesus. In the pre-critical period, interpreters never raised this question, simply assuming that all the sayings attributed to Jesus were actually spoken by him. The question arose once scholars began to recognize different classes of Son of Man sayings, classes which seemed difficult to reconcile under a single concept. With the advent of the apocalyptic explanation of "Son of Man," scholars began to see two categories of sayings represented in the Gospels: the apocalyptic sayings, which spoke of the future coming of the Son of Man, and the non-apocalyptic sayings.[1] Other scholars further subdivided the second category into sayings relating to Jesus' earthly ministry in general and those relating specifically to his death and resurrection. Thus developed the three groupings familiar today: sayings concerning the (present) earthly Son of Man, the suffering Son of Man, and the (future) coming Son of Man. Though this threefold grouping is sometimes credited to Bultmann ([1948–53] 1951–55: 1.30), it actually appears in the works of numerous earlier scholars.[2]

For those who accepted the apocalyptic origin of Son of Man, the question became how to relate the apocalyptic sayings to the non-apocalyptic sayings in the Gospels. If the Son of Man was an apocalyptic figure who would come only at the end-time, how could Jesus speak of himself as the Son of Man already in his earthly ministry? As Bousset stated the problem,

---

[1] Baldensperger [1888] 1892: 171–73; Cone 1893; Westcott 1908: 1.75–76; Holzinger 1920: 102.

[2] E.g. A. Bruce [1889] 1909: 172–77; Oort 1893 (according to Lietzmann 1896: 22); Rhees 1898: 98; Stevens 1899: 41; Rose 1900: 172; Bartmann 1904: 92; Roslaniec 1920: 78; Rawlinson 1926: 247–48.

> if the Son of Man can only mean the supra-terrestrial transcendent Messiah, as now is generally acknowledged, then we cannot explain how Jesus already in the present could claim for himself the predicate and rights of the Son of Man.   (Bousset [1913] 1970: 40)

Furthermore, if the apocalyptic Son of Man was exclusively a triumphant figure, how could Jesus use the term with reference to his suffering and death? At first many scholars did not clearly see the problem. Those who did offered differing solutions to it. One type of solution was to deny that Jesus actually spoke both kinds of sayings: either the apocalyptic or the non-apocalyptic sayings were judged creations of the church. Another type of solution was to seek a way of reconciling all types of sayings as genuine, while still another was to deny the authenticity of all the sayings.

Only non-apocalyptic sayings authentic

Hermann Samuel Reimarus ([1778] 1970) was the first to challenge the authenticity of the future Son of Man sayings. According to Reimarus, Jesus thought of himself as the Davidic Messiah in the political sense of the prophets. After this hope ended with Jesus' death, his disciples fell back on a second strand of messianic expectation: the Danielic concept of a Messiah who would come with the clouds. While the disciples created the eschatological sayings about the Son of Man, Jesus' own use of the phrase "pointed to a self-diminution and lowliness" (Reimarus [1778] 1970: 51).

In the nineteenth century, James Martineau ([1890] 1891: 335–57) and Orello Cone (1893) took the same view: Jesus himself used the term to indicate his humanity, while the church created the apocalyptic sayings. In the twentieth century, such a view was expressed by Dougall and Emmet (1922: 275–96), but is associated primarily with the name of Eduard Schweizer. According to Schweizer, Jesus drew primarily on Ezekiel for his concept of the Son of Man as a lowly, rejected, humiliated man who is nevertheless exalted by God to be the chief witness at the last judgment (Schweizer 1960: 121–22; 1970: 166–71). The parousia sayings, on the other hand, were created by a Jewish-apocalyptic group in the early church (Schweizer 1962/63: 259–60).

Several other scholars likewise accept only the non-eschatological sayings as authentic.[3] Exponents of the idiomatic/nontitular origin of "son of man" also generally accept only the present sayings as authentic and attribute the apocalyptic sayings to the church (see Chapter 8).

Only apocalyptic sayings authentic

Directly opposed to the preceding is the view that sees only the future (apocalyptic) sayings as genuine. During the nineteenth century, scholarship came increasingly to conclude that Jesus derived the title "Son of Man" from Jewish apocalyptic. This trend culminated in Albert Schweitzer's confident assertion:

> Broadly speaking . . . the Son-of-Man problem is both historically solvable and has been solved. The authentic passages are those in which the expression is used in that apocalyptic sense which goes back to Daniel.
>
> (Schweitzer [1906] 1968: 283)[4]

Following Weiss and Schweitzer, the school of Wellhausen and Bultmann (see Chapter 4) also accepted the primacy of the apocalyptic sayings. Bultmann drew a logical conclusion from these presuppositions: sayings which speak of the Son of Man as an earthly figure could only have developed after the original apocalyptic meaning of the title was forgotten. The original connection of the title to Daniel 7.13 has disappeared in these sayings. Any saying which applies the title "Son of Man" to the earthly Jesus is therefore a later Hellenistic product (Bultmann [1921] 1968: 155). For Bultmann, the Son of Man sayings concerning Jesus' earthly ministry originally referred to humans in general or used "son of man" in some other nontitular sense. The passion predictions were *vaticinia ex eventu*, created by the early church. Of the apocalyptic sayings, only those are authentic which distinguish the Son of Man as a figure different from Jesus. Thus the only occurrences of "Son of Man" as a title which go back to Jesus are Mark 8.38 (Luke 12.8–9 in Q), Luke 17.23–24, and possibly Matthew 24.37–39, 43–44.[5]

---

[3] Boman 1967: 148–83, esp. 160–63; K. Müller 1972–73; Hammerton-Kelly 1973: 95–96.

[4] Though this quotation might suggest otherwise, Schweitzer, following Johannes Weiss (1892), apparently included the passion predictions along with the future sayings as authentic sayings containing the Danielic/apocalyptic sense.

[5] Bultmann [1921] 1968: 112, 122, 128, 150–52; [1948–53] 1951–55: 1.28–31. Before Bultmann, Wellhausen ([1905] 1911) found the authentic usage, in which

Similar positions were taken by A. J. B. Higgins (1964: 185–95), Joachim Jeremias (1967; 1971: 257–76), and Carsten Colpe ([1969] 1972: 430–38), who likewise found that the only authentic titular sayings were apocalyptic. Higgins and Jeremias further agreed with Bultmann that these sayings distinguish Jesus from the Son of Man, but only in the sense that Jesus distinguished between himself in the present and the Son of Man that he would become in the future.[6]

Both apocalyptic and non-apocalyptic sayings authentic

Other scholars have accepted the apocalyptic explanation without rejecting the non-apocalyptic sayings. In the following ways, they have sought to reconcile the apocalyptic origin of the term "Son of Man" with Jesus' use of it in his earthly ministry.

Proleptic or hidden Son of Man

According to one view, in referring to himself as the Son of Man already in his earthly ministry, Jesus spoke proleptically. This theory builds on the work of Johannes Weiss (1892) and Rudolf Otto (1934), who agreed that Jesus used "Son of Man" to designate not himself in the present, but what he would become in the future. R. H. Fuller (1954: 106–108) used this idea to support the authenticity of the earthly Son of Man sayings: since Jesus already functioned in his ministry as the one who would become the Son of Man, he spoke of himself proleptically as such. Fuller later abandoned this view (Fuller 1965: 122–23).

Erik Sjöberg (1955) proposed a similar theory: Jesus spoke in his earthly ministry as the "hidden" Son of Man awaiting his future revelation. Sjöberg emphasized the idea of concealment associated with the Son of Man in 1 Enoch: he is pre-existent but remains concealed in heaven until his revelation at the end-time. So too, Jesus used language that concealed his identity on earth. He would reveal himself as the Son of Man only at the parousia.[7]

Jesus distinguished the Son of Man from himself, particularly in Mark 8.38 and 13.26. Völter (1907) found it in Luke 17.22–30 and Mark 8.38.

[6] Similarly Percy (1953: 256), who, however, takes as authentic not only the parousia sayings but also Matt. 8.20, 11.19, and 12.32.

[7] Sjöberg is criticized by Tödt [1959] 1965: 297–302; Burkill [1961] 1972: 26–38; Higgins 1964: 21.

According to another theory of prolepsis, Jesus called himself the Son of Man already in his earthly incarnation because the end-time had already come in his ministry and eschatological concepts were therefore transferred into the present.[8]

A revised Son of Man

Other scholars reconcile the different types of sayings by assuming that Jesus revised the apocalyptic Son of Man concept to include the idea of suffering. W. Baldensperger, for example, believed that Jesus took over the idea of a heavenly, pre-existent Messiah from Jewish apocalyptic but consciously revised the idea to include humiliation and suffering. He did this as a conscious protest against the elevated ideal of the Jewish sovereign (W. Baldensperger [1888] 1892: 171–73).

Scholars who take this approach most commonly assume that Jesus revised the apocalyptic Son of Man concept by combining it with the idea of the suffering Servant of God described in Isaiah 53. This suggestion, which appeared already in the work of Carl Wittichen (1868: 142–43, 145–46), is more often associated with the name of R. H. Charles (1892/93; [1893] 1912: 306–309). According to Charles, the synthesis of these two antithetical ideas explains the contrasts connected with the expression "Son of Man" in the New Testament. Charles, followed by several other scholars, explained the Gospel usage as a synthesis between the Enochic Son of Man and the suffering Servant.[9] Numerous other scholars have argued for a similar synthesis between the Danielic son of man and the suffering Servant.[10] Still others posit a combination of the suffering Servant with the Son of Man that is represented in both Daniel and 1 Enoch.[11]

While most of these authors have argued that Jesus himself

---

[8] Cullmann [1957] 1963: 159; Kümmel [1969] 1973: 83.

[9] Evans 1900; Otto [1934] 1943: 244–61; Archibald 1950/51; Sjöberg 1955; Hutchinson 1961; Paul 1961: 199–201.

[10] Klöpper 1899; Feine 1910: 48–69; A. Ross 1934; Rowley [1944] 1963: 136; Mouson 1952; Feuillet 1953; Taylor 1953: 32–35; Cruvellier 1955; France 1971: 148; Ladd 1974: 145–58; Zorn 1980; Coppens 1981: 151; Sabourin 1983; Betz 1985: 175; Simmons 1985: 95–96; Marshall [1976] 1990: 67, 77; 1991.

[11] Sanday 1908: 122–30; Moffatt 1912: 150–63; Headlam 1923: 297–306; Grand-maison [1928] 1930–34: 2.22–31, 111–13; Bowman 1943: 117–53; W. Manson 1943: 117–18; Mowinckel [1951] 1954: 346–450; Preiss 1951; Delorme 1954; Riesenfeld 1954: 91–92; Seethaler 1956; Cullmann [1957] 1963: 160–61; I. Sanders 1958; Johnson 1962: 4.415; Cambe 1963.

combined the Servant with the apocalyptic Son of Man, a few have assumed that Son of Man and suffering Servant were already connected before Jesus in Jewish apocalyptic.[12] Joachim Jeremias, who at one time held this view, subsequently withdrew his thesis, recognizing that while the Similitudes of Enoch do portray the Son of Man with traits drawn from the Servant, these traits do not include suffering.[13]

The widespread view that the Son of Man has been fused with the suffering Servant in the sayings of Jesus was challenged by C. F. D. Moule (1952; 1977). For Moule, the Son of Man in the Gospels is not a redemptive figure like the Servant, but one who is vindicated after rejection. C. K. Barrett (1959; 1972) and Morna Hooker (1959) likewise found reason to doubt the influence of the suffering Servant on the Son of Man sayings.

A Danielic son of man who suffers

From another perspective, the three types of sayings are not inconsistent, since Jesus found both future coming and present suffering already inherent in the Danielic son of man. According to W. D. Davies,

> the Son of Man in Daniel is a suffering figure – he represents the Saints of the Most High who are persecuted.
> (Davies [1948] 1980: 280 n. 1)

C. F. D. Moule developed this idea: Jesus interpreted the son of man in Daniel 7.13 in a corporate sense as a symbol for "the people of the saints of the Most High." Since the saints suffer, the Son of Man is a suffering figure. Jesus applied this corporate Son of Man symbol to himself and his followers, including the suffering associated with it. Hence, sayings which speak of Jesus' present humiliation and suffering can be explained from Daniel 7 just as adequately as the sayings concerning his future exaltation. For Moule, therefore, all types of sayings are potentially authentic, all reflecting a unified conception rooted in Daniel, a conception that

[12] Staerk 1933: 77–84, 86; Cranfield [1959] 1963: 272–77; F. Bruce 1968: 26–30, 97–99; 1982: 58–59, 61–65.
[13] J. Jeremias [1957] 1965: 61 n. 255a. For a fuller discussion of this question, see Rowley ([1952] 1965: 77–85), who finds no serious evidence that the suffering Servant was identified with Son of Man before the Christian era. Likewise Mowinckel [1951] 1954: 410–15.

is intelligible in the setting of Jesus' ministry (Moule 1952; 1974; 1977; 1995). A number of scholars have taken basically the same position.[14]

A significant objection to this theory is that it requires a corporate interpretation of the Danielic son of man: he would be a suffering figure only if he were identified with the saints who suffer in Daniel 7. Yet most of the New Testament Son of Man sayings refuse to be interpreted in a corporate sense. None of the coming Son of Man sayings can be interpreted corporately, since the Son of Man comes not *as* the saints, but to gather the saints (Mark 13.26–27). Even if all the rest of the sayings could be interpreted corporately, the coming Son of Man sayings would still reflect an unrelated interpretation.

Some of these scholars speak of the Son of Man as a "representative" figure rather than as a corporate figure. Yet this does not alleviate the difficulty, since the one like a son of man in Daniel does not appear until after the saints have suffered and therefore represents them only in their elevation to authority.[15] Furthermore, the allusions to Daniel 7.13 in the Gospel Son of Man sayings are to the triumph of the Son of Man, not to his sufferings (France 1971: 128–30).

Unifying theme

Other scholars have argued for a central theme that unifies all categories of Son of Man sayings. H. E. Tödt, for instance, found the theme of the Son of Man's "authority" running through all the sayings: "Hence we see that the bridge connecting all three groups of Son of Man sayings is Jesus' full authority" (Tödt [1959] 1965: 218). This thesis fails because, as Perrin pointed out, the only Son of Man sayings that refer to Jesus' authority are Mark 2.10 and 2.28. Tödt has to read the theme of authority into the other sayings (Perrin 1974: 69–70).

Though Tödt argued for a unifying theme, like Bultmann he accepted only certain apocalyptic sayings as genuine. Morna

---

[14] Fuller 1954: 103–106; Coppens 1961a; 1961b: 85–92; Goppelt 1963: 30–31; Hooker 1967: 27–30, 192; 1991; Longenecker 1969; 1970: 87–88; G. Stanton 1974: 160–61; Tuckett 1981; 1982: 60; E. Sanders 1985: 324 n. 7; M. de Jonge 1988: 172, 178; 1991; Davies and Allison 1988–91: 2.43–50.

[15] Rowley [1952] 1965: 64 n. 3; France 1971: 128–30; F. Bruce 1982: 58; Meeks 1993: 45–46.

Hooker (1967; 1991), on the other hand, used Tödt's theory to argue for the authenticity of all classes of sayings in Mark. She found the same uniting theme of authority in Mark that Tödt had found in the sayings in general:

> all [the Marcan sayings] are expressions of this authority, whether it is an authority which is exercised now, which is denied and so leads to suffering, or which will be acknowledged and vindicated in the future.   (Hooker 1967: 180)[16]

With respect to the theme of authority, Hooker's theory is subject to the same criticisms as those raised against Tödt's. Hooker also seeks a further means of relating the different groups of sayings: she adopts the theory of Moule (see above) that the Danielic son of man is a suffering figure (Hooker 1967: 27–30, 192). Moule believes that Jesus interpreted the Danielic son of man in a corporate sense: as a symbol for the saints of God both in their suffering and in their exaltation. Hence Jesus can speak of the Danielic son of man as both a suffering and an exalted figure. All the sayings are thus related under a single concept to Daniel 7.13. Hooker recognizes the difficulty of interpreting the New Testament sayings corporately and drops this aspect of Moule's theory: "The Son of man in the gospels, however, is not a truly corporate figure, as in Daniel" (Hooker 1967: 181). In making this move, however, she pulls the rug out from under the very theory that she wishes to maintain. If the Gospels do not equate the Son of Man with the saints, then the Gospel Son of Man is not a suffering figure, for it is the saints in Daniel's vision who do the suffering.

Robert Maddox also sees a unified conception in all three types of sayings, the theme that "the Son of Man is he who carries out ultimate judgment" (Maddox 1968: 73). This unity suggests to him that all types of sayings could be authentic. Maddox has to work hard exegetically, however, to find this theme in the sayings concerning Jesus' earthly ministry and suffering.

No sayings authentic

Since the middle of the nineteenth century, numerous scholars have argued that none of the sayings are authentic: Jesus never used the

---

[16] I. H. Marshall agrees that the theme of authority runs throughout the Son of Man sayings (Marshall [1976] 1990: 77).

expression "Son of Man." Reasons for this judgment include the absence of the expression from New Testament writings earlier than the Gospels, psychological considerations, historical considerations, and critical analysis of the Gospel traditions.

Absence of the expression outside of the Gospels

Bruno Bauer began this tradition when he affirmed that the expression "Son of Man" was created where it first appears in the literature – in the Gospel of Mark. Jesus himself did not use the term (B. Bauer 1841–42: 3.14–17). Bauer did not elaborate, but his conclusion appears to be based on the absence of "Son of Man" from New Testament writings earlier than Mark.

This reasoning was made explicit by Gustav Volkmar (1876: 197–200; 1882: 153–55). The fact that the term is absent from Paul and Revelation[17] indicated to Volkmar that it had not been developed at that time: it was created later by Mark. The title was the result of post-Easter Christian reflection on Jesus' resurrection and enthronement at God's right hand: the church saw Jesus as the man who fulfilled Daniel's vision of the Messiah. Several other scholars came to the same conclusion.[18]

Psychological considerations

Frederick Grant gave another reason for doubting that Jesus referred to himself as the Son of Man:

> For any human being to identify himself with the "Son of Man" of the visions of Enoch, taken literally and without reinterpretation, could suggest little else than an unsound mind. (Grant 1940: 63)

Grant takes the view that it was Jesus' resurrection that led the early church to view him as Messiah and to identify him with both the Son of Man and the suffering Servant (Grant 1940: 64). Other scholars have accepted the psychological argument without concluding that Jesus did not use the expression "Son of Man." John Knox (1958: 52–76, 86–102), for example, used the argument to support the view that Jesus referred not to himself but to another as

[17] The expression in Rev. 1.13 and 14.14 is not articular.
[18] Jacobsen 1886; Pfleiderer [1887] 1906–11: 2.475–84; Brandt 1893: 562–68; Lietzmann 1896: 80.

the Son of Man. Still others have questioned the validity of the argument itself (Hodgson 1961).

Historical considerations

From a historical perspective, Shirley Jackson Case argued that "It was far easier for Christians in the latter half of the first century to designate Jesus 'Son of Man' than it would have been for him in his own lifetime to so style himself" (Case 1927b: 366–67; 1927a: 17). On the one hand, it is improbable that Jesus designated himself by the title:

> The Son of Man in Jewish apocalyptic speculation was not to appear on earth until the day of judgment . . . In this imagery where would Jesus find any likeness to himself?
> (Case 1927b: 370–71; 1927a: 18)[19]

Further, it is improbable that Jesus referred to another figure as the Son of Man: if Jesus had persistently spoken of another as the coming Son of Man, the disciples would have found it more difficult than they did to substitute Jesus for this figure.

On the other hand, the disciples' motivation for identifying Jesus as the Son of Man are readily apparent. They had been ready to identify him as the Davidic political Messiah. When his death threatened to end this hope, they revised the Jewish eschatological scheme by identifying their crucified master with the apocalyptic Son of Man who would return on the clouds to establish his kingdom. They soon attributed their own perspective to Jesus himself. Case concludes:

> For Jesus himself to have made the specific revisions of Jewish messianic thinking that were effected by his disciples, would have been a glaring anachronism. He would have had to anticipate an extended series of events whose historical emergence belongs exclusively to the subsequent experiences of the disciples . . . the motives which had inspired them to revise current Jewish imagery are readily

[19] Cf. the related argument of Howard M. Teeple: "Jesus surely must not have identified himself with the Son of man, because the latter does not fit his career. If Jesus thought of himself as a human being born on earth [even by a virgin], he could not have identified himself with a heavenly, pre-existent supernatural being" (Teeple 1965: 220).

discerned . . . The ultimate problem is to discover any incentive that would have prompted him to anticipate their later way of thinking. (Case 1927b: 374–76)

B. Harvie Branscomb (1937: 146–49, 156–59) presented similar arguments.

Critical analysis of the Gospel traditions

Further arguments against the genuineness of the Son of Man tradition came from scholars who subjected the individual sayings or groups of sayings to critical analysis. In the nineteenth century, Henricus Lucas Oort (1893) judged the passion predictions to be *vaticinia ex eventu.*[20] A further series of passages could not have been spoken by Jesus in the context in which they stand. The parousia passages would make Jesus a visionary who expected divine glorification, but the picture of Jesus in the Gospels does not support such a view. As to the passages in which the emphasis is laid on Jesus' humanity, the authenticity of the formula is possible but not demonstrable.

In the early twentieth century, Wilhelm Bousset ([1913] 1970: 42) and Carl S. Patton (1922) likewise gave critical analyses that led them to attribute the entire Son of Man tradition to the Christian community.

Later Ernst Käsemann ([1954]; [1954/55]) also denied the authenticity of all the Son of Man sayings, even Mark 8.38, which his teacher Bultmann had declared genuine. In Käsemann's opinion this saying preserves the character of prophecies uttered by Palestinian Christian prophets. Jesus therefore did not speak of the Son of Man at all. The title reflects the christology of post-Easter Christianity and found its way into the Jesus tradition through the pronouncements of Christian prophets speaking in the name of the exalted Jesus.

Philipp Vielhauer (1957; 1963) mounted a two-pronged attack

---

[20] A view also expressed by Otto Pfleiderer: "The thought of a redemption through the atoning power of the death of Jesus the Messiah could not well arise until the fact of this death had become the subject of apologetic reflection with a view to removing the offence of the cross. The most obvious explanation was to suppose that the suffering and death of Jesus were determined beforehand by the divine decree, and were either permitted or brought about by the divine providence in order to test him and to prepare the way to his messianic exaltation" (Pfleiderer [1887] 1906–11: 2.485).

against the authenticity of the Son of Man tradition. First, he showed that, outside of redactional material, the two concepts of kingdom of God and Son of Man are never connected in the sayings of Jesus. They stand as two independent strands of tradition. Likewise, he maintains, the two ideas are not connected in Jewish thought. In fact, the two concepts are incompatible. He therefore infers that the concepts in the Gospels have different origins. Since sayings about the kingdom of God can more certainly be assigned to Jesus, sayings about the Son of Man stem from the church. Second, Vielhauer's tradition-historical analysis of individual Son of Man sayings comes to the same conclusion: none of the sayings originated with Jesus. He agrees with Käsemann that Mark 8.38 (Luke 12.8–9 in Q) is a community construction. It presupposes the situation of the church under persecution, a situation in which confession or denial of Jesus' person is the criterion of salvation. Though Vielhauer's work has stimulated a good measure of disagreement, the judgment of Hendrikus Boers is accepted by many: "Vielhauer's exegetical arguments have been questioned, but not disproved" (Boers 1972: 306).

Norman Perrin agreed that Jesus did not use the title Son of Man and described how the sayings might have arisen in the early church.[21] His most significant conclusions are the following:

(1) The Christian Son of Man tradition originated in christological exegesis of scripture in the early church. The heart of Perrin's work on the Synoptic Son of Man is his article on Mark 14.62 (Perrin 1974: 10–22). Here he argued that the Son of Man saying in Mark 14.62 is "the end product of a Christian pesher tradition." That is, it resulted from Christians interpreting the Old Testament in a way similar to the "pesher" method employed in the Qumran texts. Like the Qumran community, the early Christians used Old Testament passages to interpret events within their own experience, exercising significant freedom with respect to the wording of the passages. Perrin described the process as follows:

> (1) There is a point of origin in Christian experience or expectation. (2) This experience or expectation is then interpreted in terms of Old Testament passages as in the Qumran *pesharim*. This is the Christian pesher. (3) The Christian pesher can then be *historicized*, i.e., a narrative can be formed from it or it can be read back into the

[21] Perrin 1965/66; 1966; 1967: 164–99; 1967/68; 1968a; 1968b; 1974; 1976.

teaching of Jesus. (4) The pesher itself, or its historicization, can then become the basis for further theologizing.

(Perrin 1974: 10–11)

(2) The New Testament Son of Man sayings reflect two distinct
traditions of interpreting Daniel 7.13 messianically: one in which
the Son of Man goes from earth to God and one in which he comes
from God to earth. These interpretations occur in "two originally
separate strands in the Christian pesher tradition," which Perrin
calls "Pesher 1" and "Pesher 2," respectively.

Pesher 1 interpreted Daniel 7.13 as the Messiah going to God
from earth. It had its point of origin in the resurrection of Jesus.
Early Christians interpreted that event in light of Psalm 110.1:
Jesus ascended to heaven to sit at the right hand of God (Acts
2.34; Mark 12.35–37; Rom. 8.34; Eph. 1.20; Col. 3.1). In this
strand of the pesher tradition, Psalm 110.1 became linked with
Daniel 7.13, similarly interpreted as an ascent to heaven. Such a
pesher is historicized in Stephen's vision, where Stephen sees the
Son of Man (Dan. 7.13) standing at the right hand of God (Ps.
110.1). A further historicization occurs in Acts 1.9, where the
disciples see Jesus lifted up (Ps. 110.1) and taken out of their sight
in a cloud (Dan. 7.13).

Pesher 2 interpreted Daniel 7.13 as the Messiah coming to earth
from God. It originated as passion apologetic, interpreting the
crucifixion as a fulfillment of Zechariah 12.10ff.: "they will look on
him whom they have pierced." This passage was then linked with
Daniel 7.13, interpreted as a reference to Jesus' descent from
heaven at the parousia. This took the apologetic a step further: they
would see the one they crucified coming as the Son of Man. This
pesher occurs in Revelation 1.7: "Behold, he is coming with the
clouds [Dan. 7.13], and every eye will see him, every one who
pierced him; and all the tribes of the earth will wail on account of
him [Zech. 12.10–14]." The pesher has been historicized in Mark
13.26 as a word of Jesus: "And then they will see [Zech. 12.10] the
Son of Man coming in the clouds [Dan. 7.13]." It has also been
used as the basis for theologizing in John 1.51.

According to Perrin, Pesher 1 and Pesher 2 have been conflated
in Mark 14.62: "And you will see the Son of Man sitting at the
right hand of Power and coming with the clouds of heaven." Pesher
1 accounts for "the Son of Man sitting at the right hand of Power"
(Dan. 7.13 as ascent, and Ps. 110.1). To this is joined Pesher 2:

"And you will see the Son of Man . . . coming with the clouds of heaven" (Dan. 7.13 as descent, and Zech. 12.10).

According to Perrin, the church developed the present and suffering Son of Man sayings through further reflection on the Son of Man. Thus all categories of sayings arose in the church. Hendrikus Boers (1972: 310–15) and William O. Walker (1972; 1983) have supported and refined Perrin's thesis.

The analyses of Käsemann, Vielhauer, and Perrin, supplemented by other independent analyses, have thus convinced a growing number of scholars that the Son of Man sayings as a whole are formulations of the Christian community.[22] The primary objection to this conclusion has been the fact that almost all Son of Man sayings occur on the lips of Jesus. Many scholars have taken this feature of the tradition as evidence that the expression originated with Jesus himself. Such an inference, however, does not necessarily follow. As we discussed in Chapter 4, the titles "Son of God" and "Son" also appear on the lips of Jesus, especially in the Fourth Gospel. In this case, it is clear that the language of the Johannine community about Jesus has been retrojected onto the lips of Jesus himself. If these titles had not also been preserved on the lips of early Christians, we would be left with the impression that Jesus himself had originated them. Something of this sort may well have happened with the title "Son of Man." Possibly, as early Jewish Christians spoke about Jesus as the Son of Man, this title came to be retrojected onto the lips of Jesus. Unlike the title "Son of God," however, the title "Son of Man" did not continue in use once Christianity spread outside of a Jewish context. Its original use on the lips of Jewish Christians was therefore not preserved except in isolated instances, such as Acts 7.56. Its use on the lips of Jesus, however, as part of the tradition about Jesus, was preserved and even augmented in the further development of the tradition. Thus the presence of this title primarily on the lips of Jesus does not refute the conclusions of those scholars who, on various grounds, have argued that it originated in early Christianity.

[22] Conzelmann 1957; [1959] 1973: 43–46; [1968] 1969: 131–37; Marxsen [1960] 1969: 22–43; Boers 1962: 70; 1972; Ory 1964; Teeple 1965; Koester 1971: 138, 170–72, 186–87, 213–14; Walker 1972; 1983; Lohse [1974] 1984: 45–49; Edwards 1971: 87; 1976: 36; Mack 1988: 71 n. 14, 102–103; Vögtle 1989: 95; P. Hoffmann 1991: 194–97.

6

MISCELLANEOUS SONS OF MEN

Some theories about the Son of Man have gained less popularity than others. Some of the less widely held theories are those that derive the New Testament expression from Ezekiel, the Psalms, or Primal Man speculation. One theory equates the titles "Son of Man" and "Son of God." While most scholars have focused on the expression in the Synoptics, others have examined the expression in the Fourth Gospel.

Son of man in Ezekiel

In the book of Ezekiel, God addresses the prophet on numerous occasions as "son of man" (*ben adam*). Since the Reformation, some scholars have argued that Jesus employed this term (or its Aramaic equivalent) in the same way that it is employed in Ezekiel. But how is it used in Ezekiel? Depending upon the interpreter, it expresses prophetic office, human lowliness, or ideal humanity.

Ezekiel's son of man as prophet

One of the earliest interpreters to appeal to Ezekiel as a source for the Gospel expression "Son of Man" was Martin Chemnitz (d. 1586). According to Chemnitz, Ezekiel was called "son of man" by God "because he had been sent by God into public office and ministry in the congregation" (Chemnitz 1600: 2.150 at John 3.13). Thus Jesus used "Son of Man" (among other reasons) because it expressed his office as a prophet. This interpretation reappears occasionally in the seventeenth and eighteenth centuries.[1]

In the nineteenth century, Maurice Vernes (1874: 186–88) gave

---

[1] Fessel 1650–58: 2.34 (Son of Man expresses "prophetic office and ministry"); Gerhard, according to Böhme 1839: 144 n. (it expresses "prophetic office").

the same explanation: when Jesus called himself "the Son of Man," it signified "the prophet," as in Ezekiel. Like John the Baptist, Jesus was a prophet charged to announce the imminent coming of Yahweh. The early church, however, related the title to the Danielic figure, so that it took on a messianic significance that was alien to the thought of Jesus.

George Lovell Cary took this interpretation into the twentieth century. Noting that nine-tenths of all Old Testament passages containing "son of man" occur in Ezekiel, where God addresses Ezekiel as such, Cary concludes that "Jesus, in speaking of himself as 'the Son of Man,' intended to announce himself as a prophet, sent to warn his people of the danger which threatened them if they did not turn from their evil ways" (Cary 1900: 363).[2]

For Daniel Völter, too, Jesus used the term "Son of Man" to identify himself with Ezekiel (Völter 1916; cf. 1907; 1914). Like Ezekiel, he had a prophetic call. Also like Ezekiel, he had a call as a savior, a mission to seek and save the lost among his people. Eventually he came to realize that this would involve suffering and death. After Jesus' death, the Son of Man passages which allude to Daniel or Enoch were created by the church.

Pierson Parker (1941) agreed that "Son of Man" carried no messianic implication either before Jesus or as used by him. As Jesus used the title it indicated "prophetic leadership," as in pre-Christian literature, where the term is applied to Ezekiel, Daniel, and Enoch, each of whom received prophetic revelation.

Ezekiel's son of man as lowly human

For other scholars, "son of man" in Ezekiel expressed not so much prophetic office as human lowliness. According to Pierre Batiffol (1905: 194–200), Jesus combined the humble servant idea in Ezekiel with the servant of God in Isaiah. S. Vernon McCasland continues this type of interpretation: "Like Ezekiel, Jesus identified himself with man, especially with the exploited poor, the needy and sick of the common people." The apocalyptic sayings are to be taken as figurative language (McCasland 1964: 120).

Other scholars have argued that Jesus drew on Ezekiel's *ben adam* as well as Daniel's *bar enash* – the former in those passages where

---

[2] With a "moreover," Cary slips in the human Son of Man as well: Jesus, in his sympathy with human suffering, wished to be called "simply 'man,' a member of the human family, a brother to all mankind" (Cary 1900: 363).

Son of Man is a designation of lowliness or suffering, the latter in those passages where the title is a designation of sovereignty.[3]

R. K. Harrison (1951) and W. Eichrodt (1959), by contrast, saw no need to trace any part of Jesus' "Son of Man" concept to apocalyptic literature. They suggested that the usage in Ezekiel could account not only for Jesus' sayings concerning the Son of Man's lowliness and suffering, but also for those concerning his glorification and sovereignty.

Eduard Schweizer accepts only the sayings about the earthly, suffering Son of Man as authentic, tracing the expression to Ezekiel:

> Perhaps Jesus called himself "Son of Man" in the way Ezekiel did to describe the commission he had received from God to serve in lowliness and suffering.
>
> (Schweizer 1970: 169)

Yet this "title of lowliness" is at the same time a "title of majesty" because "This lowly One who has been rejected by men will be exalted to the right hand of God" (Schweizer 1970: 171).

Ezekiel's son of man as ideal human

For a few interpreters, "son of man" in Ezekiel expressed ideal humanity. According to E. A. Abbott (1909; 1910), Jesus combined the conceptions of "son of man" in Daniel 7.13 and Ezekiel. The former received prominence in the Synoptics; the latter, in the Gospel of John. Jesus' primary emphasis was on Ezekiel. From the Aramaic Targum on Ezekiel, he called himself *bar Adam* ("the son of Adam"). Since Ezekiel was so called after a vision of God in human form, the designation was related to the idea that humanity was made in the image of God. Jesus believed that humanity had fallen from that image and as "the son of Adam" saw himself as the second Adam, the new humanity created according to God's intention.

G. S. Duncan (1947: 135–205) also believed that Jesus used *bar adam*, found in the Targum of Ezekiel, in an ideal sense. Jesus used the title to express his relationship to humanity. He saw himself as "the Man," a representative of humanity as God intended it to be

---

[3] Weizsäcker 1864: 426–31; Pfleiderer 1869: 2.422–26; Blackwood 1966: 11–25; Zehrer 1974.

and as it could be when filled with God's Spirit. He found the basis
for these ideas in the prophet Ezekiel, whom God filled with his
Spirit and commissioned as his servant.

Alan Richardson (1958: 128–46) also derived Jesus' use of the
term from Ezekiel. Jesus regarded himself, like Ezekiel, as a sign to
his generation. He merged the Ezekielic son of man "with the
Isaianic Servant of the Lord and with the other prophetic types of
the Messiah who was to come." The designation identifies him as
the representative of the Israel of God, the new Adam, the new
humanity in whom the image of God is restored.

Evaluation of the Ezekielic son of man

The theory that traces the Gospel "Son of Man" to Ezekiel has
never been widespread and now appears only sporadically.
Scholten (1809: 196) criticized the idea that "Son of Man" identified Jesus as a prophet like Ezekiel, pointing out that Ezekiel was
not called "son of man" on account of his prophetic office. Later
scholars emphasized that the usage in Ezekiel cannot explain the
distinctive features of the Gospel "Son of Man" sayings:

> the Ezekielic hypothesis cannot explain the necessity of
> suffering in the predictions of the Son of man's passion
> even unto death, nor the august dignity of the Son of man
> in sayings portraying him as the heavenly witness or judge.
>   (Higgins 1964: 16; cf. Fuller 1954: 99–102)

Son of man in the Psalms

While the messianic interpretation of the term Son of Man has
centered around Daniel 7.13, other Old Testament passages have
been invoked as well. Since the term "son of man" appears not
only in Daniel 7.13, but also in Psalms 8.4 and 80.17, Jacques
Cappel (1657: at Matt. 8.20, John 5.27) appealed to all three
passages as the background to a messianic use of the term by Jesus.

Of these additional passages, it is Psalm 8.4 that has been most
frequently cited to explain "Son of Man," either in conjunction
with Daniel 7.13 or by itself. Some scholars have used the Psalm to
support the interpretation of Son of Man as a lowly human exalted
by God[4] or as the man who restored humanity's original lordship

---

[4] C. Schmid [1853] 1870: 107–15; Colani 1864: 112–21; Réville 1897: 2.190–98.

(Barrett 1967: 30–33, 95–99). Others have used it in conjunction with Daniel 7.13 to support the messianic interpretation.[5] Theodor Keim asserted that it played the primary role: Jesus derived "Son of Man" from this Psalm, understanding it in a messianic sense, and explicated it only secondarily from Daniel 7.13 (Keim [1867–72] 1876–83: 3.86–88).

Other scholars have focused on Psalm 80.17. Heinrich Holzinger (1920: 105–106) argued that this verse provides the background for the non-eschatological sayings in the Gospels. Martin Wagner (1932) likewise thought that Jesus derived his title from this passage. Several more recent scholars have appealed to the Targums as evidence for a messianic interpretation of "son of man" in Psalm 80.17[6] or Psalm 8.4 (Moloney 1981).

Evaluation

The major critique of such theories has been that no allusion to Psalm 8.4 or 80.17 appears in the Son of Man sayings, while there are allusions to Daniel 7.13 (Keil 1877: 224–25). Furthermore, the Psalm passages appear inadequate to account for the distinctive features of the Son of Man passages:

> the predicates of sovereignty which Jesus adopts as the Son of Man are totally different than those which Ps 8 would have provided, as also the lowliness of man so highly honored according to the psalm can by no means be confused with the totally heterogeneous self-denial and humble renunciation of the Son of Man as it is expressed in the saying (Matt. 8.20).   (Usteri 1886: 4)

Son of Man as Primal Man

One line of scholarship has traced the apocalyptic Son of Man to oriental speculations about a primal heavenly Man. Most scholars see these speculations as irrelevant for interpreting the Gospel passages, assuming that any influence they had on the New Testament Son of Man was mediated through Daniel or Enoch. A few

---

[5] Cellarius [1680] 1700; Hausrath [1868–] 1878–80: 2.230–31; Sanday 1908: 122–30.
[6] Gelston 1969; Hill 1973; McNeil 1979/80.

scholars, however, have seen a more direct influence on the New Testament from such speculations.

Hermann Gunkel (1899) was among the first to suggest that the designation Son of Man in the Gospels comes not only from Daniel but also from traditions which allegedly influenced Daniel, namely earlier speculations about a heavenly Man. While Gunkel did not specify the origins of such speculations, subsequent scholars developed this idea and became more specific.

According to Richard Reitzenstein, the Iranian Gayomart, or Primal Man, furnished the prototype for both the Gnostic "Anthropos" ("Man") and the apocalyptic "Bar Nasha" ("Son of Man" = "Man").[7] Jewish sects in the days of Jesus knew this figure as a messenger from God and a suffering Redeemer. Jesus, in adopting the name "Son of Man," identified himself with this expected "Man," thus designating himself as a messenger from God who would suffer. From this view, he was led to a messianic consciousness and to a use of "the Man" in an apocalyptic sense. Thus the oriental Anthropos accounts for those elements in the New Testament Son of Man which cannot be explained from Jewish apocalyptic.

F. H. Borsch (1967) drew on Iranian, Hellenistic, and Mesopotamian texts to reconstruct a myth of a Primal Man-King, a myth which he believes survived in some pre-Christian Jewish baptizing sect. The baptismal ritual of this sect symbolized that the human subject ascended to heaven to become the heavenly Man (or Son of Man). Such a sect influenced Jesus, who believed that he fulfilled the ancient myth. Borsch admits that his reconstruction is speculative, and he has been criticized for assuming that the wide variety of sources on which he draws all refer to the same mythological pattern (cf. Marshall [1976] 1990: 70).

The Son of Man as the Son of God

In earlier stages of the discussion, researchers saw "Son of Man" and "Son of God" as contrasting titles. Patristic authors understood these designations in light of the orthodox doctrine of Christ's two natures: Son of Man expressed Jesus' humanity, while Son of God expressed his divinity. Later scholarship in a certain sense reversed that evaluation. Son of God came to be recognized

---

[7] Reitzenstein 1921: 115–23, esp. 116–19 (summarized by Kraeling 1927: 13–14).

as nothing more than an epithet of the Messiah, hence of a human being, while Son of Man, in the apocalyptic sense, was understood as a pre-existent, heavenly being. The two titles remained in contrast but with a reversal of connotations (cf. Stauffer 1956).

A different line of scholarship has seen the two titles not as contrasting but as similar or identical in meaning. At the end of the nineteenth century, Heinrich Appel (1896: 127–39) expressed this view. Appel concedes that the title "Son of Man" stresses Jesus' affiliation to humanity in distinction from God. At the same time, however, many of the actions predicated of the Son of Man belong to God, not to humanity (e.g. forgiving sins, traveling on clouds, ruling over angels). This indicates that the concept "the Son of Man" stands in closest relation to the concept "the Son of God." With the expression "the Son of Man" Jesus wished to designate himself "as the godlike man" (Appel 1896: 133). Jesus derived this idea from the general teaching of scripture about the godlikeness of a son of man. In Daniel 7, for example, he found the Messiah depicted as a godlike man.

Other scholars as well have seen a close relationship between "Son of Man" and "Son of God." E. Lohmeyer, for example, affirmed that the title Son of Man "only veils what the early Christian faith confesses of the Son of God" (Marshall 1970: 87 n. 71). I. H. Marshall quotes Lohmeyer with approval and adds that the title expresses Jesus' self-consciousness as the Son of God while at the same time concealing it. The early church dropped the title in favor of the manifest title "Son of God" (Marshall 1965/66: 350–51; 1970: 81). Norman Perrin sought to show that Mark "uses Son of Man to interpret and give content to the conception of Jesus as Son of God" (Perrin 1974: 85).

Apocalyptic Son of God

A few scholars have traced the equation "Son of Man = Son of God" to pre-Christian Jewish apocalyptic. Otto Procksch (1927) affirmed that in Jewish apocalyptic, the Son of Man is a heavenly being, the Son of God. Jesus used the term in the same sense: "the riddle of the Son of Man is solved in a single stroke if one substitutes the Son of God for it" (Procksch 1927: 435). The Son of Man is Lord of the Sabbath and has authority to forgive sins, because he is the Son of God. His suffering is a paradox: he must suffer even though he is the Son of God. Eventual glorification belongs to him because he is the Son of God. When God is designated as the Father of the Son of Man (Mark 8.38), it is because the Son of Man is the Son of God. At his trial, Jesus admits that he is the Son of God, even while using the designation "Son of Man" (Mark 14.62). The fact that the Jews consider the claim blasphemy implies that Son of God is taken in a metaphysical sense.

Similarly, Seyoon Kim (1983) argues that pre-Christian Judaism already interpreted the Danielic "son of man" as the Son of God. Jesus either applied this previous interpretation to himself or developed the same interpretation independently. He supports this view by pointing to evidence in the Gospels that the Son of Man is considered the Son of God.[8]

Son of Man as a circumlocution

A few other researchers, recognizing the close relation between the titles "Son of Man" and "Son of God," have explained the former as a circumlocution for the latter. Gustav Dalman wrote that for a long time he believed that "Son of man" might be a paradoxical term for "Son of God." He adduces various Jewish phrases as possible parallels, such as the use of "bless" to mean "curse." Without further support for the thesis, however, he felt compelled to set it aside (Dalman [1898] 1902: 266–67).

The thesis was revived subsequently by J. Massingberd Ford (1968). She suggests that Son of Man was a "euphemism" for Son of God, where "God" in Greek represented "Yahweh." It was used to avoid pronouncing the divine name, an act which Jews considered blasphemy. Without referring to Dalman, she supports this view by citing the same Jewish practice of using words to say the exact opposite of what is intended. In a subsequent article (1971), Ford cites references in Jewish literature in which words meaning "man" (*ish* and *adam*) seem to refer to God. For example, on the basis of Exodus 15.3 ("God is a man [*ish*] of war"), rabbinic expositors could refer to God as *ish*. "Could not, therefore," she asks, "the reference to 'man' in the phrase 'Son of Man' also refer to God?" (Ford 1971: 76).

---

[8] For a critique of Kim's work see Burkett 1991: 104–105.

Distinctive sons of men

Some theories about the Son of Man are so distinctive as to fall into no more comprehensive category.

Johann Martin Usteri (1886) proposed that Jesus used "Son of Man" in speaking of his peculiar office or calling, as this was determined by his incarnation. This calling cannot be placed under any traditional category, such as Messiah. Though he was the promised Messiah, he was so in a higher sense than any Jew suspected, in the Christian sense of the savior of the world. The title "Son of Man," suggesting his affiliation with the human race, indicated his vocation to the whole of humanity.

According to E. Kuhnert (1917/18), in the expression "Son of Man," the element "Man" is to be taken in a generic or collective sense as "humanity, the world." "Son" means "benefactor" or "saviour" as in Greek inscriptions (e.g. "son of the city"). Thus the title means "benefactor of humanity," i.e. "the expected saviour of the world."[9]

For Gillis Gerleman (1983), the Aramaic *bar nasha* is not equivalent to *ben adam* ("son of man"). Rather *bar* means "separated," so that *bar nasha* means "separated from what is human." The phrase alludes to David as "the separated" and thus identifies Jesus as "David redivivus."

Harald Sahlin (1983) proposes that the Son of Man in Daniel, Enoch, and other Jewish and Christian literature is the angel Michael. When Jesus used the term, he meant that he fulfilled the role assigned to Michael in Jewish thought.

The Johannine Son of Man

Until the early twentieth century, scholars generally saw no major distinction between the Synoptic Son of Man and the Son of Man in the Fourth Gospel. Whatever theory they adopted for the former served as well for the latter. Among some scholars, that perspective has continued into the twentieth century, notably among scholars who derive the Johannine as well as the Synoptic Son of Man from Jewish apocalyptic.[10] Most scholars, however, have come to recognize features in the Johannine Son of Man that are difficult to

---

[9] Kuhnert's theory is reviewed and criticized by Hertlein (1920) and Dieckmann (1921).

[10] E.g. Dieckmann 1927; Bernard 1928: cxxii–cxxxiii; Preiss 1953; de Beus

explain on the basis of apocalyptic literature. Unlike the Synoptics, the Fourth Gospel portrays the Son of Man as a figure who descends from heaven and then ascends back to heaven. The centrality of this descent/ascent motif associated with the Johannine Son of Man has led scholars to comb through a wide variety of ancient literature seeking a model for it.

In the early twentieth century, scholars influenced by the history-of-religions school began to look outside of the bounds of Judaism to explain the Johannine figure. Walter Bauer, for example, while tracing the Synoptic Son of Man to Jewish apocalyptic, derived the Johannine Son of Man from speculations on a heavenly Primal Man found among Gnostics, worshipers of Hermes, Mandaeans, and Manichaeans (W. Bauer 1925: 40). Rudolf Bultmann developed this view in an influential article (Bultmann 1925). For Bultmann, John's christology was based on an oriental Gnostic myth about a Redeemer sent from heaven to free souls trapped in the world of matter.

Bultmann explained the Johannine Son of Man without reference to apocalyptic, seeing only a later apocalyptic gloss in John 5.27. Later scholars reversed the direction of this development, theorizing that an original apocalyptic concept had been overlaid in John by some non-apocalyptic influence. For some scholars, this later influence was the Gnostic Redeemer myth.[11] For others, it was the Hellenistic heavenly Man found in Hermetic literature and Philo of Alexandria.[12] Still others looked for some influence more at home in the world of Judaism, such as the personified Wisdom of the Hebrew Bible and other Jewish literature.[13] Peder Borgen (1977) found this secondary influence in Jewish traditions about God descending from heaven at Sinai, while Jan-A. Bühner found it in Jewish speculation about angels descending to incarnate themselves in prophets (Bühner 1977: 374–99, 422–29).

In my own work on this subject, I reviewed all of these suggestions, and others, in greater detail (Burkett 1991: 16–37). In the

1955–56; Héring [1937] 1959: Appendix A; Smalley 1969; Moloney 1978; Pamment 1985.

[11] Iber 1953; Schulz 1957; Kümmel [1969] 1973: 275–77.

[12] Dodd 1953: 43–44; Higgins 1964: 153–84; Colpe [1969] 1972: 470; Talbert 1975/76.

[13] Sidebottom 1957: 117; 1961: 111; F. Braun 1962: 133–47; Moeller 1963: 95; Schnackenburg 1964/65: 135–37; Dion 1967; Meeks [1972] 1986: 142, 164–65; Hammerton-Kelly 1973: 241–42; Maddox 1974: 189; Coppens 1976: 78; Martyn 1979: 141; Dunn 1983: 330–37.

constructive portion of that work, I concluded (1) that the Fourth Gospel makes no reference to an apocalyptic Son of Man;[14] (2) that the expression ὁ υἱὸς τοῦ ἀνθρώπου in the Fourth Gospel, translated as "the Son of the Man," is derived from Proverbs 30.1–4, where in one possible reading of the text, a figure designated "the Man" (*hageber*) addresses his son; (3) that the expression "the Son of the Man" is equivalent to "the Son of God"; (4) that the descent/ascent motif associated with the Son of the Man also stems from Proverbs 30.1–4, where the Man asks his son, "Who has ascended to heaven and descended?"; (5) that the Son of the Man has been identified with other descending/ascending figures in the Hebrew scriptures, such as the Word of Yahweh and Yahweh himself. Like many other historical reconstructions, this theory is possible to imagine but impossible to prove.

In that study I also suggested that this theory might help to explain the Synoptic Son of Man and even Jesus' use of the expression. Further consideration has led me to abandon this suggestion.[15] If the results of that study have any validity, they are valid only for the Fourth Gospel, not the Synoptic tradition or Jesus himself.

[14] Robert Rhea (1990) comes to the same conclusion.
[15] Cf. the review of this work by Bauckham (1993).

7

EXIT THE APOCALYPTIC SON OF MAN?

The view that Jesus spoke of an apocalyptic Son of Man presupposed that such a conception existed in Judaism prior to Jesus. This presupposition came under attack at the end of the nineteenth century and again in the 1960s. Various factors joined to cast in doubt the view that the title "Son of Man" or a unified Son of Man concept existed in pre-Christian Judaism.

The nineteenth-century consensus

A few scholars of the eighteenth and nineteenth centuries affirmed that when Jesus spoke of himself as the "Son of Man," the Jews were familiar with the title and understood him to mean the Messiah.[1] Serious objections, however, were raised against this view.

(1) First, scholars at the end of the nineteenth century pointed out that the expression "son of man" never became a title in pre-Christian Judaism.[2] In Daniel, the phrase "one like a son of man" is not a title, but a description of a manlike figure. Likewise, the human figure in 1 Enoch is introduced not with a title but with a description: "the son of man to whom belongs righteousness" (1 Enoch 46.3). Subsequently, he is called "that son of man" with reference back to his initial appearance. That this phrase never becomes a fixed title is further suggested by the fact that the Ethiopic uses three different expressions for it. Nor is there such a title in 4 Ezra 13, where the human figure is called simply "a man" or "the man" (the one referred to previously). Finally, though the

[1] E.g. Whitby [1703] 1808: at Matt. 12.8; Eckermann 1791: 1.1.78; Ewald [1855] 1883: 6.231; Baldensperger [1888] 1892: 90, 173–76; Charles [1893] 1912: 309; cf. B. Weiss 1862: 224–25.
[2] N. Schmidt 1896; Lietzmann 1896: 40–50; Dalman [1898] 1902: 241–49; Wellhausen 1899: 6.197–99.

Rabbis did interpret the figure in Daniel 7.13 as the Messiah, they did not refer to him with the title "Son of Man." Consequently, "Son of Man" first occurs as a title in the Christian tradition.

(2) Second, the Evangelists do not treat the title as a known designation. In Mark, Jesus conceals his messianic identity, yet openly refers to himself as "Son of Man" (Mark 2.10, 28). In Matthew 16.13, the Evangelist has Jesus ask, "Who do men say that the Son of Man is?" and the replies show no recognition of the title as a known messianic designation. Furthermore, Peter's reply "the Christ" is hailed as a revelation from heaven, not as a natural inference from previous knowledge of the term "Son of Man." In John 12.34, the crowd appears to be uncertain whether "Son of Man" refers to the Messiah or not.

These considerations convinced the majority of nineteenth-century scholars that "Son of Man" was not a known title for the Messiah before Jesus,[3] though some allowed that it may have been known in certain limited circles.[4] From this perspective, Jesus used the title either (1) to express his messianic consciousness while at the same time concealing it, leading people to a gradual recognition of his messiahship, or (2) to avoid the nationalistic and political ideas that the people associated with known messianic designations.

The twentieth-century consensus

At the end of the nineteenth century, the view that "Son of Man" was the title of a known figure in pre-Christian Judaism gained ground and became a general assumption of scholarship in the first half of the twentieth century. R. H. Charles paved the way for this development by challenging the argument that "son of man" in the Parables of Enoch is not a title. He pointed out that the demonstrative "that" which usually precedes it may simply be the Ethiopic translation of an underlying Greek definite article (Charles [1893] 1912: 86–87). Once it became accepted that the Parables were pre-Christian and used "Son of Man" as a messianic title, the general

---

[3] Neander [1837] 1888: 98; Weisse 1856: 101f., 210f.; Baur 1860; 1864: 75–82; Hilgenfeld 1863: 333; Colani 1864: 112–13; Weizsäcker 1864: 426–31; H. Holtzmann 1865; Keim [1867–72] 1876–83: 3.83–84; B. Weiss [1868] 1893: 1.73–74; Wittichen 1868: 141; A. Bruce [1889] 1909: 167–68; Wendt [1886–90] 1892: 2.139–51; Beyschlag [1891–92] 1894: 1.65; Holsten 1891.

[4] Stapfer [1897] 1906: 226–30; Rhees 1898: 100.

triumph of the idea that the Gospel expression was taken over from Judaism seemed inevitable.

By the middle of the twentieth century, the majority of scholars understood "Son of Man" as a pre-Christian Jewish title.[5] According to this understanding, the title referred to an expected messianic or eschatological figure familiar to first-century Judaism from apocalyptic literature, but whose ultimate origin may have been in oriental myths about a Primal Man. The figure known to Judaism was a pre-existent, heavenly being who would come to earth at the end-time to act as judge and to replace the present world-order with a transcendent kingdom of God. This apocalyptic Son of Man formed the presupposition for three primary views among scholars: (1) Jesus expressed his own conception of his messiahship by identifying himself with this figure (Cullmann et al.); (2) Jesus looked for another to come as the Son of Man, but after his death his disciples identified him with this figure (Bultmann et al.); (3) Jesus never spoke of the Son of Man, but after his death his disciples identified him with this figure (Vielhauer et al.).

Dissolution of the consensus

In the 1960s, this consensus concerning the existence of a pre-Christian apocalyptic Son of Man dissolved. Several factors led to the dissolution. First, the failure to find the Similitudes of Enoch among the fragments of 1 Enoch at Qumran renewed doubts about dating the Similitudes to the pre-Christian period. Second, Norman Perrin and others challenged the existence of a unified pre-Christian Son of Man concept. Third, Geza Vermes renewed the linguistic arguments against a pre-Christian "Son of Man" title.

Qumran and the Similitudes of Enoch

The theory that pre-Christian Judaism knew an apocalyptic Son of Man derives its primary support from the section of 1 Enoch known as the Parables or Similitudes. Though numerous scholars

---

[5] Twentieth-century scholars who continued to doubt the idea included Drummond 1901: 542; Stevens 1901: 84; Goguel 1904: 208–12; Kühl 1907: 65–87; Sanday 1908: 127; Westcott 1908: 1.75; Abbott 1909: 15–23; C. Cadoux 1943: 98; Percy 1953: 257–59; Fuller 1954: 98. Those who felt that the title may have been known in a limited circle included Driver 1902: 583–84; McNaugher 1931: 102–103; Mowinckel [1951] 1954: 445; Mouson 1952: 628.

of the nineteenth century doubted that this work came from the pre-Christian period, the judgment of R. H. Charles, who dated the Similitudes to the early first century BCE, ultimately prevailed. Later Erik Sjöberg (1946: 38) dated the work to somewhere between 38 BCE and 70 CE, but still early enough to influence Jesus.

This early dating of the Similitudes was challenged by the fragmentary copies of 1 Enoch discovered at Qumran. J. T. Milik, the editor of this material, disclosed that no trace of the Similitudes had been discovered, even though the fragments came from eleven different copies of 1 Enoch and included every chapter except those of the Similitudes (Milik 1959: 33–34; 1971; 1976: 89–100). The absence of the Similitudes from the Qumran copies of 1 Enoch suggested to Milik that this part of the Enochic corpus did not exist at the time of the Qumran community and hence must be dated after 70 CE. In his earlier work, Milik attributed the Similitudes to "a Jew or a Jewish Christian of the first or second century A.D." (Milik 1959: 33). Later, he described them as a Christian work, composed in Greek around 270 CE, which drew the title "Son of Man" from the Gospels (Milik 1971; 1976: 89–100). Thus the discoveries at Qumran raised anew three central questions concerning the Similitudes: their date, provenance (Jewish or Christian), and relation to the New Testament "Son of Man."

1. Date

Though few scholars accepted Milik's third-century date,[6] the evidence against a pre-Christian date for the Similitudes began to seem impressive. (1) As mentioned, no portions of the Similitudes appear among the Aramaic fragments of 1 Enoch discovered at Qumran, though fragments from every other chapter have been found. (2) No portions of the Similitudes appear among the Greek fragments of 1 Enoch. The Similitudes exist only in Ethiopic manuscripts of the fifteenth century or later. (3) And though Jewish and Christian works of the first four centuries abound with references and allusions to other works attributed to Enoch, none refer to the

---

[6] Matthew Black at first adopted Milik's dating: "The negative arguments, in particular the silence of Qumran and of versional and patristic tradition seems absolutely decisive for the mediaeval origins and composition of the book" (Black 1976/77: 6). Later, changing his mind, he dated the Similitudes to "the early Roman period, probably pre-70 A.D." (Black 1985: 188).

Similitudes (Milik 1976: 92). These considerations led many scholars to conclude with Ragnar Leivestad: "the Similitudes were completely unknown in the early Christian milieu, probably because at this time they did not yet exist" (Leivestad 1968: 53).[7]

Most scholars began to favor a date in the first century CE.[8] For many, this meant the late first century, since the view that the Similitudes must be post-Qumran (i.e. after 70 CE) met with wide approval.[9] Many others, however, found no significance in the absence of the Similitudes at Qumran and argued for a date in the first century CE prior to 70 CE.[10] Greenfield and Stone, for example, pointed out that Esther too is absent from Qumran and denied that this is an argument for its non-existence at this time (Greenfield and Stone 1977: 55). For some scholars the dating hinges on a possible reference to the Parthian invasion of Palestine in 40 BCE (1 Enoch 56.5) or a possible reference to Herod the Great (1 Enoch 67.8–13).

2. *Provenance*

As for the provenance of the Parables, a few scholars followed Milik in identifying them as a Jewish-Christian work[11] or as a work whose final form was influenced by Christians.[12] Most, however,

---

[7] Cf. Richard Longenecker (1970: 83): "to date there is no evidence for the pre-Christian nature" of the Similitudes. Likewise Marcus Borg (1984: 224): "there is no evidence that the Similitudes existed at the time of Jesus."

[8] E.g. the scholars attending the SNTS Seminars on Enoch in 1977 and 1978 (Charlesworth 1978/79: 322–23). J. C. Hindley (1967/68), however, proposed a date around 120 CE and was followed by Eduard Schweizer (1975: 101).

[9] E.g. Cross 1958: 150–51 n. 7; Moe 1960: 124–26; Black 1963: 312 and in Charlesworth 1978/79: 321; Hindley 1967/68; Leivestad 1968: 53; Longenecker 1970: 83–85; Gaston 1970: 375; Moule 1977: 11–22; Knibb 1978/79; Vermes et al. in Schürer 1979: 2.505, 520–23; Lindars 1983: 5; Borg 1984: 221–27.

[10] Thompson (1960/61; 1961) argues for a date in the first century CE or earlier; similarly, F. M. Wilson (1978) dates the Similitudes between 40 BCE and 70 CE. Greenfield and Stone (1977) opt for a date in the first century CE contemporaneous with the Qumran texts. Mearns (1977/78; 1978/79: 369) favors sometime in the 40s CE; Jas (1979), the years 30–40 CE; Suter (1981), the reign of Caligula (37–41 CE); Nickelsburg (1981: 223), "around the turn of the era"; Coppens (1983: 154), the first century CE sometime prior to 70 CE; Black (1985: 188), prior to 70 CE. John J. Collins (1992: 452) dates the Similitudes prior to 70 CE, since they make no reference to the fall of Jerusalem (cf. J. Collins 1984: 143: "the early or mid first century C.E."). Charlesworth (1985: 89) claims that all specialists agree that the Similitudes are Jewish, from the first century CE, and earlier than 70 CE.

[11] Longenecker 1970: 85; Mearns 1977/78.

[12] Cross 1958: 150–51 n. 7; Moe 1960: 124–26; Schweizer 1975: 102–103; Grelot 1978: 152–67.

continued to regard them as Jewish,[13] though among these were some who saw them as a Jewish reaction to Christianity.[14] The arguments for a Jewish provenance remained the same as formerly: (1) nothing in the Parables is specifically Christian, i.e. they never refer to the death or resurrection of the Messiah; (2) in chapter 71 Enoch is identified as the Son of Man, an identification no Christian would make.

3.   Relation to the New Testament

With respect to the significance of the Similitudes for the New Testament Son of Man, fewer scholars are now willing to use this work as evidence for a pre-Christian Jewish Son of Man on which Jesus might have based his concept of Son of Man. As David Suter noted,

> There seems to be a basic consensus that the Similitudes does not antedate the origins of the Christian movement and therefore does not provide *direct* evidence for a pre-Christian Jewish Son of Man.   (Suter 1981: 218)

Numerous scholars agreed with Richard Longenecker that "The evidence to date is of such a nature as to make the employment of I Enoch 37–71 in reconstructing pre-Christian thought precarious indeed" (Longenecker 1970: 84).[15]

No unified pre-Christian Son of Man concept

A second line of attack against the apocalyptic Son of Man was initiated by Norman Perrin in 1966. According to Perrin, "there is no 'Son of Man concept' but rather a variety of uses of Son of Man imagery" (Perrin 1974: 26). An examination of Daniel, 1 Enoch, 4 Ezra, and Jewish midrashic traditions led Perrin to conclude,

> What we have is not the conception of the coming of a transcendent, sovereign figure, the heavenly redeemer, the

[13] Such are the conclusions of the SNTS Seminars on Enoch in 1977 and 1978 (Charlesworth 1978/79: 322–23). So also, for example, Greenfield and Stone 1977; Suter 1981.
[14] Hindley 1967/68; Black in Charlesworth 1978/79: 321; Jas 1979; Bietenhard 1982: 322–24, 338, 343–44; J. Collins 1984: 152–53 (with respect to 1 Enoch 71).
[15] Cf. Lloyd Gaston (1970: 375): "it is clear that the burden of proof lies on him who would claim Enoch as a background for the elucidation of Daniel and the Gospels."

Son of Man. There is no sufficient relationship between the use of Son of Man in 1 Enoch and 4 Ezra for us to suppose that they are both reflections of a common conception. What we have is the imagery of Dan. 7:13 being used freely and creatively by subsequent seers and scribes. These uses are independent of one another. The common dependence is upon Dan. 7:13, on the one hand, and upon the general world of apocalyptic concepts, on the other. Similarly, the scribes of the midrashic traditions in their turn use the imagery of Dan. 7:13 in connection with the Messiah.

(Perrin 1974: 33)

Thus even if the Similitudes should prove to be pre-Christian, they provide no evidence for a generally known, unified conception of an apocalyptic Son of Man that could have been taken over by Jesus or the early church. Instead of a unified conception of a heavenly "Son of Man," the apocalyptic literature attests to a diversity of conceptions influenced by Daniel 7.13. The early church knew no ready-made "Son of Man" with which to identify Jesus; rather they developed the Son of Man sayings by a midrashic interpretation of Daniel 7.13 and other scriptures.

T. Francis Glasson also challenged the consensus that a unified "Son of Man" conception existed in pre-Christian Judaism. According to the consensus, in this unified conception the Son of Man was a celestial figure who came from heaven to judge the earth. This pre-Christian figure provided the pattern for the Gospel sayings about the coming of the Son of Man. Glasson has pointed out, however, that no pre-Christian Jewish apocalypse contains such a conception. The "one like a son of man" in Daniel comes *to* God, not *from* God, and does not exercise judicial functions, while the Enochic Son of Man is nowhere said to come or descend. As Glasson emphasizes,

Messianic beliefs become more and more diversified and there is nothing resembling the scheme put forward with such definiteness by the Schweitzer/Bultmann school. When a Messiah is mentioned he is of the warrior type. There is no transcendent figure descending in glory to conduct the last judgment.   (Glasson 1977: 299; cf. 1988)

Commenting on this statement, E. P. Sanders adds, "Glasson's statement is quite true. The picture of the Son of man coming to judge, and the like, is derived from the synoptic Gospels" (E. Sanders 1985: 124). The coming "Son of Man" who might provide a model for the New Testament figure simply does not exist in pre-Christian Judaism.

No pre-Christian Son of Man title

While Perrin and Glasson attacked the idea of a pre-Christian apocalyptic Son of Man concept, Geza Vermes renewed the attack of earlier scholars on the idea of a pre-Christian Son of Man title (Vermes 1967; 1973: 160–91; 1978a; 1978b). Vermes pointed out that in the Aramaic sources examined by him, *bar nasha* never occurred as a title for a heavenly, apocalyptic figure. He argued that Jesus used the expression not as a title but as a nontitular circumlocution for "I." The titular usage found in the Gospels was created by the church.

Not all aspects of Vermes' work can be accepted, in particular his attempt to find a nontitular circumlocution in many of the Gospel Son of Man sayings (see Chapter 8). On the other hand, his work did further challenge the view that pre-Christian Judaism knew some well-defined figure designated by the title "Son of Man." As Barnabas Lindars expressed the emerging consensus: "it has now become embarrassingly obvious that the Son of Man was not a current title in Judaism at all" (Lindars 1975/76: 52).

Exit the apocalyptic Son of Man

The developments discussed above caused numerous scholars to doubt that a pre-Christian apocalyptic Son of Man ever existed. As C. H. Dodd asked,

> As things stand at present, is there any evidence worth talking about that "Son of Man" was a title for a quasi-messianic figure in pre-Christian Judaism? I should say not.
> (Dodd 1966: 475)

Ragnar Leivestad dubbed the apocalyptic Son of Man "a theological phantom" (Leivestad 1968) and gave one article the provocative title "Exit the Apocalyptic Son of Man" (Leivestad 1971/72). Paul Winter, in a review of Perrin's work, wrote,

> If P[errin]'s interpretation of the Son of Man sayings in the Synoptic Gospels is right – and it is supported by Vermes'

. . . study of the linguistic use of the word "bar-nash(a)" in Jewish Aramaic – then the place of origin of the [Son of Man] myth must be sought neither in Iran, nor in Judea, nor even in Ugarit, but in German universities.

(Winter 1968: 784)

Maurice Casey agreed with Leivestad and Winter that the apocalyptic Son of Man was "a product of modern scholarship":

The Jews had no Son of man concept, and their use of Dan. 7 did not turn אנש בר into a title. It follows that the origin of the Gospel term ὁ υἱὸς τοῦ ἀνθρώπου must be sought in developments for which Jesus or his followers were responsible. (P. Casey 1979: 139)

Consequently numerous scholars drew the conclusion of Lloyd Gaston: "We feel justified then in eliminating completely the idea of a transcendental apocalyptic figure called Son of Man as a background for the New Testament conception" (Gaston 1970: 375).[16] More recently Marcus Borg has noted,

it is now routine to say that "Son of man" was not an apocalyptic title in Judaism. Thus Jesus could not have used this phrase as a "shorthand" way of referring to a figure of the end-time, whether to himself in a transformed state or to somebody other than himself. (Borg 1994: 53)

Responses

Responses to the apparent exit of the apocalyptic Son of Man have varied. Some scholars continue to defend the existence of a pre-Christian apocalyptic Son of Man. Others assume that Jesus or the church created the concept directly from Daniel 7.13. Still others have turned to non-apocalyptic explanations of "Son of Man."

Pre-Christian Son of Man defended

Fewer scholars now give credence to the idea that a unified concept associated with the title "Son of Man" existed in pre-Christian Judaism. The idea, however, has experienced only a decline, not a

---

[16] The same view is expressed by Dunn 1980: 95; Bietenhard 1982: 337, 338; Fuller 1985: 207; Hare 1990: 21; Davies and Allison 1988–91: 2.45–46.

demise. In 1985, Reginald Fuller complained that "German scholars continue blithely to assume without question that pre-Christian
Judaism was familiar with an apocalyptic Son of man with clearly
defined judgmental and salvific functions" (Fuller 1985: 207).[17]
   Other scholars, without ignoring scholarship's shift in perspective, have defended the idea that Judaism had a more or less unified
conception of an apocalyptic Son of Man.[18] Werner G. Kümmel,
for example, continues to believe that the Similitudes of Enoch
provide pre-Christian evidence for a heavenly figure designated by
the title "Son of Man," and that Jesus could easily have taken over
this idea (Kümmel [1969] 1973: 77–78; 1984: 20–24). As I. H.
Marshall sees it, "the evidence shows that there was considerable
fluidity in depicting the Son of Man, not that there was no Son of
Man figure" (Marshall 1970: 73; cf. 1991: 39–40). George Nickelsburg, John Collins, and Thomas Slater have also renewed arguments for a unified pre-Christian Son of Man concept. These will
be considered in Chapter 9.
   Some scholars have continued to use this presumed pre-Christian
tradition to explain the Son of Man in the New Testament.[19] Chrys
Caragounis (1986), for example, argues that Jesus inherited a pre-
Christian Jewish Son of Man tradition that included the Similitudes
of Enoch. This tradition held to a messianic hope for "a supernatural Messiah of heavenly origin and universal dimensions"
(Caragounis 1986: 143). Jesus drew primarily on Daniel in devel-
oping this tradition and applying it to himself. Sayings in all three
classes can be derived from Daniel and are authentic words of
Jesus. Ben Witherington III (1990: 233–62) presents the same view.
   Margaret Barker (1988: 91–104) gives a greater role to 1 Enoch
in her theory. She concedes that "Son of Man" was not a title in
pre-Christian Judaism and that there is no evidence that the
Similitudes are pre-Christian. She argues, nevertheless, that the
ideas in the Similitudes were widespread in pre-Christian Judaism,

---

[17] Fuller cites Merklein (1983: 152–64) as an example. One could also cite I. Tödt
(1978), Schmithals (1979), and Paul Hoffmann ([1972] 1982). Hoffmann later
corrects himself (1992: 1.452 n. 56).
[18] E.g. Thompson 1960/61; Kümmel [1969] 1973: 77–78; 1984: 20–24; Marshall
1970: 73; 1991: 39–40; F. Wilson 1978; Schade 1984: 88; Horbury 1985; Nickelsburg
1978; 1992b; J. Collins 1992; Slater 1995.
[19] Thompson 1961; Higgins 1964; 1968; 1980; Maddox 1968; Kümmel [1969]
1973; 1984; Marshall 1970; 1991; J. Jeremias 1971: 257–76; Hammerton-Kelly 1973;
Caragounis 1986; Barker 1988: 91–104; Charlesworth 1988: 39–42; Witherington
1990: 233–62.

were known to Jesus, and can be used as background for the New Testament term. Whether he used the term as a title or not, Jesus described himself as Son of Man, meaning an angelic emissary/ messiah of judgment as in Enoch.

Despite the arguments of these scholars, it is not likely that the Similitudes can account for the origin of the Christian Son of Man. On the one hand, the apocalyptic sayings in the Synoptics emphasize the coming of the Son of Man, a coming that is practically absent from the Similitudes. On the other hand, a central feature of the Enochic Son of Man is his pre-existence, a feature that has no parallel in the Synoptic sayings. More plausibly, J. Theisohn (1975: 149–201) has argued that the Similitudes first influenced the Gospels at the level of Matthean redaction. The only close parallels between the Gospels and the Similitudes occur in material unique to Matthew. These include the motif of the Son of Man sitting on "his throne of glory" (Matt. 19.28; 25.31; cf. 1 Enoch 62.5; 69.27, 29),[20] the depiction of the Son of Man as eschatological judge (Matt. 13.41–42; 16.27; 25.31–32), and the motif of a burning furnace into which rebellious angels and wicked humans are cast (Matt. 13.41–42, 49–50; 25.41; cf. 1 Enoch 54.3–6). Theisohn's view is accepted by Mearns (1977/78; 1978/79), Suter (1981), and J. J. Collins (1984: 142–43).

Apocalyptic Son of Man created by Jesus

Many who reject the idea of a pre-Christian "Son of Man" title argue that Jesus himself could have coined the expression from Daniel 7.13. Scholars who take this position differ on whether Jesus referred to himself or another messianic figure.

Among those who believe that Jesus referred to himself, some favor the view that Jesus derived all three types of sayings from Daniel 7.[21] Others explain the suffering Son of Man sayings by

[20] It is true that the "throne of glory" is mentioned in other biblical and non-biblical passages (1 Sam. 2.8; Isa. 22.23; Jer. 14.21; 17.12; Sir. 47.11; Wis. 9.10; Testament of Abraham, Rescension B, 8.5). For this reason, Hare (1990: 162–67) and Luz (1992: 8) argue that no dependence of Matthew on the Similitudes can be demonstrated from the use of this expression. Only in the Similitudes and Matthew, however, does the Son of Man sit on the throne of glory. This consideration supports Theisohn's conclusion that Matthew alludes to the Similitudes.

[21] Moule 1952; 1974; 1977: 11–22; 1995; Goppelt 1963: 30–31; Hooker 1967: 27–30, 192; 1991; Longenecker 1969; 1970: 87–88; G. Stanton 1974: 160–61; Tuckett 1981; 1982: 60; M. de Jonge 1988: 172; 1991; Hampel 1990.

theorizing that Jesus combined the Danielic son of man with the suffering Servant of Deutero-Isaiah.[22]

The once-popular theory of Wellhausen and Bultmann – that Jesus distinguished himself from a Son of Man who was expected to come – is seen only rarely today.[23] It reappears in a modified form, however, in the work of Adela Yarbro Collins (1987; 1989a; 1989b; 1990b; 1991; 1992). She agrees with the majority of scholars that no title or widespread expectation of a coming "Son of Man" existed prior to Jesus, but thinks that this argument does not negate the type of apocalyptic/messianic theory espoused by Bultmann. She believes that Jesus himself interpreted Daniel 7 as referring to a heavenly figure who would soon come. Jesus took the indefinite phrase in Daniel 7 "one like a son of man" and turned it into a definite title "the Son of Man" in order to refer to the figure in that text. While Jesus distinguished himself from that figure, his followers identified the two after his death. Only sayings such as Matthew 24.27, 24.37–39, and 24.44, which do not intrinsically identify Jesus with the Son of Man, are authentic sayings of Jesus.

Apocalyptic Son of Man created by church

Still other scholars trace the origin of the title "Son of Man" neither to pre-Christian Judaism nor to Jesus, but to the early church. The works of Käsemann, Vielhauer, and Perrin have convinced many scholars that the early church created the title (see Chapter 5).[24] Reaching the same conclusion by a different route, a number of Q scholars have argued that the Son of Man sayings were not present in the earliest stage of Q, but belong to a later level of redaction.[25] Burton L. Mack accepts this view:

[22] F. Bruce 1968: 26–30, 97–99; 1982; France 1971: 148; Ladd 1974: 145–58; Zorn 1980; Coppens 1981: 151; Sabourin 1983; Betz 1985; Simmons 1985: 95–96; Marshall [1976] 1990: 67, 77; 1991.

[23] E.g. Boring 1982: 239–42; H. de Jonge 1993; Chilton 1992; 1996. E. P. Sanders (1993: 246–48) believes that Jesus sometimes used the title of himself, but finds it unclear in the future sayings whether Jesus identified himself or another as the coming Son of Man.

[24] Marxsen [1960] 1969: 22–43; Boers 1962: 70; 1972; Ory 1964; Teeple 1965; Conzelmann [1959] 1973: 43–46; [1968] 1969: 131–37; Walker 1972; 1983; Lohse [1974] 1984: 45–49; Vögtle 1989: 95.

[25] Koester 1971: 138, 170–72, 186–87, 213–14; Edwards 1971: 87; 1976: 36; Kloppenborg 1987; Mack 1988: 71 n. 14, 102–103; P. Hoffmann 1991: 194–97. Schürmann (1975: 146–47) locates the Son of Man sayings at an early stage in the development of Q, neither in the earliest level nor in the final redaction. Schulz (1972: 481–89) traces the coming Son of Man to the older tradition and the earthly

critical work on the synoptic tradition makes it impossible to regard the Son of man sayings as early. They belong to that stage of experience within the Q tradition character-ized by pronouncements of doom and judgment upon those who rejected Jesus' teachings. (Mack 1988: 102–103)

For Mack, "the apocalyptic mythology of the Son of Man was a later development of the Q tradition" (Mack 1988: 71 n. 14). Following Käsemann and Vielhauer, he sees Luke 12.8–9, which he considers "the crucial text," as a formulation of the Christian community.

The work of the Jesus Seminar shows the extent to which current scholarship doubts the authenticity of the Son of Man sayings. Founded in 1985 by Robert Funk, the twice-yearly meetings of the Seminar generally have drawn together thirty to forty scholars, whose initial purpose was to determine the actual words of the historical Jesus.[26] Members voted on each saying in the four canonical Gospels and the Gospel of Thomas by casting one of four color-coded beads into a ballot box. A red bead indicated a strong positive vote for authenticity, while a black bead indicated a strong negative vote. Intermediate positions were indicated by pink, on the positive side, and gray, on the negative side. The colors were given a numerical value, and the values of the votes were averaged to arrive at the consensus of the members. The Seminar published the results of its work in *The Five Gospels* (Funk and Hoover 1993), which printed the words of Jesus in the four colors used in voting. Most of the Son of Man sayings appear in black, the color of a strong negative vote. Five appear in gray, indicating some uncertainty.[27] Only two appear in pink, a weak positive vote, while none appear in red. In the two pink Son of Man sayings (Mark 2.28; Luke 9.58 = Matt. 8.20), the Seminar understood the expression in a generic sense. For most of these scholars, then, Jesus did not use the title "Son of Man."

Son of Man to the later. Vaage (1991) argues precisely the opposite. Tuckett (1993) finds that Son of Man sayings are a feature of both the early tradition and the later redaction. For surveys of scholarship on the Son of Man in Q, see Neirynck 1982: 69–72; Vögtle 1982; Tuckett 1993.

[26] A roster of the Fellows of the Jesus Seminar lists seventy-four scholars (Funk and Hoover 1993: 533–37). Marcus Borg indicates that "a large number of other scholars took part in one or more meetings" (Borg 1994: 179 n. 5).

[27] Mark 10.45; Luke 6.22 (cf. Matt. 5.11); Luke 7.34 (Matt. 11.19); Luke 17.24 (Matt. 24.27); Luke 17.22.

Non-apocalyptic Son of Man

For one segment of scholarship the apparent exit of the pre-Christian apocalyptic Son of Man went hand in hand with a shift to a non-apocalyptic explanation of the title's origin. In particular the interpretation of "son of man" as a nontitular idiom gained ground. The history of this type of theory forms the subject of the following chapter.

8

THE IDIOMATIC/NONTITULAR SON OF MAN

The dissolution of the apocalyptic Son of Man consensus in the 1960s brought with it a new emphasis on the interpretation of "son of man" as a nontitular idiom. In 1990 Reginald Fuller saw a trend toward interpretations of this kind:

> There appears . . . to be a trend (it is no more) to ascribe the christological-titular use to the post-Easter community, while allowing that the earthly Jesus used it in some nontitular sense, whether generic or self-designatory.
>
> (Fuller 1990: 721–22)[1]

This type of interpretation has a long history, going back to the Reformation. While patristic and medieval authors interpreted ὁ υἱὸς τοῦ ἀνθρώπου in its Greek sense, Reformation scholars began to examine the possible Semitic background of the phrase, usually tracing it to Hebrew *ben adam* or Aramaic *bar enasha*.[2] While most scholars continued to view the expression as some sort of title, others began to see it as a nontitular idiom. Three possible idiomatic senses of the expression were investigated: the circumlocutional sense ("this man" = "I"), the generic sense ("man" in general), and the indefinite sense ("a man," someone).

A circumlocution for "I"

Phase 1: 1557–1835

As early as 1557, Theodore de Bèze (Beza) appealed to Hebrew idiom to account for the expression "son of man." Noting that

[1] For critiques of this perspective see Caragounis 1986: 9–33 and Burkett 1994. The latter forms the basis for the present chapter.

[2] The forms *bar nash(a)* and *bar enash(a)* both appear in Aramaic sources. Since some scholars have emphasized that the latter was the form current in Jesus' day, I have used it everywhere except in describing the views of scholars who employ the other form.

Jesus spoke of the son of man in the third person while apparently referring to himself, Beza suggested that the expression was a Hebrew idiom, used as a circumlocution for "I":

> since the Hebrews are accustomed to speak of themselves in the third person, this phrase is to be taken in place of a first personal pronoun in the Gospel history, in which I do not remember anyone except Christ alone called "son of man," and this exclusively when he speaks about himself.
>
> (Bèze 1557: at Matt. 8.20)

Beza thus takes "son of man" as a circumlocution for "I," without explaining what Hebrew usage he has in mind. Most likely, he had in mind the expression "this (or that) man," used as a self-reference. A more explicit form of this idea appears in the work of Joachim Camerarius (1572), who interprets "Son of Man" as "that son of man, i.e. me."[3] Johannes Cocceius (d. 1669) mentions the same explanation, with reference, however, to an Aramaic rather than a Hebrew phrase:

> With this name Christ most often invokes himself in such a way that, as far as external appearance, he seems to signify nothing other than *this man*: as Jews spoke at that time, saying הָאִי בַּר נְשָׁא [sic], *this man* for *I*.
>
> (Cocceius [1673–75] 1701: 15 at Matt. 8.20)[4]

Johann Jacob Hess ([1768–72] 1779) accepted this interpretation,[5] as did Samuel Gottlieb Lange (1796).[6]

The circumlocutional theory continued into the nineteenth century in the work of H. E. G. Paulus (1800), who believed that Jesus used the expression in the sense "this man," always pointing to himself. Only after Jesus' death did his followers take his use of "son of man" as a reference to Daniel 7.13.[7] Christian Gottlieb Kühnöl mentioned the circumlocutional interpretation as one alternative for Matthew 8.20, 10.23, and 16.13 (Kühnöl [1807] 1823: 231). K. F. A. Fritzsche likewise interpreted "son of man" to mean

---

[3] Camerarius 1572: at Matt. 9.5 [6]. Cf. at Matt. 16.13 ("me, that man"); John 12.34 ("that man").

[4] Cocceius goes on to say that the name actually had a deeper meaning for Jesus.

[5] For example, Hess interprets "son of man" at Matthew 8.20 as "this man" (Hess [1768–72] 1779: 1.539).

[6] According to Scholten 1809: 179–80.

[7] Paulus [1800] 1804: 470–71; cf. 1830–33: 1.465–66, 500. In Matthew 12.8, however, Paulus takes the phrase to mean humanity in general (1830–33: 2.23).

"that son of human parents . . . who now speaks, that man whom you well know, i.e. I" (Fritzsche 1826: 320).

The circumlocutional theory, in this first manifestation, died out after Paulus and Fritzsche. As D. F. Strauss pointed out in rejecting the view, such a usage would require a demonstrative pronoun ("*this* son of man"), whereas the Gospel expression merely has the definite article "the" (Strauss [1835–36] 1860: 293–94).[8] Strauss also found it inconceivable that Jesus would have replaced the demonstrative by always pointing to himself. Timothée Colani adduced a further argument against the theory in noticing that Jesus never used "Son of Man" for "I" in mundane statements, such as "the Son of Man wants to cross the sea," but only with reference to his coming and ministry. Such restricted usage indicates that the phrase does not serve as a simple substitute for "I," but has some connection to Jesus' vocation (Colani 1864: 112–21, esp. 117).

Phase 2: 1894–1966

Beza's suggestion revived in 1894, when a form of it was adopted by Julius Wellhausen (1894: 312 n. 1). According to Wellhausen, Jesus called himself *bar nasha* ("the man"), using the phrase as a substitute for "I." The earliest Christians, misunderstanding this peculiarity, turned the phrase into a messianic designation based on Daniel 7.13. This reinterpretation took place only after Paul, who did not use the expression. Wellhausen recognized the peculiar nature of the usage presumed in his theory[9] and subsequently abandoned this view (Wellhausen 1897: 381 n. 1).

About the same time, Arnold Meyer (1896: 91–101) recognized that the Aramaic expression for "this (or that) man," used as a self-reference, would be *hahu gabra* rather than *hahu bar nasha*. He argued, however, that the idiom *hahu gabra* might also be expressed as *hahu bar nasha* and that this would simply be a special case of a more general use of "man" for "I." He translated ὁ υἱὸς τοῦ ἀνθρώπου in Matthew 8.20 as "a man (such as I)," supposing that *bar nash* was used here instead of "I" (A. Meyer 1896: 96). Meyer's position was soundly rejected by other leading Aramaic scholars of

---

[8] Bernhard Weiss ([1868] 1893: 1.75) later made the same point: the expression cannot refer deictically to the speaker without the addition of a pronoun.

[9] "Naturally it is highly peculiar to say 'the man' instead of 'I'; but it would be no less striking to say 'the Messiah' instead of 'I'" (Wellhausen 1894: 312 n. 1).

the day.[10] These scholars pointed out that while the phrase *hahu gabra*, "this man," could be used as a self-reference, there is no evidence that *hahu bar enasha* was used in the same way. Even if it were, either of these expressions would have been translated with a demonstrative (οὗτος ὁ υἱὸς τοῦ ἀνθρώπου) and could not underlie the New Testament phrase (ὁ υἱὸς τοῦ ἀνθρώπου). The Aramaic underlying the New Testament expression would have had no demonstrative (*bar enasha*), and would thus mean "the man" (or "man" or "a man"), but not "this man." Hence it could not be used as a circumlocution for "I."

This united rejection of the theory by Aramaic scholars quenched most enthusiasm for it. Nevertheless, it continued to appear sporadically. Rush Rhees (1898: 98) saw the phrase "son of man" as the practical equivalent of "I" in Matthew 11.19 and several other passages. Paul Haupt gave the same explanation for Matthew 8.20 and Mark 2.10, affirming that *hic homo* or ὅδε ἀνήρ ("this man" = "I") would have been a better translation of the Aramaic than ὁ υἱὸς τοῦ ἀνθρώπου (Haupt 1919a; 1919b).

J. Y. Campbell (1947; 1950) also argued for a mistranslation. According to Campbell, Jesus referred to himself as *hahu bar nasha* or *bar nasha hahu*, "this (son of) man." The phrase, misunderstood when translated into Greek, should have been translated οὗτος (or ὅδε) ὁ υἱὸς τοῦ ἀνθρώπου instead of by the expression with the article. Campbell's view drew criticism from Matthew Black (1948/49b: 34). R. E. C. Formesyn (1966) followed Campbell in affirming that the Aramaic expression underlying "the Son of Man" was *hahu bar nasha*. He supposed that it could be interpreted either as a substitute for "I" or as a reference to an expected messianic Son of Man. Formesyn's thesis, like Campbell's, depended on the unlikely assumption that an Aramaic demonstrative was consistently mistranslated as an article in the Greek expression.

Other exponents of the circumlocutional theory included Eduard Schweizer (1959: 198), who adopted it to explain the present Son of Man sayings. Philipp Vielhauer (1963: 157–59) responded by recalling the objections of Dalman. Samuel Sandmel (1963) interpreted "Son of Man" as "I" in several Markan passages, theorizing that Mark invented the titular usage.

[10] Lietzmann 1896: 84; Dalman [1898] 1902: 249–50; Schmiedel 1898b: 293–94; Wellhausen 1899: 6.200; Fiebig 1901b: 74–75. Meyer's view was also rejected by W. Wrede 1904.

Phase 3: 1967–

After Meyer (1896), proponents of the circumlocutional theory received little notice until Geza Vermes argued for it (Vermes 1967). Vermes attracted more attention for two reasons. First, the publication of his work coincided with an increased skepticism concerning the previously favored apocalyptic theory based on the Similitudes of Enoch. When it became clear that the Similitudes of Enoch were absent from the fragments of Enoch found at Qumran, scholars began to reexamine the idea that a unified apocalyptic "Son of Man" concept existed in pre-Christian Judaism. Many came to a negative conclusion: there was no such idea at the time for Jesus to take over. With this conclusion came a new willingness to examine other explanations.

Second, Vermes believed that he had new evidence for the theory: he had examined a more extensive array of Aramaic sources than previous researchers. On the basis of these sources, he argued that *bar nasha*, like *hahu gabra*, could be used as a circumlocution for "I" "when (a) a speaker wishes to avoid undue or immodest emphasis on himself, or (b) when he is prompted by fear or by a dislike of asserting openly something disagreeable in relation to himself" (Vermes 1967: 320).

In a later work, Vermes applied his thesis to the Son of Man sayings in the Gospels (Vermes 1973: 160–91; cf. 1978a; 1978b). He found the circumlocutional sense in twenty sayings that are independent of Daniel 7.13. He concluded that only these sayings can be traced back to Jesus. Two other groups of sayings, which refer to Daniel 7.13 either directly or indirectly, are the work of Jesus' apocalyptically minded disciples, who eschatologized the original idiom by means of a midrash on Daniel 7.13.

While Vermes' work induced a number of scholars to accept the circumlocutional theory,[11] most continued to reject it.[12] Aramaic scholars who have examined Vermes' work generally agree that the

---

[11] Marshall 1965/66: 328 (but Marshall later backs away from this view: Marshall 1970: 70–71; [1976] 1990: 64–65); O'Neill 1968/69: 158–62; Dodd 1970: 110–13; Wansbrough 1975; M. Müller 1977; 1984a; 1984b; 1991; Schwarz 1986; Hare 1990; Kingsbury 1990: 289. Michel (1971b) finds both circumlocutional and apocalyptic roots for "Son of Man."

[12] J. Jeremias 1967: 165; 1971: 261 n. 1; Borsch 1967: 23 n. 4; Le Déaut 1968: 397–99; Colpe [1969] 1972: 403–404; Gelston 1969: 189; Boers 1972: 307; Bowker 1977: 28–32, 42; Kearns 1978: 96; P. Casey 1979: 224–26; Lindars 1983: 19–24; A. Collins 1987: 397–98; Chilton 1992: 1.203.

examples he produced show not a circumlocutional use of *bar enasha*, but a generic use ("man" in general) or an indefinite use ("a man," someone), in which a person might include himself along with others. They do not show that a speaker could use it to refer exclusively to himself. Joseph A. Fitzmyer found the circumlocutional usage convincing in one of Vermes' examples, the Geniza fragment of a Targum to Genesis 4.14, but objected to its lateness, questioning its relevance for the New Testament period.[13] As Richard Bauckham points out, however, this instance too can be regarded as the indefinite sense used in a general statement: "a man (*bar nash*) cannot hide from you, O Lord" (Bauckham 1985: 32 n. 15). There is still, therefore, no evidence of any kind that "the son of man" without a demonstrative pronoun could be used as an exclusive self-reference equivalent to "I."

Despite the lack of evidence for the theory, it continues to attract adherents. Douglas R. A. Hare (1990) believes that Jesus employed *bar enasha* as a modest self-reference in six authentic Gospel sayings which relate to Jesus' earthly ministry.[14] He realizes that no evidence exists in Aramaic sources that *bar enasha* could be used in this way, but he argues that an analysis of how the Gospel sayings function supports such a usage.[15]

Reference to "man" in general or "a man"

Besides the circumlocutional theory, scholars have offered two other explanations of ὁ υἱὸς τοῦ ἀνθρώπου based on idiomatic meanings of *bar enasha*. Used in a generic sense, the phrase can refer to "man" in general. Used in an indefinite sense, it can mean "a man" and hence be the equivalent of an indefinite pronoun, "someone, anyone." If Jesus used *bar enasha* in one of these senses, he would have been referring to himself only indirectly.

Phase 1: 248–1792

The generic interpretation appears implicitly in the *Testimonia* of Cyprian (c. 248). In commenting on Matthew 12.32 ("Whoever

---

[13] Fitzmyer 1968: 426–28; 1973/74: 397 (reprinted 1979a: 95–96); 1979a: 13–14, 152–54; 1979b; 1980: 20.

[14] Matt. 11.19 par.; Luke 12.10 par.; Luke 12.8f.; Matt. 8.20 par.; Luke 11.30; Mark 2.10. Hare also thinks it likely that an authentic statement employing the *bar enasha* idiom lies behind the passion sayings, but he declines to delineate the precise formulation of such an utterance.

[15] For a review of Hare see Burkett 1992.

speaks a word against the son of man [*filium hominis*] will be forgiven, but whoever speaks against the Holy Spirit will not be forgiven"), he adduces 1 Samuel 2.25 as a parallel: "If in being delinquent a man should sin against man, they will pray to the Lord for him; but if a man should sin against God, who will pray for him?" (Cyprian, *Testimonium* 3.28; CSEL 3.1.142). The parallel between "son of man" in Matthew 12.32 and "man" in 1 Samuel 2.25 suggests that Cyprian may have understood the former in a generic sense.

Such an interpretation of Matthew 12.32 was made explicit by Gilbert Génébrard (1569: 246–47), a noted Hebraist, who likewise cited 1 Samuel 2.25. Génébrard recognized that "son of man" in Matthew 12.32 refers not to Jesus but to "man" in general: God would forgive someone who sinned against *man*, but not someone who sinned against the Holy Spirit.

The indefinite interpretation appears in the work of Matthias Flacius (1567), who paraphrased the expression in the Gospels as "any one man."[16] Subsequent interpreters did not always strictly distinguish the generic and indefinite senses. Hugo Grotius (1641), for example, found a generic/indefinite sense for "son of man" not only in the passage noted by Génébrard (Matt. 12.32), but also in Matthew 12.8 ("any man" is lord of the Sabbath).[17] Numerous interpreters followed Grotius' explanation of the phrase in these two passages.[18]

More than a century later, Johann Adrian Bolten (1792) made a thoroughgoing attempt to interpret nearly every occurrence of "son of man" in Matthew as the equivalent of an indefinite pronoun, translating it as "a man," "one," "someone," or "another." He assumed that an original Syriac expression used by Jesus had been

---

[16] ". . . it is used only by Ezekiel and Christ, for any one man [pro uno quopiam homine] . . . In the Gospel, Christ himself, using the third for the first person, names himself thus" (Flacius 1567: s.v. *filius*).

[17] Grotius [1641] 1972: at Matt. 12.8: "But, as I said, it is well known that to the Hebrews *ben adam* [*a son of man*] signifies any man." Also at Matthew 12.32: "by υἱὸν ἀνθρώπου [*son of man*], though with the article added, is to be understood here not Christ alone, but any man, Christ, of course, not excepted. For the article is frequently the sign of generality."

[18] E.g. Episcopius (d. 1643) 1650: at Matt. 12.8 and 12.32 ("any man at all"); Le Cène [1696] 1702: at Matt. 8.20, 12.8, 12.32 ("a man in general"); S. Clarke 1701–1702: at Matt. 12.8 ("any man," including and especially Christ). Arguments against Grotius' interpretation of Matthew 12.32 were given by Quenstedt (1685: Part II, p. 86, at Matt. 12.32).

mistranslated. Later he extended this interpretation to the other Gospels, adding the circumlocutional sense in a few passages (Luke 6.22; 17.22, 26, 30). Bolten's efforts resulted in contorted interpretations of individual passages and did not explain how different translators all came to make the same mistake.[19]

Phase 2: 1896–1967

The generic/indefinite interpretation practically disappeared in the nineteenth century. At the end of the nineteenth century, Nathaniel Schmidt (1896) revived it. He argued that Jesus never referred to himself as "the Son of Man," but used *bar nasha* of "man" in a generic sense in several passages (Mark 2.10, 28; Matt. 8.20; 12.32; Mark 14.21; 9.31). Thus "man" may forgive sins, "man" may break the Sabbath: Jesus exercised this authority as one man among others. Through overliteral translation into Greek, the generic phrase came to be regarded as an exclusive self-reference, a messianic title, and with this understanding of it, the early church created the rest of the Son of Man sayings.

Following Schmidt, several other scholars likewise accepted the generic sense of the phrase as original, but also found the indefinite sense in a few authentic sayings. Julius Wellhausen (1899) found an authentic generic sense of *bar nasha* in several passages (Mark 2.10, 28; Luke 12.10) and the indefinite sense "a man" in Matthew 11.19. Georges Dupont (1924) devoted a monograph to the view that five earthly Son of Man sayings reflect an authentic Aramaic idiom, three in the generic sense of "man" (Mark 2.10; 2.28; Matt. 12.32) and two in the indefinite sense "a man," i.e. "someone" (Matt. 8.20; 11.19). Charles Guignebert (1935: 270–79) likewise argued that if Jesus used the expression "son of man," it was only in the sense "man" (Matt. 12.32; 8.20; Mark 2.28) or "a man" (Matt. 11.19; Mark 2.10). All three scholars agreed with Schmidt that the rest of the Son of Man sayings were made by the church, which misunderstood Jesus' idiomatic usage as an exclusive self-reference, a messianic title based on Daniel 7.13.

Several interpreters found a mixture of generic, indefinite, and circumlocutional senses of "son of man" in some of the present Son

---

[19] So Scholten 1809: 179. Similarly Johann Gottfried Eichhorn (1793) described Bolten's translation of "son of man" in Matthew 10.23 by "a man" (someone) as "artificial."

of Man sayings.[20] On the other hand, Erik Sjöberg registered an objection to all such views.[21]

Phase 3: 1967–

Vermes' revival of the circumlocutional theory in 1967 stimulated further discussion of *bar enash(a)*, leading to several new attempts to explain "Son of Man" in the Gospels from some idiomatic use of this Aramaic expression. A number of scholars have argued that Jesus used the expression in a generic or indefinite sense.[22]

P. M. Casey believes that Jesus used general statements (generalizations), sometimes with *bar nash*, sometimes with *bar nasha*, in order to say something about himself. For example, in Matthew 8.20 as Casey translates it, Jesus says, "The jackals have holes and the birds of the air have roosts, and a son of man has nowhere to lay his head." Here Jesus generalizes, but with the intent of applying the generalization to his own situation. Casey finds such a general sense in twelve sayings, which relate to Jesus' life on earth and his death (P. Casey 1976b; 1987).[23] These, he believes, can be considered authentic sayings of Jesus. Once such sayings were translated into Greek, the general reference was misunderstood as a title referring to Daniel 7.13, and new sayings with this title were created.

Barnabas Lindars argued for a special idiomatic use of *bar nasha*, in which the speaker refers to a limited class of persons, among whom he includes himself.[24] Lindars found this alleged idiom, in which *bar nasha* means "a man in my position," in nine of the

[20] A. Meyer 1896; O. Holtzmann [1901] 1904: 166–71; Bultmann [1921] 1968: 15, 16–17, 28, 131; Schulthess 1922; T. Manson [1931] 1935: 211–35; Héring [1937] 1959: 98–110.
[21] "It is unthinkable that Jesus would have expressed general statements about the life of man or assigned to men the right to forgive in God's place . . . The attempt to understand *bar nasha*, like *hahu gabra*, as a circumlocution for 'I' . . . founders on the fact that this use of *bar nasha* is nowhere to be found in the Aramaic sources" (Sjöberg 1955: 239 n. 3).
[22] P. Casey 1976a; 1976b; 1976c; 1979; 1985a; 1985b; 1987; 1991a: 46–54; 1991b; 1994; 1995; Polag 1977; Lindars 1980; 1981; 1983; 1985; Bauckham 1985; Fuller 1985; Mearns 1985/86; Goergen 1986: 180–202; Kearns 1988; Crossan 1991: 238–59; 1994: 49–53; Chilton 1992; 1996.
[23] Mark 2.10; 2.28; 8.38; 9.12; 10.45; 14.21 (twice); Matt. 8.20; 11.19; 12.32; Luke 12.8; 22.48.
[24] Lindars 1980; 1981; 1983. These works mark a change of opinion from his earlier view (Lindars 1975/76).

Gospel sayings.[25] Like many of his predecessors, Lindars believed that translating the Aramaic expression into Greek turned it into a phrase that could be interpreted as a title, and hence new sayings were created relating the expression to Daniel 7.13.

Unfortunately, Lindars erroneously used the term "generic" to categorize the idiom to which he refers. In a critique of Lindars' work, Richard Bauckham (1985: 26–27) suggested that he had confused generic with indefinite. In response, Lindars (1985) clarified his meaning. He uses the term "generic" in a sense that differs from the conventional meaning of that term as referring to a whole class. The idiom Lindars has in mind is described in the *Hebrew Grammar* of Gesenius-Kautzsch par. 126q. It involves the use of the definite article in Hebrew where English idiom would use an indefinite article (e.g. Amos 5.19: "as if a man fled from *the lion* and *the bear* met him"). Lindars defined this idiom as "the idiomatic use of the definite article in indefinite statements" in which the definite article denotes "a particular but unspecified member or group of members of the class" (Lindars 1985: 35).

The indefinite usage forms the basis for the proposal of Richard Bauckham (1985). He suggests that Jesus used *bar enash* in the indefinite sense ("a man," "someone"), but as a deliberately ambiguous self-reference. Jesus referred to an unidentified "someone," but those who understood him would recognize that he referred to himself. Bauckham lists sixteen passages where he finds this exclusive but implicit self-reference.

Reginald Fuller (1985) proposes basically the same theory as Bauckham. Jesus used *bar nasha* as the equivalent of an indefinite pronoun in the sense "a man," "a fellow," as we might say "Can't a guy do what he likes?" meaning "Can't I do what I like?" Thus in Matthew 8.20, Jesus says, "A fellow has nowhere to lay his head." In this way, Jesus used *bar nasha* in an indefinite sense as an exclusive self-reference. Like Bauckham, Fuller finds authentic sayings of this type in all three classes of Son of Man sayings. The post-Easter church expanded the number of sayings, but the phrase remained a nontitular self-referent.

According to Rollin Kearns (1988), Jesus used the expression in a generic sense. The early Aramaic-speaking church converted Jesus' nontitular usage into a title for Jesus as a prophet. Subse-

[25] Five in Q (Matt. 8.20; 10.32–33; 11.19; 12.32; Luke 11.30; and parallels); four in Mark (Mark 2.10 and three reconstructed forms lying behind the passion predictions).

quently, the Greek-speaking church developed the title in light of two traditions: that of the righteous man who is put to death and then glorified (Wis. 1.16–5.23; Isa. 53) and that of the reign of God revealed as judgment (Sib. Or. 3.46–50, 53–62).[26]

John Dominic Crossan (1991: 238–59; 1994: 49–53) finds one authentic Son of Man saying of Jesus (Gospel of Thomas 86 = Q/ Luke 9.57–58 = Matt. 8.19–20). He eliminates the rest by the criterion of multiple attestation: of forty complexes of Son of Man sayings, only this one has "Son of Man" attested in more than a single source. In this one authentic saying, Crossan takes "son of man" as generic. He speculates that early Christian communities had texts in which Jesus used "son of man" in a generic or indefinite sense. Such texts facilitated the transition to the titular Son of Man based on Daniel 7.13, after which the phrase was extended to other non-apocalyptic sayings put on the lips of Jesus.

Bruce Chilton (1992; 1996) thinks that Jesus used "son of man" in both a generic sense to refer to himself along with other human beings (Matt. 8.20//Luke 9.58) and an "angelic" sense to refer to an angel distinct from himself who would vindicate his teaching at the final judgment (Mark 8:38; Q/Luke 12:8–9). Chilton (1992) lists eleven sayings used in a generic sense.[27]

Critique

Our critique of the generic/indefinite theories will focus on the works of Casey, Lindars, Bauckham, and Fuller.[28] All four scholars believe that Jesus used the expression in the indefinite sense "a man," and that only sayings which can be so translated are authentic.[29] But does the translation "a man" give the best sense for the passages claimed for it by these scholars? Two considerations indicate that it does not.

To begin with, while the Aramaic bar enasha could be translated

---

[26] See the review by Fuller 1990. Kearns' earlier three-volume work (1978, 1980, 1982) is criticized by M. Müller (1984a: 27–32).

[27] Matt. 8.20; 11.19; Mark 8.31; Matt. 17.12; 17.22–23; 20.18–19; 20.28; 26.2; 26.24; Luke 22.48; Matt. 26.45; Luke 24.7; and parallels. Two other sayings, according to Chilton, have both a generic and an angelic reference (Matt. 12.8; 12.32).

[28] For reviews of Casey and Lindars see Moloney 1980 and Black 1984.

[29] In Casey's theory, "general statements" could include both the generic and indefinite senses, but in practice he consistently translates the phrase as indefinite in English.

as "a man," the Greek ὁ υἱὸς τοῦ ἀνθρώπου could not. Depending on whether the first article is individualizing or generic, the Greek expression could mean "the son of (the) man," referring to an individual, or "the human being" ("man" in a generic sense), but not "a man." Thus these scholars base their theories on neither of the two meanings of *bar enasha* that could be expressed by the Greek, but on the one meaning that could not. They have to assume that the Aramaic has been mistranslated. While this is certainly possible, it is equally possible that the translators knew their business and gave ὁ υἱὸς τοῦ ἀνθρώπου as the best equivalent of the underlying Aramaic.

Second, in order for the thesis of mistranslation to be plausible, these scholars must show that the Greek expression as it stands does not yield an adequate meaning. This they fail to do. In most sayings, the Greek expression gives the best sense when understood as a title referring to Jesus. Casey, Lindars, and Bauckham, though not Fuller, recognize that the expression must be a title in most of these sayings. They do not show why in certain sayings the titular interpretation (which is in harmony with the Greek) should be abandoned for the indefinite interpretation (which is not).

The most serious objection to all such theories is the fact that they produce implausible results when applied to particular sayings. In only one Son of Man saying is it certain that a generic use of *bar enasha* underlay the Greek translation. This is the unforgivable sin logion, which occurs in both a Markan version, which speaks of "sons of men" (Mark 3.28–29), and a Q version, which has the singular "the son of man" (Luke 12.10; Matt. 12.32). Here a generic *bar enasha* has been translated in the Q version in such a way as to permit confusion with the title "the Son of Man."[30] Yet even here it is not necessary to suppose that the overliteral translation led to the creation of a previously non-existent title. It is just as likely that the translator's familiarity with the title led him to translate the expression as such.

Besides the unforgivable sin logion, there are only two other Son of Man sayings in which the expression could plausibly be interpreted as generic. In both of these, however, the expression could just as plausibly be interpreted as a title referring exclusively to Jesus. In Mark 2.10 Jesus affirms "that ὁ υἱὸς τοῦ ἀνθρώπου has authority to forgive sins on the earth." Numerous scholars have

---

[30] Colpe [1969] 1972: 442–43; Boring 1976.

interpreted the expression here as the generic "man,"[31] while numerous others have read it as the title for Jesus.[32] The same divergence of opinion occurs concerning Mark 2.28, where Jesus says, "So ὁ υἱὸς τοῦ ἀνθρώπου is Lord even of the Sabbath." The expression has been interpreted as the generic "man,"[33] but also as the christological title.[34]

In all other Son of Man sayings besides these three, the expression is most plausibly interpreted as the christological title. Attempts to interpret the expression elsewhere as generic or indefinite have been forced and have led to implausible results. For example, Casey (1987: 37) translates Matthew 8.20 as a generalization: "The jackals have holes and the birds of the air have roosts, and a son of man has nowhere to lay his head." At first, Casey describes the generalization thus: "the divine provision of resting-places for jackals and birds is contrasted with the lack of such provision for men, who have to build houses to have anywhere to stay." In this description, however, Casey subtly changes the verb of the saying from "have" to "be provided": jackals and birds are provided with dwellings, but humans are not. Even with this change of verb, such a generalization is not true, since birds have to build their nests no less than humans have to build their homes. Nor is the generalization true with the original verb: it is not the case that animals have dwellings while humans do not.

Casey apparently recognizes the difficulty of this initial interpretation, since he then seeks to qualify it, limiting the saying's application to a social sub-group, Jesus and his disciples: animals have dwellings but Jesus and his disciples do not. Such a statement could no doubt be true, but the saying as Casey translates it will not support such a limitation. For that we would have to have something like "The jackals have holes and the birds of the air have roosts, but a son of man [who follows me] has nowhere to lay his head." The indefinite "a son of man" would have to be qualified in some such way, a qualification that is lacking in the saying as it stands.

Lindars' interpretations of particular sayings produce no more

---

[31] N. Schmidt 1896: 48; Wellhausen 1899: 6.202–203; Dupont 1924: 41–45; T. Manson [1931] 1935: 211–35; Héring [1937] 1959: 108–10; Hay 1970.

[32] Tödt [1959] 1965: 126–30; Kertelge 1973; Gnilka 1975; et al.

[33] A. Meyer 1896: 93; N. Schmidt 1896: 49; Wellhausen 1899: 6.202; Bultmann [1921] 1968: 16–17; Dupont 1924: 45–53; T. Manson [1931] 1935: 211–35; Guignebert 1935: 278; Héring [1937] 1959: 108–10; Hay 1970.

[34] Tödt [1959] 1965: 130–32; Beare 1960: 132; et al.

convincing results than those of Casey. To give an example: in
Matthew 11.19, Lindars translates,

> John came neither eating nor drinking, and they say, "He
> has a demon"; *a man* has come eating and drinking, and
> they say, "Behold, a glutton and a drunkard."

This interpretation would give a plausible sense if the adjective
"another" preceded "man." Such an adjective is lacking, however.
Furthermore, Lindars' explanation of the saying follows an extre-
mely convoluted path. He supposes that

> anyone who comes eating and drinking is contrasted with
> John the Baptist . . . The generic article [left untranslated
> before "man"] specifies one of this class who might come
> eating and drinking, and the context shows that he is to be
> identified with Jesus.   (Lindars 1985: 39)

But nothing in this saying, even if Lindars' translation is allowed,
suggests a class of eaters and drinkers. The indefinite "a man"
would indicate not one of a class of eaters and drinkers, but one of
the class of men. It is Jesus who is contrasted with John, not some
hypothetical group of gluttons. But if that is the case, there is no
reason why ὁ υἱὸς τοῦ ἀνθρώπου should not be considered a title
referring exclusively to Jesus. Lindars' interpretation introduces
unnecessary confusion and complexity into a fairly straightforward
saying.

Bauckham and Fuller differ from Casey and Lindars in seeing ὁ
υἱὸς τοῦ ἀνθρώπου as an exclusive self-reference, albeit an indefinite one. This modification, however, helps little in most instances.
Bauckham finds an example of this use in Mark 14.62: when the
high priest asks, "Are you the Christ, the Son of the Blessed One?"
Jesus replies, "I am. And you will see a man sitting at the right
hand of God." By using the indefinite phrase "a man" here,
according to Bauckham (1985: 31), "Jesus avoids a direct claim to
messiahship." But there is no reason for such obliqueness following
Jesus' direct and unequivocal "I am."

Fuller (1985: 212) finds a single authentic saying of this type
behind all the predictions of the passion: "a fellow is handed over
to the hands of men." It is no doubt a matter of judgment, but it
seems hard to imagine that Jesus would speak of his imminent
arrest in such an awkward manner. While there might be a few
sayings where an indefinite but exclusive self-reference of this sort

would be plausible, the titular sense would be just as plausible, if not more so, and the nontitular sayings would be too few to explain the Son of Man tradition as a whole.

Evaluation

The nontitular interpretation of "Son of Man" in the Gospels has been around now for about 450 years. The various theories belonging to this class have a certain appeal, because they seek to take seriously the presumed Aramaic expression underlying the Gospel phrase. They also seek to explain why the phrase appears in the third person in Jesus' mouth.

Despite their appeal, the nontitular theories lack any substantial basis. The latest manifestations, while more subtle and complex than the earliest, appear no more convincing. The basic problem with the circumlocutional theory was already pointed out by Strauss: the idiom requires a demonstrative pronoun ("*this* man") which the Gospel expression lacks. As for the generic/indefinite interpretation, its chief weakness in all of its forms lies in the fact that it produces implausible results for all but a few of the Son of Man sayings in the Gospels. Only one saying certainly reflects a generic *bar enasha* that has been translated overliterally as ὁ υἱὸς τοῦ ἀνθρώπου (Luke 12.10; Matt. 12.32). While a generic interpretation of "son of man" has also been found plausible by numerous scholars in Mark 2.10 and 2.28, applying a generic or indefinite explanation to sayings beyond these three leads to forced interpretations. If, however, no more than a few sayings can be explained as nontitular, it becomes difficult to use these to account for the remaining sayings, i.e. to explain how the Evangelists gained the impression that "Son of Man" was a characteristic titular self-designation of Jesus.

The scholars who have investigated the nontitular explanation have performed a service for the scholarly community. It was a possibility that had to be explored and has been well explored. The time has come, however, to take stock and recognize that this line of research has not led to a convincing solution. Future research will make progress only with the recognition that "Son of Man" in the bulk of its occurrences is a title rather than a nontitular idiom.

9

SON OF MAN IN APOCALYPTIC AND
RABBINIC TEXTS

In the first half of the twentieth century, scholars had reached a consensus that Jewish sources presented a unified conception of an apocalyptic "Son of Man." One of Norman Perrin's contributions to the Son of Man debate was to challenge this view (Perrin 1974: 23–40). He argued that the Similitudes of Enoch, 4 Ezra 13, and the midrashic literature reflect independent exegeses of Daniel 7.13, not a common tradition concerning an eschatological Redeemer with well-defined attributes and functions. These sources interpreted the manlike figure in Daniel 7.13 as the Messiah, but developed the figure in various ways.

Perrin's thesis has gained widespread acceptance. As Raymond Brown indicates,

> probably the majority view among scholars is that Jesus or his followers were responsible for the specification of the Son-of-Man concept, for there was no established Jewish portrait or expectation of that figure.   (Brown 1994: 1.512)

While the majority of scholars may take this view, others have argued for a greater unity in the apocalyptic "Son of Man" material than Perrin found there. As Brown further notes:

> another vein of scholarship, which now seems to be reviving, has argued that there was a 1st-cent. Jewish expectation that God would make victorious and enthrone over Israel's enemies a specific human figure who would be the instrument of divine judgment – a figure who could be appropriately designated "the Son of Man."
>
> (Brown 1994: 1.508)

Before examining the works of scholars seeking to revive this view, we will examine afresh the apocalyptic texts that allude to Daniel 7.13. These include 1 Enoch 37–70, 1 Enoch 71, and 4 Ezra

13, all of which are now generally dated to the first century CE.[1] We will attempt to determine to what extent they reflect a unity and to what extent a diversity of interpretation. We will then review the works of several scholars who have argued for a unity in this material. Following this review we will make a similar examination of the later midrashic texts that allude to Daniel 7.13.

Daniel 7.13 in 1 Enoch 37–70

The main part of the Similitudes of Enoch (1 Enoch 37–70) presents a pre-existent Messiah. This figure combines the attributes and functions of the one like a son of man in Daniel 7.13, the Davidic Messiah of Isaiah 11 and Psalm 2, the servant of the Lord in Second Isaiah, and Yahweh as eschatological judge.[2] The Similitudes explicitly identify the figure as the Messiah (1 Enoch 48.10; 52.4). From a servant passage, his primary title is "the Chosen One" (Isa. 42.1). God chose him and hid him in heaven before the world was created (1 Enoch 48.3, 6; 62.7). At the final judgment, he will sit on God's throne of glory and execute judgment for the righteous against the rebellious angels and sinners, especially the kings and rulers of earth.

What sort of being is this messianic figure in the Similitudes – human, angelic, or divine? Enoch first describes him as one "whose face had the appearance of a man, and his face (was) full of grace, like one of the holy angels" (1 Enoch 46.1).[3] This description compares his "face" to both man and angel, but identifies him as neither. Such language would be consistent with the idea of a human being who has been transformed into an angel. In the Similitudes, such a transformation is the fate of the righteous in general: "all will become angels in heaven" (1 Enoch 51.4). Like the face of the son of man, the transformed faces of the righteous receive special notice (1 Enoch 38.4; 39.14; 51.5).[4]

Chapter 46 describes the Chosen One in terms drawn from Daniel 7. Enoch, who has ascended to heaven, sees there "one who

---

[1] Generally 4 Ezra is dated to the end of the first century (Caragounis 1986: 120; Stone 1992: 612). Dates assigned to the Similitudes of Enoch (1 Enoch 37–71) range more widely, but now usually fall in the first century CE (see Chapter 7).

[2] For the first three of these see especially Nickelsburg 1992b: 138–39; cf. Nickelsburg 1981: 215; Black 1985: 189. On the last, see below.

[3] In quotations of 1 Enoch, I use the translation of Michael A. Knibb (1978).

[4] On the portrayal of a righteous human as an angel in other pseudepigraphical texts, see Charlesworth 1980.

had a head of days" and another "whose face had the appearance of a man." When Enoch asks about "that Son of Man," an angel replies that "This is the Son of Man who has righteousness" (1 Enoch 46.1, 3).

Immediately thereafter, in chapters 47–51, Enoch has an antici-patory vision of what will happen when the full number of the righteous is reached. The vision is basically a reenactment of Daniel's vision in Daniel 7.9–14. The Danielic vision provides the core of Enoch's vision:

> And in those days I saw the Head of Days sit down on the throne of his glory, and the books of the living were opened before him, and all his host, which (dwells) in the heavens above, and his council were standing before him [1 Enoch 47.3; cf. Dan. 7.9–10] . . . And at that hour that Son of Man was named in the presence of the Lord of Spirits, and his name (was named) before the Head of Days [1 Enoch 48.2; cf. Dan. 7.13] . . . All those who dwell upon the dry ground will fall down and worship before him [1 Enoch 48.5; cf. Dan. 7.14] . . . for the Chosen One stands before the Lord of the Spirits, and his glory (is) for ever and ever, and his power for all generations [1 Enoch 49.2; cf. Dan. 7.14] . . . And in those days the Chosen One will sit on his throne . . . for the Lord of Spirits has appointed him and glorified him [1 Enoch 51.3; cf. Dan. 7.14].

In Enoch's vision, as in Daniel 7.9–14, the Head of Days sits on his throne of judgment surrounded by innumerable angels, and hea-venly books are opened. One like a son of man is brought before him and given eternal power and glory and kingship, so that all on earth will serve or worship him. Enoch's vision goes beyond that of Daniel by referring to the throne on which the Son of Man will sit.[5]

Strikingly, Enoch's vision makes no mention of the Son of Man coming "with the clouds of heaven" (Dan. 7.13). That which corresponds to Daniel 7.13 in Enoch's vision (1 Enoch 48.2) is merely the naming of the Son of Man in the presence of the Head of Days (Nickelsburg 1981: 217). The interpreter apparently had difficulty working in the motif of coming to God with clouds

---

[5] "The fact that 'thrones were set' in Dan 7.9 led naturally enough to the inference that one of them was for the 'Son of Man' figure" (J. Collins 1992: 458).

because it suggested a transition from earth to heaven, whereas the Son of Man in the Similitudes was already in heaven with God, even before the creation of the world (Nickelsburg 1992b: 139).

The primary function of the Chosen One is to preside at the last judgment.[6] At that time the dead are raised (51.1–3; 61.5), and God sets the Chosen One on his throne of glory.[7] The Chosen One then judges the deeds of the angels of heaven (55.4; 61.8), the righteous (62.3 v.l.), and sinners (45.3; 62.2 v.l.; 69.27–28). Chief among the sinners are the kings, the exalted, and those who rule the earth, whose destruction receives special attention in the Similitudes.[8] Though they plead for mercy, they are turned over to the angels of punishment and tormented in the flames of Sheol (62.11; 63.10). The chosen righteous, on the other hand, are transformed into angels and dwell forever with the Son of Man on a transformed earth (51.5; 52.4; 62.14; 69.29).

The Similitudes transfer to the Messiah certain eschatological functions elsewhere attributed to Yahweh. (1) In Micah 1.4 Yahweh comes down from heaven and treads on the mountains, which melt under his feet like wax before a fire (cf. Ps. 97.5). The Similitudes transfer this theophany to the Chosen One (1 Enoch 52). (2) In Isaiah 24.21–23, it is Yahweh who punishes the host of heaven and the kings of the earth. In the Similitudes, the Chosen One performs this function. (3) The Hebrew scriptures refer to the day of judgment as the Day of Yahweh (Amos 5.20 etc.). In the Similitudes, it has become "the day of the Chosen One" (1 Enoch 61.5).

It is somewhat misleading to speak of the Enochic figure as a "Son of Man" figure, since this overemphasizes the role played by Daniel 7.13. The Similitudes generally call him "the Chosen One," and Daniel 7.13 is only one of several scriptural texts that go to make up his portrayal. The description I have given above, like most scholarship on the subject, emphasizes the Danielic element because of a desire to compare the figure with the New Testament Son of Man. In his essential nature, however, the Chosen One is a pre-existent Messiah, hidden with God in heaven and waiting to be revealed at the end-time. This concept existed in Judaism independently of Daniel 7.13.[9] In fact, when the author of the Similitudes

---

[6] ". . . and the whole judgement was given to the Son of Man" (1 Enoch 69.27).

[7] 1 Enoch 45.3; 51.3; 55.4; 61.8; 62.2, 3, 5; 69.27, 29.

[8] 1 Enoch 46.4–8; 48.8–10; 53.2–5; 54.1–2; 62.1–6, 9–12; 63.1–12.

[9] Mowinckel [1951] 1954: 304–308; Wolfson 1956: 156–61; Urbach 1979: 684–85.

tries to work Daniel 7.13 into this more central conception, he has to drop part of Daniel, the coming to God in the clouds, because this motif is inconsistent with the idea that the Messiah is in heaven with God from the beginning.

Daniel 7.13 in 1 Enoch 71

There is good reason to believe that 1 Enoch 71, the final chapter of the Similitudes, had a different origin than the earlier chapters.[10] Its use of Daniel 7.13 differs from that of the earlier chapters in two respects. First, chapter 71 identifies Enoch himself as the Danielic figure, whereas the earlier chapters distinguish between the two characters.[11] In 46.2–3 Enoch sees God and the son of man and is told, "This is the Son of Man who has righteousness, and with whom righteousness dwells." In 71.14, however, Enoch sees only God, and he is told, "You are the Son of Man who was born to righteousness, and righteousness remains over you, and the righteousness of the Head of Days will not leave you." Whereas in the earlier chapters the righteous are to dwell with the son of man that Enoch sees (45.4; 62.14), in chapter 71 they are to dwell with the son of man who is Enoch himself (71.16–17).

The second difference is that the son of man in chapter 71 (Enoch) ascends to heaven from earth, whereas the previous chapters depict a figure who exists in heaven from the beginning. Like chapters 46–51, chapter 71 reenacts the scene from Daniel 7.9–14, this time with Enoch in the role of the "one like a son of man":

> And the spirit carried Enoch off to the highest heaven, and I saw there . . . tongues of living fire. And my spirit saw a

[10] Colpe ([1969] 1972: 426–27), U. Müller (1972: 54–59), Theisohn (1975: 216 n. 4), and Nickelsburg (1981: 221; 1992a: 2.512; 1992b: 6.140) regard chapter 71 as a later redactional addition to the Similitudes. J. J. Collins earlier held this view (1980: 119–24; 1984: 151–53) but later argued for the unity of this chapter with the rest (J. Collins 1992: 455–57). M. Black (1952; 1985: 188) regards the chapter not as a later, but as an older stratum of the tradition. Vanderkam (1992: 177–85) argues for the unity of chs. 70–71 and the rest of the Similitudes.

[11] So the scholars cited in the preceding note. Collins critiques the view of Mowinckel, that chapter 71 does not identify Enoch with the messianic "son of man," and the view of Hooker, Casey, and Caquot, that the Similitudes presuppose the identification of Enoch as the son of man throughout (J. Collins 1980: 119–24; 1984: 151–53). In a later work he changes his mind and adopts the view of Mowinckel (J. Collins 1992: 455–57), but his earlier arguments remain convincing against this view.

circle of fire which surrounded that house; from its four sides (came) rivers full of living fire, and they surrounded that house. And round about (were) the Seraphim, and the Cherubim and the Ophannim; these are they who do not sleep, but keep watch over the throne of his glory. And I saw angels who could not be counted, a thousand thousands and ten thousand times ten thousand surrounding that house . . . and with them the Head of Days, his head white and pure like wool, and his garments indescribable . . . And that angel came to me, and greeted me with his voice, and said to me, You are the Son of Man who was born to righteousness.   (1 Enoch 71.5–14)

Here numerous details from Daniel 7.9–14 appear: the Head of Days, his white hair, his white garments, his throne of fiery flames, the stream of fire that comes from before him, and the tens of thousands of angels that surround him. Furthermore, as the "son of man," Enoch reenacts Daniel 7.13: "And behold with the clouds of heaven one like a son of man was coming; and he came to the Ancient of Days, and they brought him before him." Though the language of "coming with the clouds of heaven" is absent from the description, the context makes clear that this coming is fulfilled by Enoch's ascent to heaven. There he encounters the Head of Days and is acknowledged as the "son of man." Thus 1 Enoch 71 interprets the "son of man" of Daniel 7.13 as an earthly individual, and his coming as an ascent to heaven.

Does this chapter present Enoch as the Messiah? Possibly (Black 1985: 252), since the threefold emphasis on the "righteousness" of Enoch (71.14) may attach to him a feature of the Davidic Messiah, whose righteousness is emphasized in the Hebrew Bible (Isa. 9.7; 11.4–5; 32.1; Jer. 23.5–6; 33.15–16).[12]

Daniel 7.13 in 4 Ezra 13

A third interpretation of Daniel 7.13 in the apocalyptic literature appears in 4 Ezra 13. Here Ezra has a vision that incorporates imagery from Daniel 7:

and behold, a wind arose from the sea and stirred up all its waves. And I looked, and behold, this wind made some-

---

[12] It is less likely that the motif of righteousness comes from the suffering Servant of Isaiah 53.11.

thing like the figure of a man come up out of the heart of the sea. And I looked, and behold, that man flew with the clouds of heaven; and wherever he turned his face to look, everything under his gaze trembled, and whenever his voice issued from his mouth, all who heard his voice melted as wax melts when it feels the fire.   (4 Ezra 13.2–4)[13]

As the vision proceeds, this man flies up onto a mountain, destroys an army raised against him with fire from his mouth, and calls to himself another multitude that is peaceful. When Ezra seeks an interpretation, God tells him that the man is "he whom the Most High has been keeping for many ages, who will himself deliver his creation" (4 Ezra 13.26). In the last days, he will take his stand on Mount Zion, destroy an army that attacks it, and regather the ten lost tribes of Israel.

Most scholars believe that the vision in 4 Ezra 13.1–13 was not composed by the author of 4 Ezra (Pseudo-Ezra), but was an independent tradition that he took over and reinterpreted.[14] In this case, the vision may have originally expressed ideas different than those of the interpretation. P. M. Casey reviews the arguments for this view, specifically those of Michael Stone, and finds them unconvincing (P. Casey 1979: 126–29). J. J. Collins grants that "Casey shows that unity of authorship is not impossible," but still feels that probability favors Stone's arguments (J. Collins 1992: 462 n. 66). We will therefore consider the vision and Pseudo-Ezra's interpretation of it separately. The latter, if it is not a direct interpretation of Daniel 7.13, is at least an interpretation of an interpretation of that passage.

The vision as independent

As the vision begins, Ezra sees "something like the figure of a man come up out of the heart of the sea" (13.3). The manlike figure recalls the "one like a son of man" of Daniel 7.13, though the Danielic figure does not come out of the sea. Since the vision does not explain the symbolism of the sea, we can have no certainty

---

[13] For quotations of 4 Ezra (= 2 Esdras), I use the Revised Standard Version (May and Metzger, 1977).
[14] Tödt [1959] 1965: 24 n. 3; Stone 1968: 304–307; 1990: 399–400; U. Müller 1972: 108–109; J. Collins 1992: 461–62.

concerning its meaning.[15] We can, however, compare it with similar imagery in two other apocalypses. The description ultimately goes back to the vision of Daniel 7.3, where four beasts come up out of the sea. In Daniel the sea has associations with the combat myths of the ancient Near East, especially that of Israel, in which the sea represents the forces opposed to Yahweh (e.g. Pss. 74.12–15; 89.9–10). That significance is clearly not in view in 4 Ezra 13. However, another aspect of the vision in Daniel may be in view. The beasts that rise from the sea represent four kings or kingdoms that arise on the earth (Dan. 7.17, 23). By analogy, the figure in Ezra's vision may also represent a king who arises on the earth.

A second parallel occurs in an apocalypse contemporary with 4 Ezra, the book of Revelation. In Revelation 13.1, a beast arises out of the sea. Commentators generally agree that here the sea represents the underworld and that this beast represents Nero *redivivus*. Satan brings the soul of Nero up from the underworld and reincarnates it in a persecuting emperor.[16] By analogy to this vision, the "something like a figure of a man" in 4 Ezra may also be a soul brought up from the underworld and reincarnated or resurrected.[17] This figure, however, would not be an "antichrist," but the Messiah.

If we speculated on the identity of this figure, the logical choice would be David. The idea of David's return from the underworld may have come from Psalm 16.10, where the author, identified in the heading as David, says, "you will not leave my soul in Hades" (LXX Ps. 15.10). When first-century Christians used this text to prove the resurrection of Jesus, they first had to deny that it referred to David (Acts 2.27, 29). Did they perhaps deny this idea to contradict others who believed that it did refer to David? If there were such people, they could have appealed to certain scriptural passages which, if read literally, would indicate that "David" would be king over the regathered tribes of Israel (Ezek. 34.23–24; 37.24–25).[18] All of this is pure speculation, of course, but it

[15] We need not assume with Müller that the sea is a meaningless *Bildmotiv* of the vision (U. Müller 1972: 117).

[16] Caird 1966: 161, 164–65; A. Collins 1990a: 91, 97, 121; Roloff 1993: 156–57.

[17] So Gressmann, cited by Tödt 1965: 26 n. 1; similarly J. Jeremias 1929: 110.

[18] In a rabbinic tradition, Rabbi Akiba interprets the thrones of Daniel 7.9 as "one for [God] and one for David" (*b Hag.* 14a // *b Sanh.* 38b). Casey suggests that Akiba meant the historical David raised from the dead and given a throne at the last judgment (P. Casey 1979: 86–87).

develops logically from the premise of interpreting 4 Ezra 13.3 in analogy with Revelation 13.1 as a literal ascent from the abyss.

Once the figure ascends from the sea, the vision refers to him simply as a "man" (13.3, 5, 12). Yet the actions that he performs put him beyond the bounds of normal humanity. He flies with the clouds of heaven, causes everything he looks at to tremble, and melts people like wax in a fire with his voice (13.3–4). When a multitude gathers to make war against him, he carves out a great mountain and flies up onto it. From his mouth he sends forth fire, flame, and sparks that destroy his opponents (13.5–11). Scholars who interpret the vision independently of the interpretation given in the text usually take these details more literally than does Pseudo-Ezra (see below).

Most of these actions have their source in scriptural texts. Scholars generally take flying "with the clouds of heaven" as an allusion to Daniel 7.13, which links the same phrase to "one like a son of man."[19] As Stone points out, however, the Hebrew Bible also depicts Yahweh as traveling in clouds (Stone 1990: 212, esp. n. 38). The other superhuman actions of the man definitely have their roots in passages about Yahweh. In the Hebrew Bible, it is Yahweh who causes everything he looks at to tremble (Ps. 104.32; Hab. 3.6), makes the wicked melt like wax in fire (Ps. 68.2),[20] and destroys his opponents with his fiery breath.[21] Thus "the man is described using symbolic language that is drawn largely from biblical descriptions of God, particularly his epiphanies as warrior."[22]

At the conclusion of the vision, the man calls to himself another multitude that is peaceable. Some of these are joyful, others sorrowful; some are bound, and some bring others as offerings (13.12–13). Here too the original agent was Yahweh. The same pattern of Yahweh destroying his enemies by fire and then gathering the exiles of Israel to his mountain in Jerusalem occurs in Isaiah 66.15–21. The multitude of 4 Ezra 13.13 finds its closest parallel in this passage: "And they shall bring all your brethren from all the nations as an offering to the Lord . . . to my holy mountain Jerusalem" (Isa. 66.20).

From the preceding discussion, we can observe the most significant feature of the man from the sea: he is a Messiah who arises on

---

[19] On the dissenting view of Kvanvig, see J. Collins 1992: 460–61.
[20] Mountains suffer the same fate (Micah 1.4; Ps. 97.5).
[21] Ps. 18.8 // 2 Sam. 22.9; cf. Ps. 97.3; Isa. 66.15–16.
[22] Stone 1990: 212; cf. 1968: 308; J. Collins 1992: 464.

earth, possibly a reborn David, who has taken on some of the features and eschatological functions of Yahweh, particularly those of Yahweh as warrior. Daniel 7.13 adds a few details to this portrait: his initial description as "something like the figure of a man" and his action of flying "with the clouds of heaven."

Pseudo-Ezra's interpretation

We do not know for sure that anyone ever interpreted the vision in 4 Ezra 13.1–13 in the primarily literal sense that we have just considered. We do know that the author of 4 Ezra interpreted certain aspects of the vision metaphorically, and it is to his interpretation that we now turn (4 Ezra 13.25–52).

When God interprets the vision for Ezra, he says that the man is "he whom the Most High has been keeping for many ages, who will himself deliver his creation" (13.26). Later in the interpretation God calls him "my Son" (13.32), probably identifying him as the messianic king whom God calls "son" in Psalm 2.7.[23] He is thus the hidden Messiah, who will one day be "revealed" (13.32).

The interpretation does not specify where God has kept the Messiah during the ages of his concealment. In rabbinic tradition, the place could be either heaven or earth. According to *Pesikta Rabbati* 36, "God beheld the Messiah and his deeds before the creation of the world and hid him for his generation under His throne of glory" (cited by Wolfson 1956: 160).[24] In another tradition, however, the Messiah sat among the sick Jews at the gate of Rome, waiting for Israel to repent so that he could be revealed (Urbach 1979: 682–83). Other traditions thought of the hidden Messiah as living in the far north or in paradise or wandering about as a beggar.[25]

The interpretation plays down the more supernatural elements

---

[23] A number of scholars believe that the Latin "son" reflects a more original "servant" in Greek and Hebrew. Stone (1990: 207–208) sets out the textual evidence. J. J. Collins, however, has pointed out that "son" is "highly appropriate to the context" (4 Ezra 13.33–38), which alludes to Psalm 2 (J. Collins 1992: 462–63; so Nickelsburg 1992b: 141).

[24] Sjöberg (1955: 47 n. 4) locates the concealed Messiah of 4 Ezra in heaven. To this Tödt objects: "there is no reason at all to speak of the Man's concealment in heaven either in the case of the older tradition in IV Ezra 13 or in the case of its later revision. The dissimilarity to I Enoch must not be overlooked" (Tödt 1965: 26 n. 1).

[25] On the hidden Messiah, see Mowinckel 1954: 304–308.

ascribed to the figure in the vision.[26] His rise from the sea is interpreted metaphorically: "Just as no one can explore or know what is in the depths of the sea, so no one on earth can see my Son or those who are with him, except in the time of his day" (4 Ezra 13.52). The stream of fire, flaming breath, and storm of sparks from the man's mouth, which together destroy the multitude that has come against him (13.8–11), also receive a metaphorical interpretation. These signify that he will reprove them for their ungodliness, reproach them with their evil thoughts and coming punishments, and destroy them without effort by the law (13.37–38). The interpretation does not explain the motifs of flying with the clouds, causing things to tremble, or melting people like wax. Given the general non-literal tenor of the interpretation, however, the author of 4 Ezra would probably not take these literally.

The vision initially describes the Messiah as "something like the figure of a man" (13.3), which might suggest that he is something like, but other than, a man.[27] The remainder of the vision and the interpretation, however, refer to him simply as "the man" or "that man" (13.3, 4, 12, 25, 51). The author of 4 Ezra probably considered the man in the vision to be precisely that, a human being. As Stone has shown, "the Messiah presented by the author of the interpretation of chapter 13 is largely in accord with the Messiah presented elsewhere in the book" (Stone 1968: 310). An earlier passage in 4 Ezra clearly depicts the Messiah as mortal:

> For my son the Messiah shall be revealed with those who are with him, and those who remain shall rejoice four hundred years. And after these years my son the Messiah shall die, and all who draw human breath.
>
> (4 Ezra 7.28–29)

Here, as in 4 Ezra 13, God calls the Messiah his "son" and describes him as a hidden figure who will be "revealed." Yet he is a mortal human being. Like all others "who draw human breath," he will die, even though he lives for four hundred years after he is revealed. The author of 4 Ezra thus conceives the Messiah as a mortal human, though he has paranormal longevity during the ages that he is hidden and after his revelation.

[26] ". . . the cosmic features of the divine Warrior are attracted to the man. Yet in the interpretation they are all excluded or reinterpreted" (Stone 1990: 212).

[27] Michael Stone suggests that this initial description "is simply a result of the mysterious style that the apocalyptists liked to affect" (Stone 1968: 303).

In another passage, the author identifies the Messiah as a descendant of David: "this is the Messiah whom the Most High has kept until the end of days, who will arise from the posterity of David" (4 Ezra 12.32). The author leaves unclear how he would reconcile the idea of a Messiah hidden for long ages with the idea of one who will arise at the end-time from the posterity of David.

As to the function of the Messiah in 4 Ezra, he is not the judge at the final judgment like the Chosen One in 1 Enoch 37–70. Nor is he a warrior as in the vision. He is associated rather with a temporary messianic kingdom (Stone 1968: 311). At the beginning of this kingdom, he reproves the enemies of Jerusalem and then destroys them "by the law."

The man: a heavenly being?

Scholars have sometimes assumed that the figure in Ezra's vision is a "heavenly being" like the figure in the Similitudes. Several considerations, however, speak against this view. First, neither the vision nor its interpretation locates the man in heaven. In the vision, he ascends from the sea, he does not descend from heaven. The interpretation identifies him as the hidden Messiah, but does not specify whether he is hidden in heaven or on earth.

Second, the description of the man flying with the clouds of the sky does not make him a heavenly being. In the vision, his flight is neither an ascent to heaven nor a descent from heaven. The man comes not from heaven, but from the sea, and once he rises from the sea, he does not ascend to heaven.[28] Rather, he flies through the sky looking at things on the earth (4 Ezra 13:3–4). The clouds that accompany him thus apparently represent a mode of flying over the earth. The interpretation does not mention this feature of the vision, but the author probably understood it metaphorically like the other supernatural aspects of the vision.

Third, the "man" can be understood precisely as such in both vision and interpretation. In the vision he is probably a king who arises on earth, possibly a reborn David, though endowed with superhuman powers. The author of 4 Ezra understands him as a mortal human being, a descendant of David, though endowed with extraordinary longevity.

---

[28] ". . . the sixth vision [of 4 Ezra] describes no ascent into the heavenly world . . . The entire event takes place on the earth" (U. Müller 1972: 115).

A unified Son of Man tradition?

In recent years, several scholars have argued that the apocalypses just reviewed present a more unified pre-Christian Son of Man conception than Perrin allowed for. Two distinct but related claims have been made: (1) these texts attest to a "common model" of a "transcendent judge and deliverer" in Jewish eschatology of the first century CE; (2) these texts attest to certain "common assumptions" about the interpretation of Daniel 7 in the Judaism of the first century CE.

A common model: George Nickelsburg

In his article on "Son of Man" in the *Anchor Bible Dictionary*, George Nickelsburg concludes that

> the idea of a transcendent judge and deliverer was a known element in Jewish eschatology by the latter part of the 1st century C.E. The texts in question attest a common model that was composed of elements from Israelite traditions about the Davidic king, the Deutero-Isaianic servant/ chosen one, and the Danielic "son of man" . . . The texts and their sources in the Hebrew Scriptures do not represent successive developments in a single continuous process. The tradition was fluid and its components interacted with one another in different ways. The transcendent deliverer was often identified with Daniel's one like a son of man, although he was not always called "son of man."
>
> (Nickelsburg 1992b: 141)

Nickelsburg finds this transcendent judge and deliverer in the Parables of Enoch, 4 Ezra 11–13, and 2 Baruch.[29] He also finds a logically prior form of the tradition in Wisdom of Solomon 1–6, where no transcendent figure appears.

In one respect, Nickelsburg's approach represents an advance on previous discussions, since he does not focus exclusively on Daniel 7.13, but sets the interpretation of this passage within the larger context of messianic exegesis in general. He emphasizes correctly that the portraits of the Messiah in the Similitudes, 4 Ezra, and 2

---

[29] According to Nickelsburg, 2 Baruch 36–40 presupposes an identification of the Danielic son of man as the Messiah (Nickelsburg 1992b: 141). While this is possible, it is not self-evident. In any case, the text makes no explicit allusion to Daniel 7.13.

Baruch do not depend solely on Daniel 7.13, but on differing combinations of a variety of scriptural texts.

Nickelsburg goes beyond the evidence, however, when he speaks of a "common model" of the Messiah that results from this exegesis. The "common model" that Nickelsburg sees in these different portraits is a "transcendent judge and deliverer." The word "transcendent" is a somewhat ambiguous term that conceals the variety of conceptions that actually appear. The Messiah of 1 Enoch 37–70 could be called transcendent in the sense that he was created before the world and hidden in heaven. "Transcendent" would have to have a different meaning for the Messiah of 4 Ezra 13.1–13, since nothing in the text associates him with either heaven or creation prior to the world. For him the term would have to refer to his possession of supernatural abilities. The term "transcendent" would not apply to Enoch in 1 Enoch 71, who is an earthly human being. Nor would it really describe the Messiah of Pseudo-Ezra – a Messiah who, though hidden and long-lived, is ultimately mortal.

The term "judge" also fails to characterize all of the depictions of the Messiah that we have examined. The Messiah of 4 Ezra 13.1–13 is not a judge but a warrior.[30] Nor is judgment a function of Enoch in 1 Enoch 71. Furthermore, the judgment that does take place varies considerably. The Messiah of Pseudo-Ezra, on the one hand, slays the wicked at the beginning of a temporary messianic kingdom. The Messiah of 1 Enoch 37–70, on the other hand, separates the righteous from the wicked at the resurrection of the dead.

What the evidence suggests is not a common model, but a common set of building blocks – messianic and messianically interpreted passages of scripture – which are creatively combined and understood in various ways to produce a variety of constructions, i.e. a variety of portraits of the Messiah. As an example of a messianic passage used in differing portraits of the Messiah, we can take Isaiah 11.4: "with the breath of his lips he will slay the wicked." This passage refers explicitly to the Davidic Messiah. It was therefore incorporated into numerous later depictions of the Messiah. Psalm of Solomon 17, for example, ascribes this function

---

[30] "On the whole, the 'man from the sea' is very different from the Enochic Son of Man. The one is a warrior who takes his stand on a mountain, and is concerned with the restoration of Israel and Zion. The other is a judge enthroned in heaven" (J. Collins 1992: 464).

to the Davidic Messiah, interpreting it to mean that he will rid Jerusalem of colonizing Gentiles and other sinners (Ps. Sol. 17.24, 35–36). In 1 Enoch 62.2 the passage is applied to the role of an angelic/human Messiah in the destruction of sinners at the last judgment. In the vision of 4 Ezra 13.10–11 it is combined with passages about the fiery breath of Yahweh, so that the Messiah sends fire from his mouth to destroy an attacking army. In the interpretation of the author of 4 Ezra, this becomes the act of a human Messiah destroying his enemies by the law (4 Ezra 13.37–38). Each interpreter adapts the scriptural text to his own conception of the Messiah. The use of a common building block does not result in a common model of the Messiah.

Common assumptions: John Collins and Thomas Slater

Daniel 7.13 provides one of the building blocks for these messianic constructions. Is there evidence that different Jewish interpreters understood it in the same way? J. J. Collins and Thomas Slater believe so, primarily on the basis of similarities between the Messiah of the Similitudes and the Messiah of 4 Ezra 13.

J. J. Collins speaks of certain "common assumptions about the interpretation of Daniel 7 in first century Judaism," citing four correspondences that he finds between the Similitudes and 4 Ezra 13. In both works the Danielic figure (1) is an individual, not a collective figure; (2) is identified as the Messiah; (3) is pre-existent and therefore a transcendent figure of heavenly origin; and (4) takes a more active role in the destruction of the wicked than was explicit in Daniel. For Collins, "Whether these common assumptions amount to a 'Son of Man' concept is evidently a matter of definition" (J. Collins 1992: 464–66).

In this summary of the matter, Collins speaks as if we knew only two interpretations of Daniel 7.13 in first-century Judaism: the Similitudes and 4 Ezra. As we saw above, however, within the Similitudes we must distinguish between the body of the work (1 Enoch 37–70) and chapter 71. Within 4 Ezra we must distinguish between the vision of 13.1–13 and the interpretation of the author in 13.25–52. These distinctions give us at least three interpretations of Daniel 7.13 to consider, and a fourth that is an interpretation of an interpretation. Collins agrees that the vision of 4 Ezra 13.1–13 preserves a tradition independent of Pseudo-Ezra's interpretation (J. Collins 1992: 461–62), yet in his summary of "common assumptions" he fails to distinguish between their views. Collins also agreed at one time that 1 Enoch 71 preserves a different tradition than 1 Enoch 37–70. In his 1980 work he argues convincingly that 1 Enoch 71 identifies Enoch as the Danielic son of man, in contrast to 1 Enoch 37–70, which distinguishes them (J. Collins 1980: 119–24; 1984: 151–53). In his 1992 work, this identification still seems possible to him, but he finds more plausible the view that chapter 71 does not identify Enoch as the messianic son of man (J. Collins 1992: 455–57). In our discussion of 1 Enoch 71 above, we gave reasons for agreeing with Collins' earlier conclusion.

If we take all four interpretations of Daniel 7.13 into consideration, the "common assumptions" diminish. All four do treat the Danielic figure as an individual rather than as a collective figure. They all probably identify the figure as the Messiah as well.

All four do not, however, present the Messiah as a pre-existent or transcendent being of heavenly origin. This description would actually apply only to the Messiah in 1 Enoch 37–70. There the son of man is both pre-existent (created before the world) and heavenly, at least in the sense of being hidden in heaven until the final judgment. In 1 Enoch 71, however, the son of man is neither pre-existent nor of heavenly origin: he is an earthly human being, Enoch, who is raised to heaven. The man in the vision of 4 Ezra 13.1–13 is never associated with heaven, but arises on earth at the end-time. He could be pre-existent, in the sense that he may have lived previously, but that is not certain.[31] For the author of 4 Ezra, the Messiah is a mortal human being, a descendant of David, though he has been hidden by God for ages. The author does not specify whether he was hidden in heaven or on earth. With respect to pre-existence, relation to heaven, and nature of the Messiah, therefore, the four interpretations show a variety of conceptions.

The fourth common assumption about the Danielic son of man, according to Collins, is that "this figure takes a more active role in the destruction of the wicked than was explicit in Daniel." What Collins has identified, however, is not a shared assumption about the interpretation of Daniel 7.13, but a shared assumption about the Messiah. Biblical tradition gave the Messiah an active role in destroying the wicked (Isa. 11.4). Later authors incorporated this tradition into their portrayals of the Messiah, even if they did not

---

[31] ". . . the idea of pre-existence in the sense of a creation before the world, which belongs to the view of the Similitudes, is expressed by nothing in our text" (U. Müller 1972: 121–22).

make use of Daniel 7.13. For example, Psalm of Solomon 17, which does not draw on Daniel 7.13, depicts a Messiah who destroys the wicked (Ps. Sol. 17.22–25). The destruction of the wicked was thus a function of the Messiah that did not arise from an interpretation of Daniel 7.13, but developed completely independently. The Similitudes and 4 Ezra 13, as depictions of the Messiah, both incorporated this traditional function of the Messiah, as well as elements of Daniel 7.13. Yet they developed it in completely different ways. While the Chosen One sends sinners to the angels of punishment, the man from the sea personally slays an attacking army.[32]

We can agree with Collins, therefore, that first-century interpreters of Daniel 7.13, in the extant sources at least, assumed that the one like a son of man was an individual, the Messiah. They also shared certain traditions about the Messiah. Yet they combined and developed these traditions in a variety of ways.

Thomas B. Slater approves the conclusions of Collins, agreeing that there was "a common tradition in first century CE Judaism with regard to the exegeses of Dan 7.13" (Slater 1995: 197). Like Collins, Slater assumes that the manlike figure in both the Similitudes and 4 Ezra is a "heavenly being." His primary argument is that when apocalyptists likened a figure to a human being, as in the Danielic phrase "one like a son of man," that figure is always a heavenly being.

Again we can agree that in the Similitudes the one "whose face had the appearance of a man" (1 Enoch 46.1) is heavenly, in the sense that he dwells in heaven. Such is not the case, however, for the "something like the figure of a man" in 4 Ezra 13.3. As we saw above, neither the vision nor the interpretation associates this human-appearing figure with heaven. In the view of Pseudo-Ezra, he is mortal and dies like any human. Thus neither the vision nor the interpretation supports Slater's rule that "one like a son of man" would always have been understood to refer to a heavenly being. Apparently some ancient exegetes took this phrase to mean simply "a human being," just as some modern exegetes have.[33]

When we focus specifically on elements of these messianic

---

[32] "The difference in the function is clear: between the judge and revealer on the throne of glory and the fire-breathing destroyer there is no uniting function" (Theisohn 1975: 145).

[33] Casey cites modern scholars who have interpreted Daniel's "one like a son of man" as Moses, Judas Maccabeus, or Daniel himself (P. Casey 1979: 34–35).

portraits that come directly from Daniel 7.13, we find not a single interpretation but a diversity of perspectives. In 1 Enoch 37–70, the author draws on Daniel 7.9–14 to describe the enthronement of a son of man created before the world and hidden with God (1 Enoch 46–51). In 1 Enoch 71 there is a similar enthronement scene based on Daniel, but with a normal human, Enoch, in the role of the son of man. The vision of 4 Ezra 13.1–13, in contrast, has no Danielic enthronement scene, but depicts the manlike figure rising from the sea, as the beasts do in Daniel 7.3. In Pseudo-Ezra's interpretation of the vision the manlike figure becomes simply "a man," a mortal human, though one hidden for ages with God.

The motif in Daniel 7.13 of coming to God with the clouds also receives different treatment in each apocalypse. 1 Enoch 37–70 omits it entirely, presumably because the Messiah was already in heaven. In 1 Enoch 71 it is interpreted as the ascent of Enoch to heaven. The vision of 4 Ezra 13.1–13 also retains the motif, but apparently transforms it into a mode of flying over the earth. The author of 4 Ezra pays no attention to this motif in his interpretation of the vision, probably understanding it metaphorically. These distinctive uses of Daniel 7.13 make it difficult to infer that authors of the first century shared a unified interpretation of this passage, beyond identifying the one like a son of man as the Messiah.

Daniel 7.13 in rabbinic literature

Though the rabbinic literature dates to a later period than the first century CE, it may contain interpretations that existed in the earlier period. P. M. Casey has found ten references to Daniel 7.13 or 7.14 in this literature (P. Casey 1979: 80–83).

Four of these interpret the one like a son of man as the Messiah (*b. Sanh.* 98a; *Num. Rab.* 13.14; *'Ag. Ber.* 23.1; *Midr. Haggadol Gen.* 49.10). The first seeks to reconcile two apparently inconsistent scriptures:

> R. Alexandri said: R. Joshua opposed two verses: it is written, *And behold, one like the son of man came with the clouds of heaven*; whilst [elsewhere] it is written, [*behold, thy king cometh unto thee . . .*] *lowly, and riding upon an ass!* – If they are meritorious, [he will come] *with the clouds of heaven*; if not, *lowly and riding upon an ass.* (*b. Sanh.* 98a)[34]

[34] Translation from Epstein 1969.

Here the one like a son of man, as the Messiah, comes not to God but to Israel. The exegete gives two alternative manners in which the Messiah may come, either "with the clouds of heaven" (Dan. 7.13) or "riding upon an ass" (Zech. 9.9). Perrin cites the former alternative as an example of the Messiah coming from heaven to earth (Perrin 1974: 32–33). This may be what the exegete meant, but since he did not specify the Messiah's point of departure, we cannot know for sure. Since the latter alternative, "riding upon an ass," implies that the Messiah comes from elsewhere on earth, the exegete may have conceived of the clouds too merely as a mode of flying from one place to another on earth, as appears to be the case in 4 Ezra 13.3.

Two rabbinic passages cite Daniel 7.14 to show that the Messiah will have dominion:

> How do we know that he [the King Messiah] will hold sway on land? Because it is written . . . *Behold, there came with the clouds of heaven one like unto a son of man . . . and there was given unto him dominion . . . that all the peoples should serve him.*   (*Num. Rab.* 13.14)[35]

> *And to him [Judah] belongs the obedience of the peoples* (Gen. 49.10): for he will come and blunt the teeth of nations, and all of them will serve him. For it is said, *To him was given dominion and glory and kingship* (Dan. 7.14).
> (*Midr. Haggadol Gen.* 49.10, my translation)

The former passage mentions the coming with clouds, but does not specify whether the son of man comes to God or to Israel. The latter does not mention the coming with clouds, citing only a part of Daniel 7.14.

'*Aggadat Bereshit* 23.1 also interprets Daniel 7.13 messianically:

> *And you shall see and your hearts shall be glad* (Isa. 66.14). What is there, according to him, for the heart to see and to rejoice about? . . . when you see the Messiah sprung up from the gates of Rome and, lo, you rejoice. For thus Daniel says, *And behold with the clouds of the sky one like a son of man was coming* (Dan. 7.13). He beheld it. *And you shall see and your hearts shall be glad.*
> ('*Ag. Ber.* 23.1, my translation)

---

[35] Translation from Freeman and Simon 1983.

Here the exegete follows the tradition mentioned above, that the Messiah is hidden at the gates of Rome waiting to be revealed. He takes Daniel 7.13 as a vision of the Messiah's revelation. Apparently, then, he sees the coming of the son of man as the Messiah's coming to Israel rather than to God. Since the Messiah already waits on earth, this coming, even though with clouds of the sky, is neither an ascent to heaven nor a descent from heaven. It is uncertain whether the exegete understands this motif literally – as a mode of flying over the earth, as in the vision of 4 Ezra 13.3 – or metaphorically, like the author of 4 Ezra.

In contrast to these messianic interpretations, two other passages, according to Casey, interpret the manlike figure corporately, as a symbol for the people of Israel (P. Casey 1976a: 167–80; 1979: 81–83). The first is the midrash on Psalm 21.5:

> R. Berechia in the name of R. Samuel said: One time the scripture says: *He came to the Ancient of Days, and they led him before him* (Dan. 7.13), and another time the scripture says, *And I lead him to myself, so that he is near me* (Jer 30.21). How so? The angels lead them to the border of their camp, and the Holy One, blessed be he, stretches out his hand and leads them to himself. That is why it says, *I lead him to myself.*   (*Midr. Ps.* 21.5)[36]

As Casey points out, this is a standard type of midrashic passage that seeks to reconcile two apparently inconsistent scriptures. The exegete assumes that the "him" in Daniel 7.13 refers to the same entity as the "him" in Jeremiah 30.21. The problem then is to resolve the contradiction between the passages: in one the angels ("they") lead him to God, while in the other God leads him to himself. The exegete resolves the problem by having the angels lead partway, and God lead the rest of the way.

To whom, then, does this "him" refer – the Messiah or Israel? Casey gives two reasons for thinking that the exegete had Israel in mind. First, both the Septuagint and Targum translate the "him" in Jeremiah 30.21 as a plural, showing that they interpreted it as a reference to Israel. Second and more significantly, the exegete of the midrash shifts from "him" to "them" in the continuation of his exposition, showing that he had a collective entity in mind. Casey

---

[36] English translation based on the German translation of Wünsche 1967.

concludes therefore that the exegete interpreted both Jeremiah 30.21 and Daniel 7.13 corporately, as references to Israel.

Casey's explanation of this midrash may be correct. The exegete apparently believes that the two passages refer to the same entity, or there would be no inconsistency, no problem to resolve. The fact that he refers to this entity as "them" indicates that he had a collective entity in mind, presumably Israel. If so, this exegete interpreted the one like a son of man in Daniel 7.13 as a symbol for Israel. Furthermore, he regarded the coming of this corporate son of man as a coming to God.

Casey also finds a corporate interpretation in *Tanchuma Toledoth* 20. Here the exegete comments on the name "Anani," the last proper name in the list of David's descendants in 1 Chronicles 3.10–24:

> Who is Anani (1 Chron 3.24)? This is the Messianic [King], as stated: *As I was looking on . . . behold, along with Anani [of heaven, one like a son of man]* (Dan. 7.13).[37]

Where the Masoretic text reads *'anane* ("clouds") in Daniel 7.13, the exegete of *Tanhuma* found the proper name "Anani," identifying it with David's descendant in 1 Chronicles 3.24. As Casey points out, this version of Daniel 7.13 logically distinguishes the "one like a son of man" from Anani, since the former comes "along with" Anani. Since Anani is the Messiah, Casey suggests that the one like a son of man must be Israel. Again, Casey's suggestion is quite possible (contra Caragounis 1986: 135).

Four other rabbinic references to Daniel 7.13 shed little further light on its interpretation. *Gen. Rab.* 13.11 and 13.12 both discuss clouds. The former cites the phrase "with the clouds (*'anane*) of heaven" (Dan. 7.13) to prove that clouds come from above, while the latter cites it to show that *'anan* is one of five types of clouds. *Midr. Ps.* 2.9 contrasts two passages:

> Here it says: *The Eternal One said to me, You are my son* (Ps. 2.7). And in another passage it says, *And behold with the clouds of heaven he came like a son of man* (Dan. 7.13).[38]

The point is apparently that one passage speaks of a son of God, while one speaks of a son of man. Perrin cites this text as a

---

[37] Translation adapted from Townsend 1989: 167.
[38] Translation based on the German translation of Wünsche 1967.

messianic interpretation of Daniel 7.13 in which the Messiah goes to God (Perrin 1974: 33). Yet this passage does not specify whether the one like a son of man is the Messiah or Israel; nor does it indicate whether he comes to God or to Israel.[39]

In '*Aggadat Bereshit* 14.3 the exegete reflects on why Abraham is afraid when God appears to him (Gen. 15.1). He supposes that it was because God appeared in a "vision," which, according to Isaiah 21.2, can be harsh. The exegete has God reassure Abraham:

> The Lord said to him, "You are afraid because I appeared to you in a vision. As you live, I am not shown to your sons except in a vision. In the one I am punishing those who hate them." For thus Daniel saw. For it says, *I was watching in visions of the night, and behold with the clouds of the sky one like a son of man was coming, and he came to the Ancient of Days and they brought him before him* (Dan. 7.13). "You shall not fear because I was revealed to you in a vision. *Do not fear, Abram*" (Gen. 15.1).
>
> ('*Ag. Ber*. 14.3, my translation)

Casey (1979: 80) and Caragounis (1986: 132) take this passage as a messianic interpretation of Daniel 7.13, but this goes beyond the evidence. The exegete cites Daniel 7.13 as an example of a vision that is not harsh (for Israel at least), one in which God is punishing Israel's enemies. God appears in the vision as the Ancient of Days, and the punishment of Israel's enemies occurs in the larger context of the vision (the destruction of the four kingdoms) rather than in the verse quoted (Dan. 7.13). The verse quoted mentions the one like a son of man, but the author gives no clue as to how he understands this figure – whether as Israel, the Messiah, or some other entity.

Summary and conclusion

1.   Most of the passages that we have examined interpret the one like a son of man in Daniel 7.13 as an individual.[40] Such is the case for all of the relevant apocalyptic texts, generally dated to the first century CE. In the rabbinic literature, however, a corporate inter-

---

[39] "At Midr. *Ps.* 2, 9 the interpretation of the man-like figure which is presupposed is altogether uncertain" (P. Casey 1979: 80).

[40] 1 Enoch 37–70; 1 Enoch 71; 4 Ezra 13; *b. Sanh.* 98a; *Num. Rab.* 13.14; '*Ag. Ber.* 23.1; *Midr. Haggadol Gen.* 49.10.

pretation of the figure as Israel may appear in *Midr. Ps.* 21.5 and possibly also in *Tanch. Tol.* 20.[41]

2. The texts that interpret the son of man as an individual also explicitly or implicitly identify him as the Messiah.

3. As a reference to the Messiah, Daniel 7.13 becomes one element incorporated into a variety of portraits of the Messiah. These various messianic figures differ in both their nature and their function. In 1 Enoch 37–70 an angelic/human Messiah is pictured who is created before the world and hidden in heaven until he sits as judge at the last judgment. The passage draws on Daniel 7.9–14 to describe the enthronement of this Messiah. In 1 Enoch 71 the same Danielic enthronement scene is used for Enoch, a human Messiah who neither has pre-existence in heaven nor functions as judge. The Messiah in 4 Ezra 13.1–13, as in Daniel 7.13, looks like the figure of a man, but nothing in the vision suggests that he is pre-existent or heavenly or a judge. He arises on earth at the end-time and destroys an army that attacks Jerusalem. For the author of 4 Ezra, the Messiah, though hidden for ages, is a mortal human who will die after reigning over a temporary messianic kingdom for four hundred years. The rabbinic allusions to Daniel 7.13 make no references to any superhuman features of the Messiah, other than coming with clouds, though the brevity of the allusions prevents us from drawing any conclusions from this fact.

4. The interpretations of Daniel 7.13 that we have examined also show great diversity in understanding the son of man's coming to God with clouds. The author of 1 Enoch 37–70 omitted it from the enthronement scene in 1 Enoch 48.2, since this Messiah was already in heaven from the beginning. Other exegetes conceived it variously as ascent to heaven, flying over the earth, or possibly descent from heaven. The interpretations fall into two main groups: those in which it is a coming to God, as in Daniel, and those in which it is not. (a) In 1 Enoch 71 the exegete interpreted the coming as Enoch's ascent from earth to God in heaven. *Midr. Ps.* 21.5 also interprets the motif as a coming to God, though probably of Israel. In *'Ag. Ber.* 14.3 it is also a coming to God. (b) In the vision of 4 Ezra 13.3 the "flying" with clouds is not an ascent to God, but

---

[41] Traditional means of dating rabbinic sayings would place *Midr. Ps.* 21.5 at about 260 CE, though uncertainty attaches to these means of dating (P. Casey 1976a: 178–79). *Tanch. Tol.* 20 may be as late as the ninth century. Still later, the commentaries of Rashi (1045–1105) and Ibn Ezra (1089–1164) also interpret the son of man as Israel.

apparently flight over the earth, which the author of 4 Ezra probably understood metaphorically. Coming with clouds is also a mode of flying over the earth in *'Ag. Ber.* 23.1 – where the Messiah comes to Israel from the gates of Rome – if the exegete conceived the motif literally. The same is probably true for *b. Sanh.* 98a, where the Messiah also comes to Israel, though it is not impossible that here the Messiah descends from heaven to earth. *Gen. Rab.* 13.11 cites this motif to prove that clouds come from above, without referring to the one like a son of man.

5.   Diversity also appears in the other texts that Jewish exegetes combined with Daniel 7.13. The author of 1 Enoch 37–70 drew primarily on passages about the servant of the Lord in Second Isaiah, the Davidic king in Isaiah 11, and Yahweh as eschatological judge. The author of the vision in 4 Ezra 13.1–13 drew primarily on passages about Yahweh as divine warrior. Both drew on some of the same eschatological or messianic passages other than Daniel 7.13 (e.g. Isa. 11.4), but applied them in different ways.

Thus we cannot speak of a unified "Son of Man" tradition in ancient Judaism – either a common model of a transcendent deliverer or a common interpretation of Daniel 7.13. What we see instead is a shared set of messianic and messianically interpreted scriptural texts that exegetes combined and interpreted in various ways to produce a variety of portraits of the Messiah. Some exegetes used Daniel 7.13 in their portraits of the Messiah, others did not. Those who did use it interpreted the manlike figure in accord with their own particular conception of the Messiah and varied widely in their interpretation of his coming with clouds. Therefore, as Perrin recognized, when we come to the New Testament Son of Man passages we cannot presume that they reflect a unified pre-Christian tradition about a transcendent judge or a unified pre-Christian interpretation of Daniel 7.13.

10

CONCLUSIONS

Near the end of the twentieth century, F. H. Borsch summed up the status of Son of Man research: "It is clear that there is no consensus solution to the Son of Man problem on the immediate horizon" (Borsch 1992: 144). While no consensus exists, progress has been made in a number of areas, and a measure of agreement has been reached on some issues.

1. Very few proposed solutions have completely died out. Even the interpretation of the phrase as "the Son of Mary" has had its advocates in the twentieth century. Nevertheless, it is possible to distinguish between marginal proposals and those that lie at the center of the debate. Those interpretations which must now be considered marginal include genealogical interpretations (Chapter 1), the human Son of Man (Chapter 2), the corporate interpretation (Chapter 4), and derivation of the expression from Ezekiel or Primal Man speculation (Chapter 6).

2. Probably the majority of scholars have come to agree that no unified "Son of Man" title or concept existed in pre-Christian Judaism (Chapter 7). Our examination of the relevant apocalyptic and rabbinic material confirmed this view (Chapter 9). Consequently, the view that Jesus referred to some other expected messianic figure as the Son of Man must now be considered a marginal interpretation. The title "Son of Man" in all of its occurrences in the Gospels can best be understood as referring solely to Jesus.

3. The much-debated issue of the date of the Similitudes of Enoch thus turns out to be of only secondary significance for the Son of Man problem. Even if this work existed at the beginning of the Christian era, its portrait of the "Son of Man" represented only one interpretation of Daniel 7.13 among others. The significant differences between the Enochic figure and the Gospel Son of Man indicate that the latter developed independently of the former. The

evidence now suggests that the Similitudes first began to influence the Gospel Son of Man tradition at the level of Matthean redaction (Chapter 7).

4.   The bulk of scholarship is now divided between two basic alternatives, each with several variations: (a) the Christian Son of Man tradition originated with Jesus in the use of *bar enasha* as a nontitular idiom (circumlocutional, generic, or indefinite); (b) it originated as a messianic title applied to Jesus either by himself or by the early church. Other theories there are, but these two alternatives presently lie at the heart of the debate. I find myself on the latter side of this divide. I have examined the various nontitular theories in Chapter 8 and shown there my reasons for rejecting them. I find it most plausible that the expression "Son of Man" functions as a messianic title for Jesus throughout the tradition.

5.   Most scholars have found the traditional threefold classification of the sayings useful: sayings concerning the ministry, suffering, and coming of the Son of Man. The work of Norman Perrin, however, indicates the need to add a fourth category: sayings concerning the exalted Son of Man (Acts 7.56; Luke 22.69). The sayings thus portray Jesus as the earthly, suffering, exalted, and coming Son of Man.

The fact that the title "Son of Man" occurs in all of these categories suggests that those who used it felt it to be an appropriate messianic title for Jesus at any stage of his career. Early Christianity, in identifying Jesus of Nazareth as the Christ, developed a distinctive non-Jewish conception of the Messiah. In this conception, the Messiah (1) had already appeared on the earth, (2) had been killed and raised from the dead, (3) had ascended to heaven, and (4) would come from heaven at the end-time to exercise messianic functions. The sayings identify Jesus as the Son of Man in all four of these stages. The title thus appears to function as a general title for Jesus as the Christian Messiah. If this is the case, the distinctive associations of the different categories of sayings must come from the context, not from the title itself. The title seems to function in much the same way as "Christ," as a title for the Christian Messiah that can refer to Jesus at any stage of his career, past, present, or future.

6.   Perhaps the widest measure of agreement attaches to the view that the titular use of "Son of Man" originated in a christological interpretation of Daniel 7.13. This text has the strongest claim to be the source of the title, for two reasons. First, Judaism in the

first century CE and later interpreted Daniel 7.13 messianically. While Jewish interpreters developed no title and no unified messianic conception from this passage, they did generally regard the "one like a son of man" as the Messiah. Early Christianity therefore could easily have drawn "Son of Man" from this text to create a title for the Christian conception of the Messiah. Second, allusions to Daniel 7.13 occur in Mark 14.62 and in Matthew's redaction of Mark 13.26 (Matt. 24.30b). While both these allusions could be secondary developments within the tradition, they still represent the earliest known interpretation of the Gospel title. They show that at the time these sayings were formulated, the title was associated with Daniel 7.13.

If Daniel 7.13 provided the source for the title, we need not assume that the title originally had a purely future reference. Even if the "coming" of the Danielic figure were interpreted as a coming from heaven to earth at the end-time, the fact that the coming figure was identified as Jesus would automatically imply that he had a previous history. The Son of Man who came at the end-time would have been the same Son of Man who appeared on earth, suffered and died, and ascended to heaven. As a title for Jesus, "Son of Man" would not have been strictly limited to an association with the future, but would have been appropriate for referring to Jesus as the Christian Messiah in any of the categories of sayings.

7.   The absence of the title "Son of Man" in the New Testament outside of the Gospels and Acts can best be explained if the title had currency primarily in Palestinian Christianity. While most of the New Testament represents the legacy of Hellenistic Christianity outside of Palestine, the Gospels and the early chapters of Acts retain traces of Palestinian tradition. If the title "Son of the Man" arose in a Palestinian context, it should appear precisely where it does (Branscomb 1937: 149).

8.   Why do the sayings have Jesus refer to the Son of Man in the third person? Bultmann's answer, that Jesus referred to a Messiah other than himself, no longer commands general assent. Nor is it clear why a Christian prophet speaking as the voice of Jesus would use the third person rather than the first. If the theory that Jesus referred to himself with a nontitular idiom cannot be accepted, then the likeliest solution is that the third-person speech represents the voice of the church rather than that of Jesus. The church's language about Jesus has been retrojected onto the lips of Jesus himself. The

similar usage of "Son" and "Son of God" on the lips of Jesus points in the same direction (Chapter 4).

9.   In agreement with this conclusion, critical scholarship has increasingly tended to dissociate the Son of Man sayings from Jesus and attribute them to the early church (Chapter 5). Wellhausen and Bultmann had already reduced the number of authentic sayings to a handful, and the subsequent work of Käsemann, Vielhauer, and Perrin eliminated these as well. The primary challenge to this line of scholarship has come from scholars who find in some of the sayings a nontitular idiom used by Jesus. Yet our analysis of these nontitular theories suggests that this challenge has been less than successful (Chapter 8).

Even if it were certain, however, that all of the Son of Man sayings originated in the early church, we could not be certain about the title "Son of Man" itself. The title may well have existed prior to any of the sayings in which it appears. If so, we would have no way of tracing the title to its point of origin in the Christian tradition. Its origin would lie beyond the horizon of our vision.

10.   The Son of Man debate thus serves as a prime illustration of the limits of New Testament scholarship. Those limits lie both in our own inevitable subjectivity as scholars and in the intractable nature of the sources at our disposal. Because of these limits, some questions may never be fully resolved, at least to everyone's satisfaction. At the end of the twentieth century, it appears that the Son of Man problem may be one of those questions.

APPENDIX: SURVEYS OF RESEARCH ON "THE SON OF MAN"

(in chronological order)

Wolf [1725] 1739: 1.159; Köcher 1766: 191–93; Scholten 1809: 141–209; H. Holtzmann 1865; Appel 1896: 1–27; Lietzmann 1896: 1–29; Baldensperger 1900; Schmiedel 1901; Croskery 1901/1902; Driver 1902; Mouren 1903: 11–32; N. Schmidt 1903; Schweitzer [1906] 1968: 267–69, 277–86; Tillmann 1907a: 9–60; H. Holtzmann [1897] 1911: 1.313–35; Foakes Jackson and Lake 1920: 1.368–84; Roslaniec 1920: 4–33; Dupont 1924: 1–6; Peake 1924; Rawlinson 1926: 242–50; N. Schmidt 1926; Kraeling 1927: 6–16; Riesenfeld 1947: 307–13; McCown 1948; Preiss 1951: 11–14; Higgins 1959; Fuller 1962: 37–43; Black 1963; Perrin 1963: 90–129; Higgins 1964: 20–25; Marshall 1965/66; Haufe 1966; Hindley 1966; Marlow 1966; Jüngel 1967: 215–34; Vermes 1967: 311–15; Higgins 1969; Birdsall 1970; Marshall 1970; Van Cangh 1970; Maddox 1971; Boers 1972; Weist 1972; Coppens 1973; Legasse 1977; Black 1978; Vermes 1978a; 1978b; Coppens 1980; Higgins 1980: 1–53; Kümmel 1980; Colpe 1981; Tuckett 1981; Neirynck 1982: 69–72; Vögtle 1982; Walker 1983; M. Müller 1984a; Don Jackson 1985/86; Caragounis 1986: 9–33; Donahue 1986; P. Casey 1991b; Borsch 1992; Aufrecht 1993; Tuckett 1993; Burkett 1994.

REFERENCES

(The original date of publication is given in brackets if this differs from the date of the edition cited.)

Abbott, Edwin A. 1909. *The Message of the Son of Man.* London: Black.
    1910. *"The Son of Man" or Contributions to the Study of the Thought of Jesus.* Diatessarica VIII. Cambridge: Cambridge University Press.
Alexander, Gross. 1900. *The Son of Man: Studies in His Life and Teachings.* Nashville/Dallas: Publishing House of the M.E. Church, South.
Alford, Henry. [1849–61] 1874. *The Greek Testament.* 7th ed. 4 vols. London: Rivington's.
Alting, Jakob. 1685–87(?). *Comm. in loca quaedam selecta novi testamenti.* Cited by Scholten 1809: 203–204.
Anger, Rudolf. 1873. *Vorlesungen über die Geschichte der messianischen Idee.* Ed. Max Krenkel. Berlin: Henschel.
Appel, Heinrich. 1896. *Die Selbstbezeichnung Jesu: Der Sohn des Menschen.* Stavenhagen: Beholtz.
Archibald, D. Y. 1950/51. "The Son of Man." *ExpT* 62: 348–49.
Aretius, Benedict. 1577. *Commentarii in quatuor evangelistas.* Lausanne. Reprinted as part 1 of *Commentarii in Domini nostri Iesu Christi novum testamentum.* Bern: Le Preux, 1607.
Arnoldi, Matthias. 1856. *Commentar zum Evangelium des h. Matthäus.* Trier: Liutz.
Ashby, Eric. 1960/61. "The Coming of the Son of Man." *ExpT* 72: 360–63.
Aufrecht, Walter E. 1993. "The Son of Man Problem as an Illustration of the *Techne* of New Testament Studies." In *Origins and Method: Towards a New Understanding of Judaism and Christianity,* ed. Bradley H. McLean, 282–94. JSNTSS 86. Sheffield: JSOT Press.
Bacon, B. W. 1922. "The 'Son of Man' in the Usage of Jesus." *JBL* 41: 143–82.
Badham, F. P. 1911. "The Title 'Son of Man.'" *ThT* 45: 395–448.
Baeck, Leo. 1937. "Der 'Menschensohn.'" *MGWJ* 81: 12–24.
Baldensperger, W. [1888] 1892. *Das Selbstbewusstsein Jesu im Lichte der messianischen Hoffnungen seiner Zeit.* 2nd ed. Strasburg: Heitz & Mündel.
    1900. "Die neueste Forschung über den Menschensohn." *TRu* 3: 201–10, 243–55.

Balz, Horst Robert. 1967. *Methodische Probleme der neutestamentlichen Christologie.* WMANT 25. Neukirchen-Vluyn: Neukirchener Verlag.

Bard, Friedrich. [1908] 1915. *Der Sohn des Menschen: Eine Untersuchung über Begriff und Inhalt und Absicht solcher Jesusbezeichnung.* 2nd ed. Gütersloh: Bertelsmann.

Barker, Margaret. 1988. *The Lost Prophet: The Book of Enoch and its Influence on Christianity.* Nashville: Abingdon.

Barrett, C. K. 1959. "The Background of Mark 10:45." In *New Testament Essays: Studies in Memory of Thomas Walter Manson,* ed. A. J. B. Higgins, 1–18. Manchester: Manchester University Press.

1967. *Jesus and the Gospel Tradition.* London: SPCK.

1972. "Mark 10.45: A Ransom for Many." In C. K. Barrett, *New Testament Essays,* 20–26. London: SPCK.

Bartlet, Vernon. 1892. "Christ's Use of the Term 'Son of Man.'" *Expositor* ser. 4, vol. 6, pp. 427–43.

1892/93. "Christ's Use of 'The Son of Man.'" *ExpT* 4: 403.

1893/94. "The Son of Man: A Rejoinder." *ExpT* 5: 41–42.

Bartmann, Bernhard. 1904. *Das Himmelreich und sein König.* Paderborn: Schöning.

Batiffol, Pierre. 1905. *L'enseignement de Jésus.* Paris: Bloud.

Bauckham, Richard. 1985. "The Son of Man: 'A Man in My Position' or 'Someone'?" *JSNT* 23: 23–33.

1993. Review of *The Son of the Man in the Gospel of John,* by Delbert Burkett. In *EvQ* 65: 266–68.

Bauer, Bruno. 1841–42. *Kritik der evangelischen Geschichte der Synoptiker und des Johannes.* 3 vols. Leipzig: Wigand; Braunschweig: Otto.

Bauer, Walter. 1925. *Das Johannesevangelium.* 2nd ed. HNT 6. Tübingen: Mohr.

Baumgarten-Crusius, Ludwig Friedrich Otto. 1843–45. *Theologische Auslegung der johanneischen Schriften.* Ed. E. J. Kümmel. 2 vols. Jena: Luden.

Baur, Ferdinand Christian. 1860. "Die Bedeutung des Ausdrucks: ὁ υἱὸς τοῦ ἀνθρώπου." *ZWT* 3: 274–92.

1864. *Vorlesungen über neutestamentliche Theologie.* Leipzig: Fues. Reprinted with an introduction by W. G. Kümmel. Darmstadt: Wissenschaftliche Buchgesellschaft, 1973.

Baxter, Richard. 1685. *A Paraphrase on the New Testament, with Notes . . .* London: Simmons and Simmons.

Beare, Francis Wright. 1960. "The Sabbath Was Made for Man?" *JBL* 79: 130–36.

Beausobre, Isaac de and Lenfant. 1718. *Le Nouveau Testament . . . traduit en français . . . avec des notes.* Amsterdam: Humbert. English translation (of Matthew only): *A New Version of the Gospel According to Saint Matthew.* London: Whittaker; Cambridge: Deighton, 1819.

Ben-Chorin, Schalom. 1967. *Bruder Jesus: Der Nazarener in jüdischer Sicht.* Munich: List.

Bengel, Johann Albrecht. [1742] 1893. *Gnomon of the New Testament,* ed. Blackley and Hawes. 3 vols. Vol. 1: *The Gospels.* New York: Revell. Translation of *Gnomon novi testamenti.* 2nd ed. Tübingen: Schramm, 1759.

128   List of references

Bernard, J. H. 1928. *A Critical and Exegetical Commentary on the Gospel According to John.* Ed. A. H. McNeile. 2 vols. ICC. Edinburgh: Clark.
Betz, Otto. 1985. *Jesus und das Danielbuch.* Vol. 2: *Die Menschensohnworte Jesu und die Zukunftserwartung des Paulus (Daniel 7,13–14).* Frankfurt-on-Main: Lang.
Beus, Ch. de. 1955–56. "Het gebruik en de betekenis van de uitdrukking 'de Zoon des Mensen' in het Evangelie van Johannes." *NTT* 10: 237–51.
Beyschlag, Willibald. 1866. *Die Christologie des Neuen Testaments: Ein biblisch-theologischer Versuch.* Berlin: Rauh.
[1885–86] 1901–1902. *Das Leben Jesu.* 4th ed. 2 vols. Halle: Strien.
[1891–92]. 1894. *New Testament Theology.* 2 vols. Edinburgh: Clark. Translation of *Neutestamentliche Theologie.* Halle: Strien, 1891–92.
Bèze, Theodore de. 1557. *Novum D[omini] n[ostri] Iesu Christi testamentum.* [Geneva]: Stephanus.
Bietenhard, Hans. 1982. "'Der Menschensohn' – ὁ υἱὸς τοῦ ἀνθρώπου. Sprachliche und religionsgeschichtliche Untersuchungen zu einem Begriff der synoptischen Evangelien. I. Sprachlicher und religionsgeschichtlicher Teil." In *Aufstieg und Niedergang der römischen Welt* II.25.1, ed. W. Haase, 265–350. Berlin: De Gruyter.
Billerbeck, P. 1905. "Hat die Synagoge einen präexistenten Menschensohn gekannt?" *Nathanael* 21: 89–150.
Birdsall, J. Nevell. 1970. "Who Is This Son of Man?" *EvQ* 42: 7–17.
Black, Matthew. 1948/49a. "Unsolved NT Problems: The 'Son of Man' in the Old Biblical Literature." *ExpT* 60: 11–15.
1948/49b. "Unsolved NT Problems: 'The Son of Man' in the Teaching of Jesus." *ExpT* 60: 32–36.
1952. "The Eschatology of the Similitudes of Enoch." *JTS* n.s. 3: 1–10.
1953. "Servant of the Lord and Son of Man." *SJT* 6: 1–11.
1963. "The Son of Man Problem in Recent Research and Debate." *BJRL* 45: 305–18.
1969. "The 'Son of Man' Passion Sayings in the Gospel Tradition." *ZNW* 60: 1–8.
1976. "The Throne-Theophany Prophetic Commission and the 'Son of Man': A Study in Tradition History." In *Jews, Greeks and Christians: Essays in Honor of William David Davies*, ed. R. Hammerton-Kelly and Robin Scroggs, 57–73. Leiden: Brill.
1976/77. "The 'Parables' of Enoch (1 En. 37–71) and the 'Son of Man.'" *ExpT* 88: 5–8.
1978. "Jesus and the Son of Man." *JSNT* 1: 4–18.
1984. "Aramaic Barnāshā and the 'Son of Man.'" *ExpT* 95: 200–206.
1985. *The Book of Enoch or I Enoch: A New English Edition with Commentary and Textual Notes.* Leiden: Brill.
1992. "The Messianism of the Parables of Enoch: Their Date and Contributions to Christological Origins." In *The Messiah: Developments in Earliest Judaism and Christianity*, ed. James H. Charlesworth, 145–68. Minneapolis: Fortress.
Blackwood, Andrew W. 1966. *The Other Son of Man: Ezekiel/Jesus.* Grand Rapids: Baker.

Bleibtreu, Walther. 1926. "Jesu Selbstbenennung als der Menschensohn." *TSK* 99: 164–211.

Boers, Hendrikus. 1962. *The Diversity of New Testament Christological Concepts and the Confession of Faith.* Bonn: Rheinische Friedrich-Wilhelms-Universität.

1972. "Where Christology is Real: A Survey of Recent Research on New Testament Christology." *Interpretation* 26: 300–27 (esp. 302–15).

Böhme, Christian Friedrich. 1839. *Versuch das Geheimnis des Menschensohn zu enthüllen.* Neustadt: Orla.

Bolten, Johann Adrian. 1792. *Der Bericht des Matthäus von Jesu dem Messia.* Summarized by Scholten 1809: 174–79.

Boman, Thorlief. 1967. *Die Jesus-Überlieferung im Lichte der neueren Volkskunde.* Göttingen: Vandenhoeck & Ruprecht.

Borg, Marcus J. 1984. *Conflict, Holiness, and Politics in the Teachings of Jesus.* New York: Mellen.

1994. *Jesus in Contemporary Scholarship.* Valley Forge, PA: Trinity.

Borgen, Peder. 1977. "Some Jewish Exegetical Traditions as Background for Son of Man Sayings in John's Gospel (Jn 3,13–14 and Context)." In *L'Evangile de Jean: sources, rédaction, théologie,* ed. M. de Jonge, 243–58. BETL 44. Gembloux: Duculot; Leuven: Leuven University Press.

Boring, M. Eugene. 1976. "The Unforgivable Sin Logion Mark III 28–29/ Matt XII 31–32/Luke XII 10: Formal Analysis and History of the Tradition." *NovT* 18: 258–79.

1982. *Sayings of the Risen Jesus: Christian Prophecy in the Synoptic Tradition.* Cambridge: Cambridge University Press.

Bornkamm, Günther. [1956] 1960. *Jesus of Nazareth.* New York: Harper & Row. Translation of *Jesus von Nazareth.* 3rd ed. 1959.

Borsch, Frederick Houk. 1963. "The Son of Man." *ATR* 45: 174–90.

1967. *The Son of Man in Myth and History.* NTL. Philadelphia: Westminster.

1970. *The Christian and Gnostic Son of Man.* SBT, 2nd ser., 14. London: SCM.

1992. "Further Reflections on 'The Son of Man': The Origins and Development of the Title." In *The Messiah: Developments in Earliest Judaism and Christianity,* ed. James H. Charlesworth, 130–44. Minneapolis: Fortress.

Bousset, Wilhelm. 1903. *Die jüdische Apokalyptik: Ihre religionsgeschichtliche Herkunft und ihre Bedeutung für das Neue Testament.* Berlin: Reuther & Reichard.

1907. *Hauptprobleme der Gnosis.* Göttingen: Vandenhoeck & Ruprecht.

1926. *Die Religion des Judentums im späthellenistischen Zeitalter.* Ed. Hugo Gressmann. Tübingen: Mohr.

[1913] 1970. *Kyrios Christos.* Translated from the 5th German edition of 1965. New York: Abingdon.

Bowker, John. 1977. "The Son of Man." *JTS* n.s. 28: 19–48.

Bowman, John Wick. 1943. *The Intention of Jesus.* Philadelphia: Westminster.

1947/48. "The Background of the Term 'Son of Man.'" *ExpT* 59: 283–88.

1989. "David, Jesus Son of David and Son of Man." *Abr-Nahrain* 27: 1–22.

Brandt, W[ilhelm]. 1893. *Die evangelische Geschichte und der Ursprung des Christentums*. Leipzig: Reisland.

Branscomb, B. Harvie. 1937. *The Gospel of Mark*. New York/London: Harper.

Braun, F.-M. 1962. "Messie, Logos et Fils de l'homme." In *La venue du Messie*, ed. E. Massaux, 133–47. Bruges: Desclée de Brouwer.

Braun, Herbert. 1969. *Jesus: Der Mann aus Nazareth und seine Zeit*. Stuttgart/Berlin: Kreuz-Verlag.

Brown, John Pairman. 1977. "The Son of Man: 'This Fellow.'" *Biblica* 58: 361–87.

Brown, Raymond E. 1994. *The Death of the Messiah*. 2 vols. New York: Doubleday.

Bruce, Alexander Balmain. [1889] 1909. *The Kingdom of God or Christ's Teaching According to the Synoptical Gospels*. 9th ed. Edinburgh: Clark.

Bruce, F. F. 1968. *This is That: The New Testament Development of Some Old Testament Themes*. Exeter: Paternoster.

1982. "The Background to the Son of Man Sayings." In *Christ the Lord: Studies in Christology presented to Donald Guthrie*, ed. H. H. Rowden, 50–70. Leicester: Inter-Varsity.

Bruce, James. [1790] 1813. *Travels to Discover the Source of the Nile*. 3rd ed. 5 vols. Edinburgh: Ramsay.

Brückner, Wilhelm. 1886. "Jesus 'des Menschen Sohn.'" *JPT* 12: 254–78.

Buber, Salomon, ed. 1972 or 1973. *'Aggadat Bereshit*. Jerusalem.

Bucer (Butzer), Martin. 1527. *Ennarrationum in evangelia Matthaei, Marci, & Lucae*. Argentorati: Hervag. Cited by Scholten 1809: 172.

Bühner, Jan-A. 1977. *Der Gesandte und sein Weg im 4. Evangelium*. WUNT 2 Reihe, 2. Tübingen: Mohr.

Bulcock, H. 1945. "Was the Double Use of 'Son of Man' a Factor in the Deification of Jesus?" *Congregational Quarterly* 17: 44–55.

Bullinger, Heinrich. 1542. *In sacrosanctum Iesu Christi Domini nostri evangelium secundum Matthaeum, commentariorum libri xii*. Tiguri: Froschover.

Bultmann, Rudolf. 1925. "Die Bedeutung der neuerschlossenen mandäischen und manichäischen Quellen für das Verständnis des Johannesevangeliums." *ZNW* 24: 100–46. Reprinted in *Exegetica*, ed. E. Dinkler, 55–104. Tübingen: Mohr, 1967.

1937. Review of *Reich Gottes und Menschensohn*, by Rudolf Otto. In *TRu* n.s. 9: 1–35.

[1948–53] 1951–55. *Theology of the New Testament*. 2 vols. New York: Scribner. Translation of *Theologie des Neuen Testaments*. Tübingen: Mohr, 1948–53.

[1921] 1968. *The History of the Synoptic Tradition*. Rev. ed. New York: Harper & Row. Translation of *Die Geschichte der synoptischen Tradition*. 3rd ed. Göttingen: Vandenhoeck & Ruprecht, 1958.

Burkett, Delbert. 1991. *The Son of the Man in the Gospel of John*. JSNTSS 56. Sheffield: JSOT Press.

1992. Review of *The Son of Man Tradition*, by Douglas A. Hare. In *Heythrop Journal* 33: 447–48.

1994. "The Nontitular Son of Man: A History and Critique." *NTS* 40: 504–21.

Burkill, T. A. 1944/45. "The Son of Man: A Brief General Statement." *ExpT* 56: 305–306.

[1961] 1972. "The Hidden Son of Man in St. Mark's Gospel." In T. A. Burkill, *New Light on the Earliest Gospel: Seven Markan Studies*, 1–38. Ithaca: Cornell University Press. Reprinted from *ZNW* 52 (1961) 189–213.

Bynaeus, Anthony. 1691–98. *De morte Jesu Christi.* 3 vols. Amsterdam: Borst.

Cadoux, A. T. 1920. "The Son of Man." *The Interpreter* 18: 202–14.

Cadoux, Cecil John. 1943. *The Historic Mission of Jesus.* New York: Harper & Bros.

Caird, G. B. 1966. *A Commentary on the Revelation of St. John the Divine.* London: Black.

Calixtus, Georg. [1624] 1638. *Quatuor evangelicorum scriptorum concordia & locorum, quae in iis occurrunt, difficilium ac dubiorum explicatio.* Goslariae: Duncker & Gruber.

Calov(ius), Abraham. [1676] 1719. *Biblia novi testamenti illustrata.* 2nd ed. Dresden/Leipzig: Zimmermann.

Calvin, Jean. [1559] 1960. *Institutes of the Christian Religion*, ed. John T. McNeill and Ford Lewis Battles. 2 vols. Library of Christian Classics 20–21. Philadelphia: Westminster.

[1561] 1948. *Commentaries on the Book of the Prophet Daniel.* 2 vols. Grand Rapids: Eerdmans. Translation of *Praelectiones in librum Danielis.* Geneva, 1561.

Cambe, Michel. 1963. "Le Fils de l'homme dans les Evangiles synoptiques." *LumVie* 12: 32–64.

Camerarius, Joachim. 1572. *Notatio figurarum sermonis in libris quatuor evangeliorum* . . . Reprinted as *Commentarius in novum foedus* along with Beza's NT and Annotations. Cambridge: Daniel, 1642.

Cameron, John (d. 1625). 1632. *Myrothecium evangelicum.* Geneva: Aubert.

Campbell, George. 1789. *The Four Gospels.* 4 vols. Reprinted, Boston: Wells and Wait, 1811.

Campbell, J. Y. 1947. "The Origin and Meaning of the Term Son of Man." *JTS* 48: 145–55. Reprinted in J. Y. Campbell, *Three New Testament Studies*, 29–40. Leiden, 1965.

1950. "Son of Man." In *A Theological Wordbook of the Bible*, ed. Alan Richardson, 230–32. New York: Macmillan.

Cangh, Jean-Marie Van. 1970. "Le Fils de l'homme dans la tradition synoptique." *RTL* 1: 411–19.

Cappel, Jacques (d. 1624). 1657. *Observationes in novum testamentum. Una cum eiusdem Ludovici Cappelli Spicilegio.* Amsterdam: Elzevir.

Caragounis, Chrys C. 1986. *The Son of Man: Vision and Interpretation.* WUNT 38. Tübingen: Mohr.

Carpenter, J. Estlin. 1890. *The First Three Gospels: Their Origin and Relations.* 2nd ed. Boston: American Unitarian Association.

Carrairon, Emile. 1886. *Essai historique et critique sur le titre de Fils de l'homme*. Nîmes: Chastanier.

Cary, George Lovell. 1900. *The Synoptic Gospels*. New York/London: Putnam's.

Case, Shirley Jackson. 1927a. "The Alleged Messianic Consciousness of Jesus." *JBL* 46: 1–19 (esp. 16–19).

1927b. *Jesus: A New Biography*. New York: Greenwood.

Casey, P. Maurice. 1976a. "The Corporate Interpretation of 'One Like a Son of Man' (Dan. VII 13) at the Time of Jesus." *NovT* 18: 167–80.

1976b. "The Son of Man Problem." *ZNW* 67: 147–54.

1976c. "The Use of the Term 'Son of Man' in the Similitudes of Enoch." *JSJ* 7: 11–29.

1979. *Son of Man: The Interpretation and Influence of Daniel 7*. London: SPCK.

1985a. "Aramaic Idiom and Son of Man Sayings." *ExpT* 96: 233–36.

1985b. "The Jackals and the Son of Man (Matt. 8.20//Luke 9.58)." *JSNT* 23: 3–22.

1987. "General, Generic, and Indefinite: The Use of the Term 'Son of Man' in Aramaic Sources and in the Teaching of Jesus." *JSNT* 29: 21–56.

1991a. *From Jewish Prophet to Gentile God: The Origins and Development of New Testament Christology*. Cambridge: James Clarke; Louisville: John Knox/Westminster.

1991b. "Method in Our Madness and Madness in Their Methods: Some Approaches to the Son of Man Problem in Recent Scholarship." *JSNT* 42: 17–43.

1994. "The Use of the Term (א) נשׁ (א) בר in the Aramaic Translations of the Hebrew Bible." *JSNT* 54: 87–118.

1995. "Idiom and Translation: Some Aspects of the Son of Man Problem." *NTS* 41: 164–82.

Casey, R. P. 1958. "The Earliest Christologies." *JTS* n.s. 9: 253–77 (esp. 263–65).

Cavalier, H. O. 1923. "The Gospel of the Son of Man." *Theology* 6: 218–21.

Cellarius, Christoph. [1680] 1700. *Programma exercitii oratorii de humana Christi natura contra haereticos quosvis defendenda*. In *Opuscula: christologia mosaica*, ed. Salomon Glass, 588–92. Lugduni-Batavorum: Swart.

Chamberlain, William D. 1953. "Till the Son of Man Be Come." *Interpretation* 7: 3–13.

Charles, R. H. 1892/93. "The Son of Man." *ExpT* 4: 504.

[1893] 1912. *The Book of Enoch*. 2nd ed. Oxford: Clarendon Press.

Charlesworth, James H. 1978/79. "The SNTS Pseudepigrapha Seminars at Tübingen and Paris on the Books of Enoch." *NTS* 25: 315–23.

1980. "The Portrayal of the Righteous as an Angel." In *Ideal Figures in Ancient Judaism: Profiles and Paradigms*, ed. J. Collins and G. Nickelsburg, 135–51. Chico, CA: Scholars.

1985. *The Old Testament Pseudepigrapha and the New Testament*. Cambridge: Cambridge University Press.

1988. *Jesus Within Judaism: New Light from Exciting Archaeological Discoveries.* New York: Doubleday.

Châteillon, Sébastien. 1551. *Biblia interprete Sebastiano Castalione: una cum eiusdem annotationibus.* Basle: Oporinus.

Chemnitz, Martin (d. 1586). 1600. *Libri tres harmoniae evangelicae.* Ed. Polycarp Lyser. 3 vols. in 1. Frankfurt-on-Main: Spiess.

Chilton, Bruce D. 1992. "The Son of Man: Human and Heavenly." In *The Four Gospels 1992: Festschrift Frans Neirynck*, ed. F. Van Segbroeck et al., 1.203–18. 3 vols. Leuven: Leuven University Press. Also published in *Approaches to Ancient Judaism: Religious and Theological Studies*, ed. Jacob Neusner, 97–114. Atlanta: Scholars, 1993.

1996. "The Son of Man: Who Was He?" *Bible Review* 12 (August 1996) 35–39, 45–47.

Ciholas, Paul. 1981. "Son of Man in the Synoptic Gospels." *BTB* 11: 17–20.

1982. "'Son of Man' and Hellenistic Christology." *RevExp* 79: 487–501.

Clarke, Adam. 1810–17. *The Holy Bible . . . with a Commentary and Critical Notes.* Reprinted as *The Holy Bible*, 6 vols. London: Tegg, 1836.

Clarke, Samuel. 1701–1702. *A Paraphrase on the Four Evangelists . . . Together with Critical Notes on the More Difficult Passages.* 2 vols. London: Knapton.

Clemen, Carl. 1909. *Religionsgeschichtliche Erklärung des Neuen Testaments.* Giessen: Töpelmann.

Cocceius, Johannes (d. 1669). [1673–75] 1701. *Scholia in evangelia secundum Matthaeum, Marcum, Lucam et Johannem, utet in Acta Apostolorum.* In vol. 4 of his *Opera omnia.* 3rd ed. Amsterdam: Someren.

Colani, Timothée. 1864. *Jésus-Christ et les croyances messianiques de son temps.* 2nd ed. Strasburg: Treuttel et Wurtz.

Collins, Adela Yarbro. 1987. "The Origin of the Designation of Jesus as 'Son of Man.'" *HTR* 80: 391–407.

1989a. "Daniel 7 and Jesus." *Journal of Theology* 93: 5–19.

1989b. "The Son of Man Sayings in the Sayings Source." In *To Touch the Text: Biblical and Related Studies in Honor of Joseph A. Fitzmeyer, S.J.*, ed. Maurya P. Horgan and Paul J. Kobelski, 369–89. NY: Crossroad.

1990a. *The Apocalypse.* Collegeville, MN: Liturgical Press.

1990b. "Daniel 7 and the Historical Jesus." In *Of Scribes and Scrolls*, ed. Harold W. Attridge et al., 187–93. Lanham, MD: University Press of America.

1991. "The Apocalyptic Son of Man Sayings." In *The Future of Early Christianity*, ed. Birger A. Pearson, 220–28. Minneapolis: Fortress.

1992. "The 'Son of Man' Tradition and the Book of Revelation." In *The Messiah: Developments in Earliest Judaism and Christianity*, ed. James H. Charlesworth, 536–68. Minneapolis: Fortress. Reprinted in Adela Yarbro Collins, *Cosmology and Eschatology in Jewish and Christian Apocalypticism*, 159–97. Leiden: Brill, 1996.

Collins, John J. 1980. "The Heavenly Representative: The 'Son of Man' in the Similitudes of Enoch." In *Ideal Figures in Ancient Judaism: Profiles and Paradigms*, ed. J. Collins and G. Nickelsburg, 111–33. Chico, CA: Scholars.

1984. *The Apocalyptic Imagination: An Introduction to the Jewish Matrix of Christianity*. New York: Crossroad.

1992. "The Son of Man in First-Century Judaism." *NTS* 38: 448–66.

Cölln, Daniel Georg Conrad von. 1836. *Biblische Theologie*. Ed. David Schulz. 2 vols. Leipzig: Barth.

Colpe, Carsten. 1969–72. "Der Begriff 'Menschensohn' und die Methode der Erforschung messianischer Prototypen." *Kairos* 11,4 (1969) 241–63; 12,2 (1970) 81–112; 13,1 (1971) 1–17; 14,4 (1972) 241–57.

[1969] 1972. "ὁ υἱὸς τοῦ ἀνθρώπου." *TDNT* 8: 400–77.

1981. "Neue Untersuchungen zum Menschensohn-Problem." *TRev* 77: 353–72.

Cone, Orello. 1893. "Jesus' Self-designation in the Synoptic Gospels." *The New World* 2: 492–518.

Conzelmann, Hans. 1957. "Gegenwart und Zukunft in der synoptischen Tradition." *ZTK* 54: 277–96 (esp. 281–83).

[1959] 1973. *Jesus*. Philadelphia: Fortress. Expanded translation of "Jesus Christus." In *RGG* vol. 3 (1959) cols. 619–53.

[1968] 1969. *An Outline of the Theology of the New Testament*. London: SCM. Translation of *Grundriss der Theologie des Neuen Testaments*. 2nd ed. Munich: Kaiser, 1968.

Coppens, Joseph. 1961a. "Le Fils d'homme daniélique et les relectures de Dan. VII, 13 dans les apocryphes et les écrits du Nouveau Testament." *ETL* 37: 5–51.

1961b. *Le Fils de l'homme et les Saints du Très-Haut en Daniel, VII, dans les apocryphes et dans le Nouveau Testament*. With Luc Dequeker. 2nd ed. Gembloux: Duculot.

1973. *De Menschenzoon-logia in het Markus-evangelie: avec un résumé, des notes et une bibliographie en français*. Brussels: Paleis der Academiën.

1974. "Les logia du Fils de l'homme dans l'Evangile de Marc." In *L'Evangile selon Marc: tradition et rédaction*, ed. M. Sabbe, 487–528. BETL 34. Gembloux. Reprinted in Coppens 1981: 109–49.

1975/76. "Le Fils de l'homme dans le judaïsme de l'époque néotestamentaire." In *Orientalia lovaniensia periodica* 6–7, ed. P. Naster, 59–73.

1976. "Le Fils de l'homme dans l'Evangile johannique." *ETL* 52: 28–81.

1980. "Où en est le problème de Jésus 'Fils de l'homme.'" *ETL* 56: 282–302. Reprinted in Coppens 1981: 1–21.

1981. *Le Fils de l'homme néotestamentaire*. BETL 55. Leuven: Peeters; Leuven University Press.

1983. *Le Fils d'homme vétéro- et intertestamentaire*. Leuven: Peeters; Leuven University Press.

Cortés, Juan B. and Florence M. Gatti. 1968. "The Son of Man or the Son of Adam." *Biblica* 49: 457–502.

Cranfield, C. E. B. [1959] 1963. *The Gospel According to Saint Mark*. 2nd ed. Cambridge: Cambridge University Press.

Creed, J. M. 1925. "The Heavenly Man." *JTS* 26: 113–36.

Cremer, Hermann. [1867] 1895. *Biblico-Theological Lexicon of New Testament Greek*. 4th ed. Edinburgh: Clark. Reprinted 1954. Translation of *Biblisch-theologisches Wörterbuch der neutestamentlichen Gräcität*.

Croskery, J. 1901/1902. "Recent Discussions on the Meaning of the Title 'Son of Man.'" *ExpT* 13: 351–55.

Cross, Frank M. 1958. *The Ancient Library of Qumran and Modern Biblical Studies*. Garden City, NY: Doubleday.

Crossan, John Dominic. 1991. *The Historical Jesus: The Life of a Mediterranean Jewish Peasant*. HarperSanFrancisco.

1994. *Jesus: A Revolutionary Biography*. HarperSanFrancisco.

Cruvellier, Jean. 1955. "La notion de 'Fils de l'homme' dans les Evangiles." *Etudes évangéliques* 15: 31–50.

Cullmann, Oscar. [1957] 1963. *The Christology of the New Testament*. Rev. ed. Philadelphia: Westminster. Translated from *Die Christologie des Neuen Testaments*. Tübingen: Mohr, 1957.

Dalman, Gustav. [1898] 1902. *The Words of Jesus*. Edinburgh: Clark. Translation of *Die Worte Jesu*. Leipzig: Hinrichs, 1898.

Davies, W. D. [1948] 1980. *Paul and Rabbinic Judaism*. 4th ed. Philadelphia: Fortress.

Davies, W. D. and Dale C. Allison. 1988–91. *A Critical and Exegetical Commentary on the Gospel According to Saint Matthew*. Vols. 1–2. ICC. Edinburgh: Clark.

Davis, H. Francis. 1961. "The Son of Man – I: The Image of the Father." *The Furrow* 12: 39–48.

Del Rio, Martin Anton. 1614. *Adagialia sacra veteris et novi testamenti*. 2nd ed. Lugduni: Cardon.

Delorme, Jean. 1954. *Le Fils de l'homme*. "Evangile" 16. Paris: Tournon.

Denney, James. 1909. *Jesus and the Gospel*. London: Hodder & Stoughton.

Derambure, Jean. 1908–1909. "Le 'Fils de l'homme' dans les Evangiles." *RevAug* 13: 708–20; 14: 319–40.

Dewick, E. C. 1912. *Primitive Christian Eschatology*. Cambridge: Cambridge University Press.

Dieckmann, Hermann. 1921. "Ὁ υἱὸς τοῦ ἀνθρώπου." *Biblica* 2: 69–71.

1927. "'Der Sohn des Menschen' im Johannesevangelium." *Scholastik* 2: 229–47.

1928. "De nomine 'Filii hominis.'" *Verbum Domini* 8: 295–301.

Díez Macho, A. 1981. "L'usage de la troisième personne au lieu de la première dans le Targum." In *Mélanges Dominique Barthélemy*, ed. P. Casetti et al., 61–89. Göttingen: Vandenhoeck & Ruprecht.

1982. "La Cristología del Hijo del Hombre y el uso de la tercera persona en vez de la primera." *Scripta theologica* 14: 189–201.

Dillmann, August. 1853. *Das Buch Henoch*. Leipzig: Vogel.

Dion, H.-M. 1967. "Quelques traits originaux de la conception johannique du Fils de l'homme." *ScEc* 19: 49–65.

Dodd, C. H. 1953. *The Interpretation of the Fourth Gospel*. Cambridge: Cambridge University Press.

1966. Review of *Invitation to the New Testament*, by W. D. Davies. In *USQR* 21: 474–76.

1970. *The Founder of Christianity*. London: Macmillan.

Donahue, John R. 1986. "Recent Studies on the Origin of 'Son of Man' in the Gospels." *CBQ* 48: 484–98.

Donker Curtius, Hendrik Herman. 1799. *Specimen hermeneutico-theologicum, de Apocalypsi*. Traiecti Batavorum: Paddenburg.

Dorner, Isaak August. [1839] 1861–63. *History of the Development of the Doctrine of the Person of Christ*. 5 vols. Edinburgh: Clark. Translation of *Entwicklungsgeschichte der Lehre von der Person Christi*. 2nd ed. 3 vols. Stuttgart: Liesching, 1845.

Dougall, Lily and Cyril W. Emmet. 1922. *The Lord of Thought*. London: SCM.

Dowman, John et al. 1645. *Annotations Upon all the Books of the Old and New Testament*. 2 vols. London: Legatt and Raworth.

Driver, S. R. 1902. "Son of Man." In *A Dictionary of the Bible*, ed. James Hastings, 4.579–89.

Drummond, James. 1877. *The Jewish Messiah*. London: Longmans, Green.
    1901. "The Use and Meaning of the Phrase 'The Son of Man' in the Synoptic Gospels." *JTS* 11: 350–58, 539–71.

Drusius, Johannes. 1612. *Annotationum in totum Jesu Christi testamentum*. Franeker: Radaeus.

Duncan, George S. 1947. *Jesus, Son of Man: Studies Contributory to a Modern Portrait*. London: Nisbet.

Dunn, James D. G. 1980. *Christology in the Making: A New Testament Inquiry into the Origins of the Doctrine of the Incarnation*. Philadelphia: Westminster.
    1983. "Let John be John: A Gospel for its Time." In *Das Evangelium und die Evangelien: Vorträge vom Tübinger Symposium 1982*, ed. P. Stuhlmacher, 309–39. WUNT 28. Tübingen: Mohr.

Dupont, Georges. 1924. *Le Fils de l'Homme: essai historique et critique*. Paris: Fischbacher.

Eaton, David. 1898/99. "Prof. Dalman on 'The Son of Man.'" *ExpT* 10: 438–43.

Ebrard, Johannes Heinrich August. [1851–52] 1862–63. *Christliche Dogmatik*. 2nd ed. 2 vols. Königsberg: Unzer.

Eckermann, Jacob Christoph Rudolph. 1791. *Theologische Beyträge*. Altona: Hammerich.

Edwards, Richard. A. 1971. *The Sign of Jonah in the Theology of the Evangelists and Q*. SBT, 2nd ser., 18. London: SCM.
    1976. *A Theology of Q: Eschatology, Prophecy, and Wisdom*. Philadelphia: Fortress.

Eerdmans, B. D. 1894. "De Oorsprong van de uitdrukking 'Zoon des Menschen' als evangelische Messiastitel." *Theologische Tijdschrift* 28: 153–76.

Eichhorn, Johann Gottfried. 1791. *Commentarius in apocalypsin Joannis*. Göttingen: Dieterich.
    1793. *Allgemeine Bibliothek der biblischen Literatur* 5: 524.
    1795. *Allgemeine Bibliothek der biblischen Literatur* 7: 961.

Eichrodt, Walther. 1959. "Zum Problem des Menschensohnes." *EvT* 19: 1–3.

Elliott, John H. 1970. "Man and the Son of Man in the Gospel According to Mark." In *Humane Gesellschaft: Beiträge zu ihrer sozialen Gestaltung*, 47–59. Zurich: Zwingli.

Elsner, Jakob. 1767–69. *Commentarius critico-philologicus in evangelium Matthaei.* Ed. Ferdinand Stosch. 2 vols. Zwolla: Clement.

Emerton, John A. 1958. "The Origin of the Son of Man Imagery." *JTS* n.s. 9: 225–42.

Enslin, Morton Scott. 1961. *The Prophet from Nazareth.* New York: Schocken.

Episcopius, Simon (d. 1643). 1650. *Notae breves in xxiv. priora capita Matthaei.* In vol. 2 of his *Opera theologica.* Amsterdam: Blaev.

Epstein, I., ed. 1969. *Hebrew–English Edition of the Babylonian Talmud.* London: Soncino Press.

Erasmus, Desiderius (d. 1536). 1705. *Novum testamentum, cui in hac editione, subjectae sunt singulis paginis adnotationes.* In vol. 6 of his *Opera omnia.* Lugduni-Batavorum: Vander.

Evans, Milton G. 1900. "The Title 'The Son of Man.'" *BSac* 57: 680–95.

Ewald, Heinrich. 1828. *Commentarius in apocalypsin Johannis, exegeticus et criticus.* Leipzig: Hahn.

1854. *Abhandlung über des Äthiopischen Buches Henókh.* Göttingen: Dieterich.

[1855] 1883. *The History of Israel.* Vol. 6: *The Life and Times of Christ.* London: Longmans, Green. Translated from *Geschichte des Volkes Israel bis Christus.* Vol. 5: *Geschichte Christus' und seiner Zeit.* 2nd ed. Göttingen: Dieterich, 1857.

Feine, Paul. 1910. *Theologie des Neuen Testaments.* Leipzig: Hinrichs.

Fessel, Daniel. 1650–58. *Adversariorum sacrorum.* 2 vols in 1. Wittenberg: Fincel.

Feuillet, André. 1953. "Le Fils de l'homme de Daniel et la tradition biblique." *RB* 60: 170–202, 321–46.

Fiebig, Paul. 1901a. "Der 'Menschensohn' als Geheimname." *PM* 5: 333–51.

1901b. *Der Menschensohn: Jesu Selbstbezeichnung.* Tübingen: Mohr.

1904. "Der Menschensohn und Wellhausen." *PM* 8: 12–26.

Fitzmyer, Joseph A. 1968. Review of *An Aramaic Approach to the Gospels and Acts*, by M. Black, 3rd ed. In *CBQ* 30: 417–28 (esp. 424–28).

1973/74. "The Contribution of Qumran Aramaic to the Study of the New Testament." *NTS* 20: 382–407. Reprinted in Fitzmyer 1979a: 85–113.

1979a. *A Wandering Aramean: Collected Aramaic Essays.* SBLMS 25. Missoula, MT: Scholars Press, 1979.

1979b. "Another View of the 'Son of Man' Debate." *JSNT* 4: 58–65.

1979c. "The New Testament Title 'Son of Man' Philologically Considered." In Fitzmyer 1979a: 143–60.

1980. "The Aramaic Language and the Study of the New Testament." *JBL* 99: 5–21.

Flacius, Matthias (Illyricus). 1567. *Clavis scripturae, sive, De sermone sacrarum literarum.* Basle: Quecum.

Flusser, David. [1968] 1969. *Jesus.* New York: Herder and Herder. Translation of *Jesus in Selbstzeugnissen und Bilddokumenten.* Hamburg: Rowohlt, 1968.

Foakes Jackson, F. J. and Kirsopp Lake, eds. 1920. *The Beginnings of Christianity. Part I: The Acts of the Apostles*. 5 vols. London: Macmillan.

Ford, J. Massingberd. 1968. "'The Son of Man' – A Euphemism?" *JBL* 87: 257–66.

1971. "The Epithet 'Man' for God." *ITQ* 38: 72–76.

Formesyn, R. E. C. 1966. "Was There a Pronominal Connection for the 'Bar Nasha' Self-Designation?" *NovT* 8: 1–35.

France, R. T. 1971. *Jesus and the Old Testament*. Grand Rapids: Baker.

Freeman, H. and Maurice Simon. 1983. *Midrash Rabbah*. 3rd ed. London/ New York: Soncino Press.

Fritzsche, Karl Friedrich August. 1826. *Quatuor N.T. evangelia*. Vol. 1: *Evangelium Matthaei*. Leipzig: Fleischer.

Fuller, Reginald H. 1954. *The Mission and Achievement of Jesus*. London: SCM.

1962. *The New Testament in Current Study*. New York: Scribner.

1965. *The Foundations of New Testament Christology*. New York: Scribner's.

1985. "The Son of Man: A Reconsideration." In *The Living Text: Essays in Honor of Ernest W. Saunders*, ed. Dennis E. Groh and Robert Jewett, 207–17. Lanham, MD: University Press of America.

1990. Review of *Die Entchristologisierung des Menschensohnes*, by Rollin Kearns. In *JBL* 109: 721–23.

Funk, Robert W. 1996. *Honest to Jesus: Jesus for a New Millennium*. HarperSanFrancisco.

Funk, Robert W. and Roy W. Hoover. 1993. *The Five Gospels: The Search for the Authentic Words of Jesus*. New York: Polebridge Press.

Gaillard, Jacques. 1684. *Specimen quaestionum in novum instrumentum de filio hominis*. Lugduni-Batavorum. Summarized by Köcher 1766: 191 and Scholten 1809: 202–203.

Gall, August Freiherrn von. 1926. βασιλεία τοῦ θεοῦ: *Eine religionsgeschichtliche Studie zur vorkirchlichen Eschatologie*. Heidelberg: Winter.

Gass, Fr. Wilhelm. 1839. *De utroque Jesu Christi nomine in novo testamento obvio Dei filii et hominis*. Vratislavia: Friedländer.

Gaston, Lloyd. 1970. *No Stone on Another: Studies in the Significance of the Fall of Jerusalem in the Synoptic Gospels*. Leiden: Brill.

Geist, Heinz. 1986. *Menschensohn und Gemeinde: Eine redaktionskritische Untersuchung zur Menschensohnprädikation im Matthäusevangelium*. Würzburg: Echter Verlag.

Gelston, A. 1969. "A Sidelight on the 'Son of Man.'" *SJT* 22: 189–96.

Génébrard, Gilbert. 1569. *De S. Trinitate: libri III contra hujus aevi trinitarios, antitrinitarios et autotheanos*. Paris. Cited by Legasse 1977: 272 n. 3.

Gerleman, Gillis. 1983. *Der Menschensohn*. Studia Biblica 1. Leiden: Brill.

Gese, Hartmut. 1981. "Wisdom, Son of Man, and the Origins of Christology: The Consistent Development of Biblical Theology." *HBT* 3: 23–57 (esp. 38–41).

Gess, Wolfgang Friedrich. 1870. *Christi Person und Werk*. Vol. 1: *Christi Zeugniss von seiner Person und seinem Werk*. Basle: Bahnmaier.

Gfrörer, August Friedrich. 1838. *Das Jahrhundert des Heils*. Stuttgart: Schweizerbart.
Gill, John. 1744. *An Exposition of the New Testament*. Reprinted in 2 vols. London: Collingridge, 1852–53.
Glass, Salomon. [1623] 1705. *Philologiae sacrae*. Leipzig: Gleditsch.
Glasson, T. Francis. [1945] 1963. *The Second Advent: The Origin of the New Testament Doctrine*. 3rd ed. London: Epworth.
 1977. "Schweitzer's Influence – Blessing or Bane?" *JTS* n.s. 28: 289–302.
 1988. "Theophany and Parousia." *NTS* 34: 259–70.
Gnilka, Joachim. 1975. "Das Elend vor dem Menschensohn (Mk 2, 1–12)." In Pesch and Schnackenburg 1975: 196–209.
Godet, Frédéric. [1871] 1875. *A Commentary on the Gospel of St. Luke*. 2 vols. Edinburgh: Clark. Translation of *Commentaire sur l'Evangile de saint Luc*. 2nd ed. Neuchâtel/Paris: Sandoz, 1872.
Goergen, Donald J. 1986. *The Mission and Ministry of Jesus*. Wilmington, DE: Glazier.
Goguel, Maurice. 1904. *L'Apôtre Paul et Jésus-Christ*. Paris: Fischbacher.
Goppelt, Leonhard. 1963. "Zum Problem des Menschensohns: Das Verhältnis von Leidens- und Parusieankündigung." In *Mensch und Menschensohn: Festschrift für Bischof Professor D. Karl Witte*, ed. H. Sierig, 20–32. Hamburg: Wittig. Reprinted in L. Goppelt, *Christologie und Ethik: Aufsätze zum Neuen Testament*, 66–78. Göttingen, 1969.
Gottsched, H. 1908. *Der Menschensohn*. Gütersloh: Bertelsmann.
Graham, E. A. 1931. "The Heavenly Man." *Church Quarterly Review* 113: 224–39.
Grandmaison, Léonce de. [1928] 1930–34. *Jesus Christ: His Person, His Message, His Credentials*. 3 vols. London: Sheed & Ward. Translation of *Jésus Christ, sa personne, son message, ses preuves*. 2 vols. Paris: Beauchesne, 1928.
Grant, Frederick C. 1940. *The Gospel of the Kingdom*. New York: Macmillan.
Grau, Rudolf Friedrich. 1887. *Das Selbstbewusstsein Jesu*. Nördlingen: Beck.
Greenfield, Jonas C. and Michael E. Stone. 1977. "The Enochic Pentateuch and the Date of the Similitudes." *HTR* 70: 51–65.
Grelot, Pierre. 1978. *L'espérance juive à l'heure de Jésus*. Paris: Desclée.
Grotius, Hugo. [1641] 1972. *Annotationes in libros evangeliorum*. In his *Opera omnia theologica*. Amsterdam, 1679. Reprinted, Stuttgart/Bad Cannstatt: Frommann, 1972.
Guignebert, Charles Alfred Honoré. [1933] 1935. *Jesus*. New York: Knopf. Reprinted, New York: University Books, 1956. Translation of *Jésus*. Paris: La Renaissance du livre, 1933.
Guillet, Jacques. 1961. "A propos des titres de Jésus: Christ, Fils de l'homme, Fils de Dieu." In *A la rencontre de Dieu: mémorial Albert Gelin*, by M. Jourjon et al., 309–17. Le Puy: Mappus.
Gunkel, Hermann. 1899. "Aus Wellhausen's neuesten apokalyptischen Forschungen." *ZWT* 42 (= N.F. 7) 581–611 (esp. 582–90).
Guy, H. A. 1970. "Did Jesus Call Himself the Son of Man?" *The Modern Free Churchman* 91: 30–34.

Hackspan, Theodor. 1664. *Notarum philologico-theologicarum in varia et difficilia scripturae loca pars prima [secunda, tertia].* 3 vols. Altdorff: Hagen.

Hahn, Ferdinand. [1963] 1969. *The Titles of Jesus in Christology.* London: Lutterworth Press. Translation of *Christologische Hoheitstitel.* Göttingen: Vandenhoeck & Ruprecht, 1963.

Hammerton-Kelly, R. G. 1973. *Pre-existence, Wisdom, and the Son of Man: A Study of the Idea of Pre-existence in the New Testament.* SNTSMS 21. Cambridge: Cambridge University Press.

Hammond, Henry. 1639. *A Paraphrase and Annotations upon All the Books of the New Testament.* Reprinted in 4 vols. Oxford: Oxford University Press, 1845.

Hampel, Volker. 1990. *Menschensohn und historischer Jesus: Ein Rätselwort als Schlüssel zum messianischen Selbstverständnis Jesu.* Neukirchen-Vluyn: Neukirchener.

Hardouin, Jean. 1741. *Commentarius in novum testamentum.* Amsterdam: Sauzet.

Hare, Douglas R. A. 1990. *The Son of Man Tradition.* Minneapolis: Fortress.

Harnack, Adolf. [1907] 1908. *New Testament Studies II: Sayings of Jesus.* New York: Putnam's. Translation of *Sprüche und Reden Jesu.* Leipzig: Hinrichs, 1907.

Harrison, R. K. 1951. "The Son of Man." *EvQ* 23: 46–50.

Hartl, Vinzenz. 1909. "Anfang und Ende des Titels 'Menschensohn': Ein Beitrag zur Lösung der johanneischen Frage." *BZ* 7: 342–54.

Hase, Karl von. [1829] 1860. *Life of Jesus: A Manual for Academic Study.* Translated from the 3rd and 4th German editions. Boston: Walker, Wise.

  [1876] 1891. *Geschichte Jesu nach akademische Vorlesungen.* 2nd ed. Leipzig: Breitkopf und Härtel.

Haufe, Günter. 1966. "Das Menschensohn-Problem in der gegenwärtigen wissenschaftlichen Diskussion." *EvT* 26: 130–41. Published in French as "Le problème du Fils de l'homme." *ETR* 42 (1967) 311–22.

Haupt, Paul. 1919a. "Hidalgo and Filius Hominis." *JBL* 40: 167–70.

  1919b. "The Son of Man = *hic homo – ego.*" *JBL* 40: 183.

Hausrath, Adolf. [1868–] 1878–80. *A History of the New Testament Times.* Translated from the 2nd and 3rd German editions. 2 vols. London: Williams and Norgate. Translation of *Neutestamentliche Zeitgeschichte.* 4 vols. Heidelberg: Basserman, ²1873, ³1879.

Hay, Lewis S. 1970. "The Son of Man in Mark 2:10 and 2:28." *JBL* 89: 69–75.

Headlam, Arthur C. 1923. *The Life and Teaching of Jesus the Christ.* New York: Oxford University Press.

Heinsius, Daniel. [1639] 1640. *Sacrarum exercitationum ad novum testamentum.* 2nd ed. Lugduni-Batavorum/Cambridge.

Hengstenberg, Ernst Wilhelm. [1854–57] 1858. *Christology of the Old Testament.* 2nd ed. 4 vols. Edinburgh: Clark. Translation of *Christologie des Alten Testaments.* 2nd ed. 1854–57.

Henze, Clemens M. 1956. "Der Sohn des Menschen." *Theologisch-Praktische Quartalschaft* 104: 70–75.

Herder, Johann Gottfried von. [1796] 1880. *Christliche Schriften. Zweite Sammlung: Vom Erlöser der Menschen*. Vol. 19 in *Herders sämmtliche Werke*. Ed. Bernard Suphan. Berlin: Weidmann.

Héring, Jean. [1937] 1959. *Le royaume de Dieu et sa venue*. 2nd ed. Neuchâtel: Delachaux & Niestlé.

Hertlein, E. 1920. "'Ο υἱὸς τοῦ ἀνθρώπου." *ZNW* 19: 46–48.

Hess, Johann Jacob. [1768–72] 1779. *Geschichte der drey letzten Lebensjahre Jesu*. 4th ed. 2 vols. Tübingen: Frank & Schramm.

Heumann, Christoph August. 1740. "Programma de quaestione, cur filius Dei perfrequenter se appellaverit filium hominis?" In *Dissertationum sylloge diligenter recognitarum novisque illustratarum accessionibus*, 1.4.488ff. Göttingen, 1743–50. Summarized by Köcher 1766: 191 and Scholten 1809: 157–58.

Higgins, A. J. B. 1959. "Son of Man – *Forschung* since 'The Teaching of Jesus.'" In *New Testament Essays: Studies in Memory of Thomas Walter Manson 1893–1958*, ed. A. J. B. Higgins, 119–35. Manchester: Manchester University Press.

1964. *Jesus and the Son of Man*. London: Lutterworth; Philadelphia: Fortress.

1965. *Menschensohn Studien: Franz Delitsch-Vorlesungen 1961*. Stuttgart: Kohlhammer.

1968. "The Son of Man Concept and the Historical Jesus." *SE* 5 (= TU 103): 14–20.

1969. "Is the Son of Man Problem Insoluble?" In *Neotestamentica et Semitica: Studies in Honour of Matthew Black*, ed. E. Earle Ellis and Max Wilcox, 70–87. Edinburgh: Clark.

1980. *The Son of Man in the Teaching of Jesus*. SNTSMS 39. Cambridge: Cambridge University Press.

Hilgenfeld, Adolf. 1857. *Die jüdische Apokalyptik in ihrer geschichtlichen Entwickelung*. Jena. Reprinted, Amsterdam: Rodopi, 1966.

1863. "Die Evangelien und die geschichtlichen Gestalt Jesu." *ZWT* 6: 311–40 (esp. 327–34).

1888. "Jüdische Apokalyptik und Christentum." *ZWT* 31: 488–98.

1892. "Der Menschensohn-Messias." *ZWT* 35: 445–64.

1899. "Noch ein Wort über den Menschensohn." *ZWT* 42: 149–51.

Hill, D. 1973. "'Son of Man' in Psalm 80 v. 17." *NovT* 15: 261–69.

Hindley, J. C. 1966. "The Son of Man: A Recent Analysis." *Indian Journal of Theology* 15: 172–78.

1967/68 "Towards a Date for the Similitudes of Enoch: An Historical Approach." *NTS* 14: 551–65.

Hitzig, Ferdinand. 1843. *Über Johannes Marcus und seine Schriften, oder: Welcher Johannes hat die Offenbarung verfasst?* Zurich: Orell, Füssli.

Hodgson, Peter C. 1961. "The Son of Man and the Problem of Historical Knowledge." *JR* 41: 91–108.

Hoekstra, Sytse. 1866. *De benaming "de Zoon des menschen."* Amsterdam: van Kampen. Summarized by M. Müller 1984a: 158.

Hoffmann, Andreas Gottlieb. 1833–38. *Das Buch Henoch*. Jena: Croeker.

Hoffmann, Paul. [1972] 1982. *Studien zur Theologie der Logienquelle*. 3rd. ed. Münster: Aschendorff.

1991. "Jesus versus Menschensohn: Mt 10,32f und die synoptische Menschensohnüberlieferung." In *Salz der Erde – Licht der Welt: Exegetische Studien zum Matthäusevangelium*, ed. L. Oberlinner and P. Fiedler, 165–202. Stuttgart: Katholisches Bibelwerk.

1992. "QR und der Menschensohn: Eine vorläufige Skizze." In *The Four Gospels 1992: Festschrift Frans Neirynck*, ed. F. Van Segbroeck et al., 1.421–56. 3 vols. Leuven: Leuven University Press.

Hofmann, Johann Christian Konrad von. 1852. "Ueber die Entstehungszeit des Buch Henoch." *ZDMG* 6: 87–91.

[1853] 1857–60. *Der Schriftbeweis: Ein theologischer Versuch*. 2nd ed. 2 vols. in 3. Nördlingen: Beck.

1886. *Biblische Theologie des neuen Testaments*. Ed. W. Volck. Nördlingen: Beck.

Holsten, Carl. 1868. *Zum Evangelium des Paulus und des Petrus*. Rostock: Stiller.

1891. "Die Bedeutung der Ausdrucksform ὁ υἱὸς τοῦ ἀνθρώπου im Bewusstsein Jesu." *ZWT* 34: 1–79.

Holtzmann, Heinrich Julius. 1865. "Ueber den NTlichen Ausdruck 'Menschensohn.'" *ZWT* 8: 212–37.

[1897] 1911. *Lehrbuch der neutestamentlichen Theologie*. 2nd ed. 2 vols. Tübingen: Mohr.

Holtzmann, Oskar. [1901] 1904. *The Life of Jesus*. London: Black. Translation of *Das Leben Jesu*. Tübingen, 1901.

Holzinger, Heinrich. 1920. "Zur Menschensohnfrage." In *Beiträge zur alttestamentlichen Wissenschaft: Karl Budde zum siebzigsten Geburtstag*, ed. Karl Marti, 102–106. BZAW 34. Giessen: Töpelmann.

Hommel, Fritz. 1899/1900. "The Apocalyptic Origin of the Expression 'Son of Man.'" *ExpT* 11: 341–45.

Hooker, Morna D. 1959. *Jesus and the Servant: The Influence of the Servant Concept of Deutero-Isaiah in the New Testament*. London: SPCK.

1967. *The Son of Man in Mark: A Study of the Background of the Term "Son of Man" and its Use in St Mark's Gospel*. Montreal: McGill University Press.

1979. "Is the Son of Man Problem Really Insoluble?" In *Text and Interpretation: Studies in the New Testament, Presented to Matthew Black*, ed. E. Best and R. M. Wilson, 155–68. Cambridge: Cambridge University Press.

1991. *The Gospel According to Saint Mark*. Peabody, MA: Hendrickson.

Horbury, W. 1985. "The Messianic Associations of 'The Son of Man.'" *JTS* n.s. 36: 34–55.

Hutchinson, Harry. 1961. "Who Does He Think He Is?" *SJT* 14: 234–47.

Iber, Gerhard. 1953. "Ueberlieferungsgeschichtliche Untersuchungen zum Begriff des Menschensohns im Neuen Testament." Dissertation, Heidelberg.

Jackson, David R. 1985. "The Priority of the Son of Man Sayings." *WTJ* 47: 83–96.

Jackson, Don. 1985/86. "A Survey of the 1967–1981 Study of the Son of Man." *ResQ* 28: 67–78.

Jacobsen, August. 1886. "Die Johannes-Apocalypse und die canonischen Evangelien." *Protestantische Kirchenzeitung für das evangelische Deutschland* 33: 563–68.

Jacobson, Arland D. 1992. *The First Gospel: An Introduction to Q.* Sonoma, CA: Polebridge Press.

James, J. Courtenay. 1924/25. "The Son of Man: Origin and Uses of the Title." *ExpT* 36: 309–14.

Jansen, Cornelius (d. 1576). 1576. *Commentariorum in suam concordiam, ac totam historiam evangelicam partes quatuor.* Louvain: Zangrium.

Jansen, Cornelius (d. 1638). 1639. *Tetrateuchus, sive commentarius in sancta Iesu Christi evangelia.* Louvain: Zeger.

Jansen, Herman Ludin. 1939. *Die Henochgestalt: Eine vergleichende religionsgeschichtliche Untersuchung.* Oslo: Dybwad.

Jas, Michel. 1979. "Hénoch et le fils de l'homme: datation du livre des paraboles pour une situation de l'origine du Gnosticisme." *La revue réformée* 30: 105–19.

Jay, E. G. 1965. *Son of Man, Son of God.* Montreal: McGill University Press.

Jennings, Theodore W., Jr. 1990. "The Martyrdom of the Son of Man." In *Text and Logos: The Humanistic Interpretation of the New Testament,* ed. T. Jennings, 229–43. Atlanta: Scholars Press.

Jeremias, A. 1899. "Oannes." In *Ausfürliches Lexikon der griechischen und römischen Mythologie,* ed. Wilhelm Heinrich Roscher, vol. 3, cols. 577–93. Leipzig: Teubner.

Jeremias, Joachim. 1929. "Erlöser und Erlösung im Spätjudentum und Urchristentum." In *Der Erlösungsgedanke,* ed. D. E. Pfennigsdorf, 106–19. Deutsche Theologie 2. Göttingen: Vandenhoeck & Ruprecht.

[1957] 1965. *The Servant of God,* by Walther Zimmerli and Joachim Jeremias. 2nd ed. SBT 20. London: SCM. Revision of "παῖς θεοῦ." *TWNT* 5 (1954) 653–713.

1967. "Die älteste Schicht der Menschensohn-Logien." *ZNW* 58: 159–72.

1971. *New Testament Theology.* Vol. I: *The Proclamation of Jesus.* London: SCM Press. Translation of *Neutestamentliche Theologie.* Vol. I: *Die Verkündigung Jesu,* 1971.

Johnson, S. E. 1962. "Son of Man." In *The Interpreter's Dictionary of the Bible,* 4.413–20. Nashville: Abingdon.

Johnston, L. 1954. "The Son of Man." *Scripture* 6: 181–83.

Jones, C. W. 1948. "The Use of the Title 'Son of Man' in Mark." Dissertation, Southern Baptist Theological Seminary.

Jonge, H. J. de. 1993. "The Historical Jesus' View of Himself and His Mission." In *From Jesus to John: Essays on Jesus and New Testament Christology in Honour of Marinus de Jonge,* ed. Martinus C. De Boer, 21–37. JSNTSS 84. Sheffield: JSOT Press.

Jonge, Marinus de. 1988. *Christology in Context: The Earliest Christian Response to Jesus.* Philadelphia: Westminster.

1991. *Jesus, the Servant-Messiah.* New Haven: Yale University Press.

Joüon, Paul. 1930. "Appendice A: le Fils de l'homme." In Paul Joüon, *L'Evangile de Notre-Seigneur Jésus-Christ,* 601–604. 2nd ed. Paris: Beauchesne.

Jüngel, Eberhard. 1967. *Paulus und Jesus: Eine Untersuchung zur Präzisierung der Frage nach dem Ursprung der Christologie.* 3rd ed. Tübingen: Mohr.

Käsemann, Ernst. [1954] 1964. "The Problem of the Historical Jesus." In Ernst Käsemann, *Essays on New Testament Themes*, 15–47 (esp. 43–44). SBT 41. London: SCM Press. Translated from "Das Problem des Historischen Jesus." *ZTK* 51 (1954) 125–53.

[1954/55]. 1969. "Sentences of Holy Law in the New Testament." In Käsemann 1969: 66–81 (esp. 77). Translated from "Satze Heiligen Rechtes im Neuen Testament." *NTS* 1 (1954/55) 248–60.

1969. *New Testament Questions of Today.* Philadelphia: Fortress.

Kearns, Rollin. 1978. *Vorfragen zur Christologie.* Vol. 1: *Morphologische und semasiologische Studie zur Vorgeschichte eines eschatologischen Hoheitstitel.* Tübingen: Mohr.

1980. *Vorfragen zur Christologie.* Vol. 2: *Überlieferungsgeschichtliche und Rezeptionsgeschichtliche Studie zur Vorgeschichte eines christologischen Hoheitstitel.* Tübingen: Mohr.

1982. *Vorfragen zur Christologie.* Vol. 3: *Religionsgeschichtliche und Traditionsgeschichtliche Studie zur Vorgeschichte eines christologischen Hoheitstitel.* Tübingen: Mohr.

1986. *Das Traditionsgefüge um den Menschensohn.* Tübingen: Mohr.

1988. *Die Entchristologisierung des Menschensohnes.* Tübingen: Mohr.

Keerl, Philipp Friedrich. 1866. *Der Mensch, das Ebenbild Gottes.* Vol. 2: *Der Gottmensch, das Ebenbild des unsichtbaren Gottes.* Basle: Bahnmaier.

Keil, Carl Friedrich. 1877. *Commentar über das Evangelium des Matthäus.* Leipzig: Dörffling und Franke.

Keim, Theodor. [1867–72] 1876–83. *The History of Jesus of Nazara.* 6 vols. London: Williams and Norgate. Translation of *Die Geschichte Jesu von Nazara*, 1867–72.

Kellner, Wendelin. 1985. *Der Traum vom Menschensohn: Die politisch-theologische Botschaft Jesu.* Munich: Kösel.

Kertelge, Karl. 1973. "Die Vollmacht des Menschensohnes zur Sündenvergebung (Mk 2,10)." In *Orientierung an Jesus: Zur Theologie der Synoptiker* (FS Josef Schmid), ed. Paul Hoffmann et al., 205–13. Freiburg: Herder.

Kim, Seyoon. 1983. *"The 'Son of Man'" as the Son of God.* WUNT 30. Tübingen: Mohr.

Kingsbury, Jack Dean. 1975. "The Title 'Son of Man' in Matthew's Gospel." *CBQ* 37: 193–202.

1990. "Observations on 'the Son of Man' in the Gospel According to Luke." *CurTM* 17: 283–90.

Kipp, J. 1904. "Des Menschen Sohn." *Evangelische Kirchenzeitung.* Pp. 437–45, 459–63.

Kloppenborg, John S. 1987. *The Formation of Q: Trajectories in Ancient Wisdom Collections.* Philadelphia: Fortress.

Klöpper, A. 1899. "Der Sohn des Menschen in den synoptischen Evangelien." *ZWT* 42 (= N.F. 7) 161–86.

Knibb, M. A. 1978. *The Ethiopic Book of Enoch: A New Edition in the*

Light of the Aramaic Dead Sea Fragments. 2 vols. Oxford: Clarendon Press.

1978/79. "The Date of the Parables of Enoch: A Critical Review." *NTS* 25: 345–59.

Knox, John. 1958. *The Death of Christ.* New York: Abingdon.

Köcher, Johann Christoph. 1766. *Analecta philologica et exegetica in quatuor ss. evangelia.* Altenburg: Richter.

Koester, Helmut. 1971. In *Trajectories Through Early Christianity*, by James M. Robinson and Helmut Koester, 138, 170–72, 186–87, 213–14. Philadelphia: Fortress.

Köstlin, Julius. 1858. "Die Einheit und Mannigfaltigkeit in der neutestamentlichen Lehre." In *Jahrbücher für deutsche Theologie* 3: 85–154 (esp. 90).

Kraeling, Carl H. 1927. *Anthropos and Son of Man: A Study in the Religious Syncretism of the Hellenistic Orient.* CUOS 25. Columbia University Press. Reprinted, New York: AMS Press, 1966.

Krop, Frédéric. 1897. *La pensée de Jésus sur le Royaume de Dieu d'après les Evangiles synoptiques, avec un appendice sur la question du "Fils de l'homme."* Paris: Fischbacher.

Kühl, Ernst. 1907. *Das Selbstbewusstsein Jesu.* Berlin: Runge.

Kuhnert, E. 1917/18. "'Ο υἱὸς τοῦ ἀνθρώπου." *ZNW* 18: 165–76.

Kühnöl, Christian Gottlieb. [1807] 1823. *Commentarius in libros novi testamenti historicos.* Vol 1: *Evangelium Matthaei.* 3rd ed. Leipzig: Barth.

Kümmel, Werner Georg. [1969] 1973. *The Theology of the New Testament According to its Major Witnesses.* Nashville: Abingdon. Translation of *Die Theologie des Neuen Testaments nach seinen Hauptzeugen.* Göttingen, 1969.

1975. "Das Verhalten Jesus gegenüber und das Verhalten des Menschensohns: Markus 8,38 par und Lukas 12,8f par Mattäus 10,32f." In Pesch and Schnackenburg 1975: 210–24.

1980. "Jesusforschung seit 1965; V. Der persönliche Anspruch Jesu." *TRu* N.F. 45: 40–84.

1984. *Jesus der Menschensohn?* Stuttgart: Steiner.

Küttner, Christian Gottfried. 1780. *Hypomnemata in novum testamentum.* Leipzig: Breitkopf.

Ladd, George Eldon. 1974. *A Theology of the New Testament.* Grand Rapids: Eerdmans.

Lagrange, Marie-Joseph. 1931. *Le judaïsme avant Jésus-Christ.* 2nd ed. Paris: Gabalda.

Lampe, Friedrich Adolf. 1724–26. *Commentarius analytico-exegeticus tam literalis quam realis evangelii secundum Joannem.* Amsterdam: Schoonenburg. Cited by Scholten 1809: 204–205.

Lange, Joachim. 1743. *Biblia parenthetica . . . In Biblisches Licht und Recht.* 2 vols. Leipzig: Gleditsch.

Langen, Joseph. 1866. *Das Judenthum in Palästina zur Zeit Christi.* Freiburg i.B.: Herder.

Lapide, Cornelius à (d. 1637). [1638] 1891–96. *The Great Commentary of Cornelius à Lapide.* 3rd ed. London: Hodges. Translation of *Commentarii in quatuor evangelia*, 1638.

Larsen, A. C. 1902. "Om Menneskesønnen." Summarized by M. Müller 1984a: 158.

Laurence, Richard. 1821. *The Book of Enoch the Prophet . . . Now First Translated.* Oxford: Parker.

Le Cène, Charles. [1696] 1702. *An Essay for a New Translation of the Bible.* London: Nutt. Translation of *Projet d'une nouvelle version françoise de la Bible,* 1696.

Le Clerc, Jean. [1699]. 1701. *The Harmony of the Evangelists.* London: Buckley. Translation of *Harmonia evangelica.* Amsterdam: Huguetani, 1699.

Le Déaut, R. 1968. "Le substrat araméen des Evangiles: scolies en marge de l'*Aramaic Approach* de Matthew Black." *Biblica* 50: 388–99 (esp. 397–99).

Legasse, Simon. 1977. "Jésus historique et le Fils de l'homme: aperçu sur les opinions contemporaines." In *Apocalypses et théologie de l'espérance: Congrès de Toulouse 1975,* Association Catholique Française pour L'Etude de la Bible, 271–98. Paris: Cerf.

Leigh, Edward. 1650. *Annotations upon All the New Testament Philologicall and Theologicall.* London: Lee.

Leivestad, Ragnar. 1968. "Der apokalyptische Menschensohn ein theologisches Phantom." *ASTI* 6: 49–105.

1971/72. "Exit the Apocalyptic Son of Man." *NTS* 18: 243–67.

1982. "Jesus – Messias – Menschensohn: Die jüdischen Heilandserwartungen zur Zeit der ersten römischen Kaiser und die Frage nach dem messianischen Selbstbewusstsein Jesu." In *Aufstieg und Niedergang der römischen Welt* II.25.1, ed. W. Haase, 220–64. Berlin: De Gruyter.

Less, Gottfried. 1776. *Nonnulla de FILIO HOMINIS praefatus.* Göttingen: Rosenbusch.

Lietzmann, Hans. 1896. *Der Menschensohn.* Freiburg/Leipzig: Mohr.

1899. *Zur Menschensohnfrage.* Freiburg i.B.: Mohr.

Lightfoot, John. 1675. *Horae Hebraicae et talmudicae in quatuor evangelistas.* Ed. J. B. Carpzov. Leipzig: Lanckis. Reprinted in *A Commentary on the New Testament from the Talmud and Hebraica: Matthew–I Corinthians.* Vol. 2: *Matthew–Mark.* Grand Rapids: Baker, 1979.

Lindars, Barnabas. 1975/76. "Re-enter the Apocalyptic Son of Man." *NTS* 22: 52–72.

1980. "Jesus as Advocate: A Contribution to the Christology Debate." *BJRL* 62: 476–97.

1981. "The New Look on the Son of Man." *BJRL* 63: 437–62.

1983. *Jesus Son of Man: A Fresh Examination of the Son of Man Sayings in the Gospels in the Light of Recent Research.* London: SPCK.

1985. "Response to Richard Bauckham: The Idiomatic Use of Bar Enasha." *JSNT* 23: 35–41.

Lindeskog, Gösta. 1968. "Das Rätsel des Menschensohnes." *ST* 22: 149–75.

Lohse, Eduard. [1974] 1984. *Grundriss der neutestamentlichen Theologie.* 3rd ed. Stuttgart: Kohlhammer.

Loisy, Alfred. 1907. *Les Evangiles synoptiques.* 2 vols. Ceffonds.

Longenecker, Richard N. 1969. "'Son of Man' as a Self-Designation of Jesus." *JETS* 12: 151–58.

1970. *The Christology of Early Jewish Christianity.* SBT, 2nd ser., 17. Napierville, IL: Allenson, 1970.

Lucas, Franciscus. 1606. *In sacrosancta quatuor Iesu Christi evangelia . . . commentarius.* 3 vols. Antwerp: Plantin, Moretus.

Lücke, Friedrich. [1820] 1840–43. *Commentar über die Schriften des Evangelisten Johannes.* 3rd ed. 4 vols. Vols. 1–2: *Commentar über das Evangelium des Johannes.* Bonn: Weber.

[1832] 1852. *Commentar über die Schriften des Evangelisten Johannes.* Vol. 4: *Versuch einer vollständigen Einleitung in die Offenbarung des Johannes.* 2nd ed. Bonn: Weber.

Luthardt, Christoph Ernst. [1852–53] 1876–78. *St. John's Gospel Described and Explained According to its Peculiar Character.* 3 vols. Edinburgh: Clark. Translation of *Das johanneische Evangelium nach seiner Eigenthümlichkeit geschildert und erklärt.* 2nd ed. 2 vols. Nuremberg: Geiger, 1875–76.

Luther, Martin. [1530–32] 1959. *Luther's Works.* Vol. 23: *Sermons on the Gospel of St. John, Chapters 6–8.* Ed. Jaroslav Pelikan and Daniel E. Poellot. St. Louis: Concordia. Translation of *Auslegung des sechsten, siebenten und achten Capitels St. Johannis,* 1530–32.

Lutz, Johann Ludwig Samuel. [1847] 1861. *Biblische Dogmatik.* Ed. Rudolf Rüetschi. 2nd ed. Pforzheim: Flammer.

Luz, Ulrich. 1992. "The Son of Man in Matthew: Heavenly Judge or Human Christ." *JSNT* 48: 3–21.

McCasland, S. Vernon. 1964. *The Pioneer of Our Faith: A New Life of Jesus.* New York: McGraw-Hill.

McCown, C. C. 1948. "Jesus Son of Man: A Survey of Recent Discussion." *JR* 28: 1–12.

Mack, Burton L. 1988. *A Myth of Innocence: Mark and Christian Origins.* Philadelphia: Fortress.

MacKnight, James. [1756] 1950. *Harmony of the Four Gospels . . . With a Paraphrase and Notes.* Reprinted from 1819 ed. Grand Rapids: Baker.

McNaugher, John. 1931. "The Son of Man." *BSac* 88: 90–104.

McNeil, Brian. 1979/80. "The Son of Man and the Messiah: A Footnote." *NTS* 26: 419–21.

MacRory, J. 1915. "The Son of Man." *ITQ* 10: 50–63.

Maddox, Robert. 1968. "The Function of the Son of Man According to the Synoptic Gospels." *NTS* 15: 45–74.

1971. "The Quest for Valid Methods in 'Son of Man' Research." *AusBR* 19: 36–51. German translation: "Methodenfragen in der Menschensohnforschung." *EvT* 32 (1972) 143–60.

1974. "The Function of the Son of Man in the Gospel of John." In *Reconciliation and Hope: New Testament Essays on Atonement and Eschatology,* ed. R. Banks, 186–204. Grand Rapids: Eerdmans.

Maldonado, Juan (d. 1583). [1596–97] 1888. *A Commentary on the Holy Gospels: S. Matthew's Gospel.* London: Hodges. Translated from *Commentarii in quatuor evangelistas.* 2 vols. Mussiponti, 1596–97.

Mangold, W. 1877. "Über die Bedeutung des Ausdrucks ὁ υἱὸς τοῦ ἀνθρώπου." In *Theologische Arbeiten aus dem rheinisch-wissenschaftlichen Predigerverein* 3: 1–25.

148   List of references

Manson, T. W. [1931] 1935. *The Teaching of Jesus: Studies of its Form and Content*. 2nd ed. Cambridge: Cambridge University Press.
1950. "The Son of Man in Daniel, Enoch, and the Gospels." *BJRL* 32: 171–93. Reprinted in *Studies in the Gospels and Epistles*, ed. Matthew Black, 123–45. Manchester: Manchester University Press, 1962.
1953. *The Servant-Messiah*. Cambridge: Cambridge University Press.
Manson, William. 1943. *Jesus the Messiah*. London: Hodder & Stoughton.
Margulies, Mordecai, ed. [1966]. *Midrash Haggadol on the Pentateuch: Genesis*. Jerusalem: Mosad Haraw Kook.
Mariana, Juan de. 1619. *Scholia in vetus et novum testamentum*. Madrid.
Marlorat, Augustin. 1561. *Novi testamenti catholica expositio ecclesiastica*. [Paris]: Stephanus.
Marlow, Ransom. 1966. "The *Son of Man* in Recent Journal Literature." *CBQ* 28: 20–30.
Marshall, I. Howard. 1965/66. "The Synoptic Son of Man Sayings in Recent Discussion." *NTS* 12: 327–51.
1970. "The Son of Man in Contemporary Debate." *EvQ* 42: 67–87.
[1976] 1990. *The Origins of New Testament Christology*. 2nd ed. Downer's Grove, IL: Intervarsity Press.
1991. "The Son of Man and the Incarnation." *Ex Auditu* 7: 29–43.
Martineau, James. [1890] 1891. *The Seat of Authority in Religion*. 3rd ed. London: Longmans, Green.
Martyn, J. Louis. 1979. *History and Theology in the Fourth Gospel*. 2nd ed. Nashville: Abingdon.
Marxsen, Willi. [1960] 1969. *The Beginnings of Christology: A Study in its Problems*. Philadelphia: Fortress. Translation of *Anfangsprobleme der Christologie*. Gütersloh, 1960.
May, Herbert G. and Bruce M. Metzger, eds. 1977. *The New Oxford Annotated Bible with the Apocrypha: Revised Standard Version*. New York: Oxford University Press.
Mearns, Christopher L. 1977/78. "The Parables of Enoch – Origin and Date." *ExpT* 89: 118–19.
1978/79 "Dating the Similitudes of Enoch." *NTS* 25: 360–69.
1985/86 "The Son of Man Trajectory and Eschatological Development." *ExpT* 97: 8–12.
Meeks, Wayne A. [1972] 1986. "The Man from Heaven in Johannine Sectarianism." In *The Interpretation of John*, ed. John Ashton, 141–73. Philadelphia: Fortress. Reprinted from *JBL* 91 (1972) 44–72.
1993. "Asking Back to Jesus' Identity." In *From Jesus to John: Essays on Jesus and New Testament Christology in Honour of Marinus de Jonge*, ed. Martinus C. De Boer, 38–50. JSNTSS 84. Sheffield: JSOT Press.
Meloni, G. 1913. "Filius hominis." In *Saggi di Filologia Semitica*, 315–19. Rome.
Menochio, Giovanni Stefano. 1630. *Brevis explicatio sensus literalis totius s. scripturae*. 2 vols. Colon: Kinch. Reprinted as *Commentarii totius sacrae scripturae*. 2 vols. Venice: Recurti, 1722.
Mercken, Johann Caspar. 1722. *Observationes criticae in passionem Domini nostri Iesu Christi*. Cited by Scholten 1809: 205.

Merklein, Helmut. 1983. *Jesu Botschaft von der Gottesherrschaft: Eine Skizze*. Stuttgart: Katholisches Bibelwerk.

Messel, Nils. 1922. *Der Menschensohn in den Bilderreden des Henoch*. Giessen: Töpelmann.

Meyer, Arnold. 1896. *Jesu Muttersprache*. Freiburg i. B./Leipzig: Mohr.

Meyer, Heinrich August Wilhelm. 1832. *Kritisch exegetischer Kommentar über das Neue Testament*. Vol. 1: *Kritisch exegetisches Handbuch über die Evangelien des Matthäus, Markus und Lukas*. Göttingen: Vandenhoeck & Ruprecht.

[1876] 1884. *Critical and Exegetical Hand-Book to the Gospel of Matthew*. New York/London: Funk & Wagnalls. Translation of *Kritisch exegetisches Handbuch über das Evangelium Matthäus*. 6th ed. Göttingen: Vandenhoeck & Ruprecht.

Michaelis, Johann David. [1773–90] 1790–92. *Anmerkungen für Ungelehrte zu seiner Uebersetzung des Neuen Testaments*. 4 vols. Göttingen: Vandenhoeck & Ruprecht. Comments from *Deutsche Uebersetzung des Alten und des Neuen Testaments, mit Anmerkungen für Ungelehrte*. Göttingen: Dieterich, 1773–90.

1792. *Supplementa ad lexica Hebraica*. 2 vols. Göttingen: Rosenbusch.

Michel, Otto. 1971a. "Der Menschensohn. Die eschatologische Hinweisung. Die apokalyptische Aussage. Bemerkungen zum Menschensohnverständnis des Neuen Testaments." *TZ* 27: 81–104.

1971b. "Der Menschensohn in der Jesusüberlieferung." *TBei* 2: 119–28.

1971c. "υἱὸς τοῦ ἀνθρώπου." *Theologisches Begriffslexicon zum Neuen Testament* II 2.1153–66. Wuppertal: Brockhaus.

1971d. "Der Umbruch: Messianität = Menschensohn: Fragen zu Markus 8,31." In *Tradition und Glaube: Das frühe Christentum in seiner Umwelt*, ed. G. Jeremias et al., 311–16. Göttingen: Vandenhoeck & Ruprecht.

Micklem, N. 1929. "The Son of Man." *Queen's Quarterly*. 36: 205–24.

Milik, J. T. 1959. *Ten Years of Discovery in the Wilderness of Judea*. SBT 26. London: SCM.

1971. "Problèmes de la littérature hénochique à la lumière des fragments araméens de Qumrân." *HTR* 64: 333–78.

1976. *The Books of Enoch: Aramaic Fragments of Qumrân Cave 4*. With the collaboration of Matthew Black. Oxford: Clarendon Press.

Milligan, G. 1902. "The Messianic Consciousness of Jesus." *Expositor* ser. 6, vol. 5, pp. 72–80.

Moe, Olaf. 1960. "Der Menschensohn und der Urmensch." *ST* 14: 119–29.

Moeller, H. R. 1963. "Wisdom Motifs and John's Gospel." *BETS* 6: 92–100.

Moffatt, James. 1912. *The Theology of the Gospels*. London: Duckworth.

Moloney, Francis J. 1978. *The Johannine Son of Man*. 2nd ed. Rome: LAS.

1980. "The End of the Son of Man?" *Downside Review* 98: 280–90.

1981. "The Re-interpretation of Psalm VIII and the Son of Man Debate." *NTS* 27: 656–72.

Montefiore, C. G. [1909] 1927. *The Synoptic Gospels*. 2nd ed. 2 vols. Reprinted, New York: Ktav, 1968.

Morgenstern, Julian. 1960. "The King-God Among the Western Semites and the Meaning of Epiphanes." *VT* 10: 138–97.

1961. "The 'Son of Man' of Daniel 7:13f.: A New Interpretation." *JBL* 80: 65–77.

Morus, Samuel Friedrich Nathanael. 1796. *Recitationes in evangelium Joannis.* Ed. Theoph. Immanuel Dindorf. Leipzig: Herrl. Cited by Scholten 1809: 200.

Mosche, Gabriel Christoph Benjamin. 1788–90. *Erklärung aller Sonn-und Festtags-Episteln.* 2nd ed. 2 vols. Frankfurt: Fleischer.

Moule, C. F. D. 1952. "From Defendant to Judge – and Deliverer." *Bulletin of the Studiorum Novi Testamenti Societas* 3: 40–53. Reprinted in C. F. D. Moule, *The Phenomenon of the New Testament,* 82–99. SBT, 2nd ser., 1. Napierville, IL: Allenson, 1967.

1974. "Neglected Features in the Problem of 'the Son of Man.'" In *Neues Testament und Kirche: Für Rudolf Schnackenburg,* ed. Joachim Gnilka, 413–28. Freiburg: Herder.

1977. *The Origin of Christology.* Cambridge: Cambridge University Press.

1995. "'The Son of Man': Some of the Facts." *NTS* 41: 277–79.

Mouren, J. 1903. *Le Fils de l'homme: étude historique et critique.* Lyons: Paquet.

Mouson, J. 1952. "De locutione 'filius hominis' apud Matthaeum." *Collectanea mechliniensia* 22: 627–31.

Mowinckel, Sigmund. [1951] 1954. *He That Cometh.* New York: Abingdon. Translation of *Han som kommer,* 1951.

Muirhead, L. A. 1899/1900. "The Name 'Son of Man' and the Messianic Consciousness of Jesus." *ExpT* 11: 62–65.

Müller, Karlheinz. 1972–73. "Menschensohn und Messias: Religions-geschichtliche Vorüberlegungen zum Menschensohnproblem in den synoptischen Evangelien." *BZ* N.F. 16 (1972) 161–87; 17 (1973) 52–66.

Müller, Mogens. 1977. "Über den Ausdruck 'Menschensohn' in den Evangelien." *ST* 31: 65–82.

1984a. *Der Ausdruck "Menschensohn" in den Evangelien: Voraussetzungen und Bedeutung.* Leiden: Brill.

1984b. "The Expression 'the Son of Man' as Used by Jesus." *ST* 38: 47–64.

1991. "Have You Faith in the Son of Man? (John 9.35)." *NTS* 37: 291–94.

Müller, Ulrich B. 1972. *Messias und Menschensohn in jüdischen Apokalypsen und in der Offenbarung des Johannes.* Gütersloh: Mohn.

Münster, Sebastian. 1537. *Torat Hammashiach: Evangelium secundum Matthaeum in lingua Hebraica, cum versione Latina atque succinctis annotationibus.* Basle: Petrus.

Musculus, Wolfgang. 1544. *In evangelistam Matthaeum commentarii.* Basle: Hervag.

Neander, Augustus Wilhelm. [1837] 1888. *The Life of Jesus Christ in its Historical Connexion and Historical Development.* London: Bell. Translation of *Das Leben Jesu-Christi.* 4th ed. Hamburg.

Neirynck, Frans. 1982. "Recent Developments in the Study of Q." In *Logia – Les paroles de Jésus – The Sayings of Jesus*, ed. J. Delobel, 29–75, esp. 69–72. BETL 59. Leuven: Peeters.

Neugebauer, Fritz. 1972. *Jesus der Menschensohn: Ein Beitrag zur Klärung der Wege historischer Wahrheitsfindung im Bereich der Evangelien.* Stuttgart: Calwer.

1974/75. "Die Davidssohnfrage (Mark xii. 35–7 parr.) und der Menschensohn." *NTS* 21: 81–108 (esp. 91–96).

Newman, Barclay M. 1970. "Towards a Translation of 'The Son of Man' in the Gospels." *BT* 21: 141–46.

Nickelsburg, George W. E. 1978. Review of *The Books of Enoch*, by J. T. Milik. In *CBQ* 40: 411–19 (esp. 417–18).

1981. *Jewish Literature Between the Bible and the Mishnah.* Philadelphia: Fortress.

1992a. "Enoch, First Book of." *ABD* 2.508–16.

1992b. "Son of Man." *ABD* 6.137–50.

Nösgen, Karl Friedrich. 1869. *Christus der Menschen- und Gottessohn.* Gotha: Perthes.

1891. *Geschichte Jesu Christi.* Munich: Beck.

Novarini, Luigi. 1642. *Matthaeus et Marcus expensi.* Lugduni: Boissat & Anisson.

Oehler, Gustavus Franz. [1854–68] 1883. "Messiah, Messianic Prophecy." In *A Religious Encyclopedia*, ed. Philip Schaff, 2.1479–84. Translation of "Messias." In *Realencyklopädie für protestantische Theologie und Kirche*, ed. Johann Jacob Herzog, 1854–68.

Olearius, Johannes. [1699] 1721. *De stilo novi testamenti.* Coburg: Pfotenhauer.

Olshausen, Hermann. [1830] 1858. *Biblical Commentary on the New Testament.* New York: Sheldon, Blakeman. Translation of *Biblischer Commentar über sämmtliche Schriften des Neuen Testaments*, vol. 1. 3rd ed. Königsberg: Unzer, 1837.

O'Neill, J. C. 1968/69. "The Silence of Jesus." *NTS* 15: 153–67.

Oort, Henricus Lucas. 1893. *Die uitdrukking ὁ υἱὸς τοῦ ἀνθρώπου in het Nieuwe Testament.* Leiden: Brill.

Ory, Georges. 1964. "L'intrusion du Fils de l'homme dans nos Evangiles." *Bulletin du Cercle Ernest-Renan* 104: 1–3.

Otto, Rudolf. [1934] 1943. *The Kingdom of God and the Son of Man.* 2nd ed. London: Lutterworth. Reprinted, Boston: Starr King Press, 1957. Translation of *Reich Gottes und Menschensohn.* 2nd ed. Munich: Beck, 1940.

Pamment, Margaret. 1983. "The Son of Man in the First Gospel." *NTS* 29: 116–29.

1985. "The Son of Man in the Fourth Gospel." *JTS* n.s. 36: 56–66.

Parker, Pierson. 1941. "The Meaning of 'Son of Man.'" *JBL* 60: 151–57.

Patton, Carl S. 1922. "Did Jesus Call Himself the Son of Man?" *JR* 2: 501–11.

Paul, Leslie. 1961. *Son of Man: The Life of Christ.* London: Hodder & Stoughton.

Paulus, Heinrich Eberhard Gottlobb. [1800] 1804. *Philologisch-kritischer*

und historischer Commentar über das neue Testament. Vol. 1: *Der drey ersten Evangelien erster Hälfte.* 2nd ed. Lübeck: Bohn.
1830–33. *Exegetisches Handbuch über die drei ersten Evangelien.* 3 vols. Heidelberg: Universitäts-Buchhandlung.
Peake, Arthur Samuel. 1924. "The Messiah and the Son of Man." *BJRL* 8: 52–81. Reprinted in *The Servant of Yahweh*, 220–37. Manchester: Manchester University Press, 1931.
Percy, Ernst. 1953. *Die Botschaft Jesu.* Lund: Gleerup.
Perrin, Norman. 1963. *The Kingdom of God in the Teaching of Jesus.* Philadelphia: Westminster.
1965/66. "Mark 14:62: The End Product of a Christian Pesher Tradition?" *NTS* 12: 150–55. Reprinted with a postscript in Perrin 1974: 10–22.
1966. "The Son of Man in Ancient Judaism and Primitive Christianity: A Suggestion." *BR* 11: 17–28. Reprinted with a postscript in Perrin 1974: 23–40.
1967. *Rediscovering the Teaching of Jesus.* New York: Harper & Row.
1967/68. "The Creative Use of the Son of Man Traditions by Mark." *USQR* 23: 237–65. Reprinted in Perrin 1974: 84–93.
1968a. "Recent Trends in Research in the Christology of the New Testament." In *Transitions in Biblical Scholarship*, ed. J. Coert Rylaarsdam, 217–33. Chicago: University of Chicago Press. Reprinted in Perrin 1974: 41–56.
1968b. "The Son of Man in the Synoptic Tradition." *BR* 13: 3–25. Reprinted with a postscript in Perrin 1974: 57–83.
1974. *A Modern Pilgrimage in New Testament Christology.* Philadelphia: Fortress.
1976. "Son of Man." In *The Interpreter's Dictionary of the Bible*: *Supplementary Volume*, 833–36. Nashville: Abingdon.
Pesch, Rudolf and Rudolf Schnackenburg, eds. 1975. *Jesus und der Menschensohn: Für Anton Vögtle.* Freiburg i.B: Herder.
Pfleiderer, Otto. 1869. *Die Religion, ihr Wesen und ihre Geschichte.* 2 vols. Leipzig: Fues.
[1887] 1906–11. *Primitive Christianity: Its Writings and Teachings in their Historical Connections.* New York: G. P. Putnam's Sons. Reprinted in 4 vols., Clifton, NJ: Reference Book, 1965. Translation of *Das Urchristentum: Seine Schriften und Lehren in geschichtlichem Zusammenhang.* 2nd ed. Berlin: Reimer, 1902.
Philippi, Ferdinand. 1868. *Das Buch Henoch, sein Zeitalter und sein Verhältniss zum Judasbriefe.* Stuttgart: Liesching.
Philippi, Friedrich Adolf. 1868. *Kirchliche Glaubenslehre.* Vol. 4, first half: *Die Lehre von der Erwählung und von Christi Person.* 2nd ed. Stuttgart: Liesching.
Piscator, Johannes. 1613. *Commentarii in omnes libros novi testamenti.* Herbornae Nassoviorum.
Polag, Athanasius. 1977. *Die Christologie der Logienquelle.* WMANT 45. Neukirchen-Vluyn: Neukirchener-Verlag.
Poussines, Pierre (d. c. 1650). 1713. *Spicilegium evangelicum.* In *Observationes selectae in varia loca novi testamenti.* Ed. Johann Albrecht Fabricius. Hamburg: Liebezeit.

Preiss, Théo. 1947. "Le mystère du Fils de l'Homme." *Dieu Vivant* 8: 15–36.
1951. *Le Fils de l'Homme*. Etudes théologiques et religieuses. Montpellier.
1953. "Le Fils de l'Homme dans le IVe Evangile." *ETR* 28: 7–61.
Procksch, Otto. 1927. "Der Menschensohn als Gottessohn." *Christentum und Wissenschaft* 3: 425–43, 473–81.
Proudman, C. L. J. 1966. "Remarks on the 'Son of Man.'" *CJT* 12: 128–31.
Pseudo-Justin. Before 1583. *Quaestionum et responsionum ad orthodoxos*. Quaest. 66. Cited by Scholten 1809: 155–56.
Quenstedt, Johann Andreas. 1685. *Theologia didactico-polemica*. Wittenberg: Quenstedt & Haeredes.
Rawlinson, A. E. J. 1926. *The New Testament Doctrine of the Christ*. London: Longmans, Green.
Rechenberg, Adam. 1714. *Hierolexicon reale*. Leipzig/Frankfurt: Klos.
Reimarus, Hermann Samuel. [1778] 1970. *The Goal of Jesus and His Disciples*. Leiden: Brill. Translation of *Von dem Zwecke Jesu und seiner Jünger: Noch ein Fragment des Wolfenbüttelschen Ungennanten*. Ed. Gotthold Ephraim Lessing. 2nd ed. Braunschweig, 1788.
Reitzenstein, Richard. 1921. *Das iranische Erlösungsmysterium*. Bonn: Weber. Summarized by Kraeling 1927: 13–14.
Renan, Ernest. [1863] 1936. *The Life of Jesus*. London/New York: Brentano's. Reprinted, [New York:] Boni, 1936. Translation of *Vie de Jésus*. Paris: Lévy, 1863.
Reuss, Edouard. [1852] 1860. *Histoire de la théologie chrétienne au siècle apostolique*. 2nd ed. 2 vols. Strasburg/Paris: Treuttel et Wurtz.
Reuss, Joseph, ed. 1966. *Johannes-Kommentare aus der Griechischen Kirche*. TU 89. Berlin: Akademie-Verlag.
Réville, Albert. 1897. *Jésus de Nazareth*. 2 vols. Paris: Fischbacher.
Rhea, Robert. 1990. *The Johannine Son of Man*. Zurich: Theologischer Verlag.
Rhees, Rush. 1898. "A 'Striking Monotony' in the Synoptic Gospels." *JBL* 17: 87–102.
Richardson, Alan. 1958. *An Introduction to the Theology of the New Testament*. New York: Harper & Row.
Riesenfeld, Harald. 1947. *Jésus transfiguré*. Copenhagen: Munksgaard.
1954. "The Mythological Background of New Testament Christology." In *The Background of the New Testament and its Eschatology*, ed. W. D. Davies and D. Daube, 81–95. Cambridge: Cambridge University Press.
Robinson, J. Armitage. 1906. *The Study of the Gospels*. Longmans, Green.
Robinson, James M., ed. 1990. *The Nag Hammadi Library in English*. 3rd ed. San Francisco: Harper.
Roloff, Jürgen. 1993. *The Revelation of John: A Continental Commentary*. Minneapolis: Fortress.
Rose, Vincent. 1900. "Fils de l'homme et Fils de Dieu." *RB* 9: 169–99 (esp. 172–83). Reprinted in Vincent Rose, *Etudes sur les Evangiles*, 157–82. Paris: Welter, 1902.
Rosenmüller, Johann Georg. [1777] 1815. *Scholia in novum testamentum*. Vol. 1: *Evangelia Matthaei et Marci*. 6th ed. Nuremberg: Felsecker.

154   List of references

Roslaniec, Franciszek. 1920. *Sensus genuinus et plenus locutionis "Filius hominis" a Christo Domino adhibitae.* Rome: Typis Polyglottis Vaticanis.

Ross, Alexander. 1934. "The Title 'Son of Man.'" *EvQ* 6: 36–49.

Ross, J. M. 1991. "The Son of Man." *IBS* 13: 186–98.

Rowley, H. H. [1944] 1963. *The Relevance of Apocalyptic.* 3rd ed. New York: Association Press.

[1952] 1965. "The Suffering Servant and the Davidic Messiah." In H. H. Rowley, *The Servant of the Lord*, 63–93. 2nd ed. Oxford: Blackwell.

Sabourin, Leopold. 1983. "About Jesus' Self-Understanding." *Religious Studies Bulletin* 3: 129–34.

Sacy, Silvestre de. 1822. Review of *The Book of Enoch*, by Richard Laurence. In *Journal des savans* 7: 587–95.

Sahlin, Harald. 1983. "Wie wurde ursprünglich die Benennung 'Der Menschensohn' verstanden?" *ST* 37: 147–79.

Sanday, William. 1891. "On the Title, 'Son of Man.'" *Expositor* ser. 4, vol. 3, pp. 18–32.

1908. *The Life of Christ in Recent Research.* New York: Oxford University Press.

Sanders, E. P. 1985. *Jesus and Judaism.* Philadelphia: Fortress.

1993. *The Historical Figure of Jesus.* Harmondsworth: Penguin.

Sanders, Ian L. 1958. "The Origin and Significance of the Title 'The Son of Man' as Used in the Gospels." *Scripture* 10: 49–56.

Sandmel, Samuel. 1963. "Son of Man." In *In the Time of Harvest: Essays in Honor of Abba Hillel Silver*, ed. Daniel Jeremy Silver, 355–67. New York: Macmillan.

Sanford, A. M. 1923. "Did Jesus Call Himself the Son of Man? Another Point of View." *JR* 3: 308–13.

Schade, Hans-Heinrich. 1984. *Apokalyptische Christologie bei Paulus.* 2nd. ed. Göttingen: Vandenhoeck & Ruprecht.

Schenke, Hans-Martin. 1962. *Der Gott "Mensch" in der Gnosis.* Göttingen: Vandenhoeck & Ruprecht.

Schenkel, Daniel. [1864] 1869. *A Sketch of the Character of Jesus.* London: Longmans, Green. Translation of *Das Characterbild Jesu.* 3rd ed. Wiesbaden: Kreidel, 1864.

1872. "Menschensohn." In Daniel Schenkel, *Bibel-Lexicon: Realwörterbuch zum Handgebrauch für Geistliche und Gemeindeglieder*, 4.170–75. 5 vols. Leipzig: Brockhaus, 1869–75.

Schlatter, A. 1921. *Die Geschichte des Christus.* Stuttgart: Calwer.

Schleiermacher, Friedrich. [1821–22] 1928. *The Christian Faith.* Edinburgh: Clark. Reprinted, New York: Harper & Row, 1963. Translation of *Der christliche Glaube.* 2nd ed. Halle a.d.S.: Hendel, 1830–31.

Schleusner, Johann Friedrich. [1792] 1824. *Novum lexicon Graeco-Latinum in novum testamentum.* 4th ed. 2 vols. London: Priestley.

Schlichting, Jonas (d. 1564). After 1656. *Commentaria posthuma in plerosque novi testamenti libros.* 2 vols. Irenopolis: Philaleth.

Schmid, Christian Friedrich. [1853] 1870. *Biblical Theology of the New Testament.* Translated from the 4th German edition. Edinburgh: Clark.

List of references   155

Schmid, Erasmus (d. 1637). 1658. *Opus sacrum posthumum, in quo continentur versio novi testamenti nova . . . et notae ac animadversiones in idem.* Nuremberg: Endter.

Schmidt, Hans and Gerhard Kittel. 1929. "Menschensohn." In *RGG*, 3.2117–21. 2nd ed. Tübingen.

Schmidt, Hermann. 1889. "Bildung und Gehalt des messianischen Bewusstseins Jesu." *TSK* 62: 423–507 (esp. 502).

Schmidt, Karl Christian Ludwig. 1798. "Ueber den Ausdruck 'ὁ υἱὸς τοῦ ἀνθρώπου' im Neuen Testament." *Neues Magazin für Religionsphilosophie, Exegese und Kirchengeschichte* 2: 507–26.

Schmidt, Nathaniel. 1896. "Was בר נשא a Messianic Title?" *JBL* 15: 36–53.

1903. "Son of Man." In *Encyclopedia Biblica*, ed. T. K. Cheyne and J. Sutherland Black, vol. 4, cols. 4705–40.

1926. "Recent Study of the Term 'Son of Man.'" *JBL* 45: 326–49.

Schmiedel, Paul Wilhelm. 1898a. "Der Name 'Menschensohn' und das Messiasbewusstsein Jesu." *PM* 2: 252–67.

1898b. "Bezeichnet Jesus den Menschen als solchen durch 'Menschensohn'?" *PM* 2: 291–308.

1901. "Die neusten Auffassungen des Namens 'Menschensohn.'" *PM* 5: 333–51.

Schmithals, Walter. 1979. "Die Worte vom leidenden Menschensohn: Ein Schlüssel zum Lösung des Menschensohns-Problems." In *Theologia Crucis – Signum Crucis: Festschrift für Erich Dinkler zum 70 Geburtstag*, ed. C. Andreson and G. Klein, 417–45. Tübingen: Mohr.

Schnackenburg, Rudolf. 1959. "Das kommende Reich Gottes und der Menschensohn." In Rudolf Schnackenburg, *Gottes Herrschaft und Reich*, 110–22. Freiburg i.B.: Herder.

1964/65. "Der Menschensohn im Johannesevangelium." *NTS* 11: 123–37.

Schnedermann, Georg. 1893–95. *Jesu Verkündigung und Lehre vom Reiche Gottes in ihrer geschichtlichen Bedeutung.* 2 vols. Leipzig: Deichert.

Schodde, George Henry. 1882. *The Book of Enoch.* Andover: Draper. Summarized by Charles [1893] 1912: xxxviii–xxxix.

Scholten, Wessel. 1809. *Specimen hermeneutico-theologicum: De appellatione τοῦ υἱοῦ τοῦ ἀνθρώπου, qua Jesus se Messiam professus est.* Trajecti ad Rhenum: Paddenburg & Schoonhoven.

Schöttgen, Christian. 1717. *[Georgii Pasoris] Lexicon Graeco-Latinum in novum testamentum.* Leipzig: Gleditsch.

1765. *Novum lexicon Graeco-Latinum in novum D.n.J.C. testamentum.* Ed. Johann Tobias Krebs. Leipzig: Breitkopf.

Schulthess, F. 1922. "Zur Sprache der Evangelien." *ZNW* 21: 241–58 (esp. 247–50).

Schulz, Siegfried. 1957. *Untersuchungen zur Menschensohn-Christologie im Johannesevangelium.* Göttingen: Vandenhoeck & Ruprecht.

1972. *Q: Die Spruchquelle der Evangelisten.* Zurich: Theologischer Verlag.

Schulze, Ludwig. 1867. *Vom Menschensohn und vom Logos: Ein Beitrag zur biblischen Christologie.* Gotha: Perthes.

Schürer, Emil. 1979. *The History of the Jewish People in the Age of Jesus Christ (175 B.C.–A.D. 135)*. Revised and edited by Geza Vermes, Fergus Millar, and Matthew Black. Edinburgh: Clark.

Schürmann, Heinz. 1975. "Beobachtungen zum Menschensohn-Titel in der Redequelle: Sein Vorkommen in Abschluss- und Einleitungswendungen." In Pesch and Schnackenburg 1975: 124–47.

Schwarz, Günther. 1986. *Jesus "der Menschensohn": Aramaistische Untersuchungen zu den synoptischen Menschensohnworten Jesu*. BWANT 119. Stuttgart: Kohlhammer.

Schweitzer, Albert. [1906] 1968. *The Quest of the Historical Jesus*. New York: Macmillan. Translation of *Von Reimarus zu Wrede*, 1906.

Schweizer, Eduard. 1959. "Der Menschensohn (Zur eschatologischen Erwartung Jesu)." *ZNW* 50: 185–209.

1960. "The Son of Man." *JBL* 79: 119–29.

1962/63. "The Son of Man Again." *NTS* 9: 256–61.

1963. "Menschensohn." *Die Zeichen der Zeit* 22: 361–63.

1970. *The Good News According to Mark*. Richmond, VA: John Knox.

1975. "Menschensohn und eschatologischer Mensch im Frühjudentum." In Pesch and Schnackenburg 1975: 100–16.

Scott, R. B. Y. 1958/59. "'Behold, He Cometh with Clouds.'" *NTS* 5: 127–32.

Seethaler, Paula. 1956. "Kleine Studie über den 'Menschensohn.'" *BK* 11: 85–87.

Sharman, Henry Burton. 1944. *Son of Man and Kingdom of God*. 2nd ed. New York: Harper & Bros.

Sidebottom, E. M. 1957. "The Ascent and Descent of the Son of Man in the Gospel of St. John." *ATR* 39: 115–22.

1961. *The Christ of the Fourth Gospel in the Light of First-Century Thought*. London: SPCK.

Sieffert, Friedrich. 1867. *De apocryphi libri Henochi origine et argumento*. Regimonti. Summarized by Charles [1893] 1912: xxxiv.

Simmons, Billy E. 1985. "A New Look at an Old Christology." *Theological Educator* 32: 93–107.

Sjöberg, Erik. 1946. *Der Menschensohn im äthiopischen Henochbuch*. Lund: Gleerup.

1953. "*Ben 'adam* und *bar 'enash* im Hebräischen und Aramäischen." *Acta orientalia* 21: 57–65, 91–107.

1955. *Der verborgene Menschensohn in den Evangelien*. Lund: Gleerup.

Skibniewski, St. de. 1908. *De bar naša Filio hominis*. Vienne: Méchitaristes.

Slater, Thomas B. 1995. "One Like a Son of Man in First-Century CE Judaism." *NTS* 41: 183–98.

Smalley, Stephen S. 1969. "The Johannine Son of Man Sayings." *NTS* 15: 278–301.

Smith, David. 1906/1907. "The Nickname 'Son of Man.'" *ExpT* 18: 553–55.

Staerk, Willy. 1933. *Soter: Die biblische Erlösererwartung als religionsgeschichtliches Problem*. Gütersloh: Bertelsmann.

Stalker, James. 1899. *The Christology of Jesus*. New York: Armstrong.

Stanley, David. 1968. "The Quest of the Son of Man." *Way* 8: 3–17.

Stanton, G. N. 1974. *Jesus of Nazareth in New Testament Preaching.* SNTSMS 27. Cambridge: Cambridge University Press.

Stanton, Vincent Henry. 1886. *The Jewish and the Christian Messiah: A Study in the Earliest History of Christianity.* Edinburgh: Clark.

Stapfer, Edmond. [1897] 1906. *Jesus Christ During His Ministry.* New York: Scribner's. Translation of *Jésus-Christ pendant son ministère.* Paris: Fischbacher, 1897.

Stauffer, Ethelbert. [1941] 1955. *New Testament Theology.* New York: Macmillan. Translation of *Die Theologie des Neuen Testaments,* 1941.

1956. "Messias oder Menschensohn." *NovT* 1: 81–102.

Stephanus, Robert. 1553. *In evangelium secundum Matthaeum, Marcum et Lucam commentarii.* Cited by Scholten 1809: 162–63.

Stephenson, T. 1917/18. "The Title 'Son of Man.'" *ExpT* 29: 377–78.

Stevens, George Barker. 1899. *The Theology of the New Testament.* New York: Scribner's.

1901. *The Teaching of Jesus.* Reprinted, New York: Macmillan, 1929.

Stier, Ewald Rudolf. [1843–48] 1855–58. *The Words of the Lord Jesus.* 8 vols. Edinburgh: Clark. Translation of *Die Reden des Herrn Jesu,* 2nd ed.

Stock, Christian. 1725. *Clavis linguae sanctae novi testamenti.* Jena: Bielck.

Stolz, Johann Jakob. 1796–1802. *Erläuterungen zum neuen Testamente.* Hanover: Hahn.

Stone, Michael. 1968. "The Concept of the Messiah in IV Ezra." In *Religions in Antiquity,* ed. Jacob Neusner, 295–312. Leiden: Brill.

1990. *Fourth Ezra: A Commentary on the Book of Fourth Ezra.* Hermeneia. Minneapolis: Fortress.

1992. "Esdras, Second Book of." *ABD* 2.611–14.

Storr, Gottlob Christian. 1793. *Doctrinae christianae pars theoretica e sacris literis repetita.* Stuttgart: Mezler.

Stott, Wilfrid. 1972. "'Son of Man' – A Title of Abasement." *ExpT* 83: 278–81.

Strauss, David Friedrich. [1835–36] 1860. *The Life of Jesus Critically Examined.* New York: Blanchard. Translated from *Das Leben Jesu kritisch bearbeitet.* 4th ed. Tübingen, 1840.

Sturch, R. L. 1983. "The Replacement of 'Son of Man' by a Pronoun." *ExpT* 94: 333.

Sulzbach, Maria Fuerth. 1961. "Who was Jesus? The Theology of the Son of Man." *Religion in Life* 30: 179–86.

Suter, David. 1981. "Weighed in the Balance: The Similitudes of Enoch in Recent Discussion." *RelSRev* 7: 217–21.

Talbert, Charles H. 1975/76. "The Myth of a Descending–Ascending Redeemer in Mediterranean Antiquity." *NTS* 22: 418–40.

Taylor, Vincent. 1946/47. "The 'Son of Man' Sayings Relating to the Parousia." *ExpT* 58: 12–15. Reprinted in Vincent Taylor, *New Testament Essays,* 119–26. London, 1970.

1953. *The Names of Jesus.* London: Macmillan.

Teeple, Howard M. 1965. "The Origin of the Son of Man Christology." *JBL* 84: 213–50.

Theisohn, Johannes. 1975. *Der auserwählte Richter: Untersuchungen zum traditionsgeschichtlichen Ort der Menschensohngestalt der Bilderreden des Äthiopischen Henoch.* Göttingen: Vandenhoeck & Ruprecht.

Theophylactus. 1631. Ἑρμηνεία εἰς τὰ τέσσαρα εὐαγγέλια . . . *Commentarii in quatuor evangelia.* Lutetiae Parisiorum: Morell.

Tholuck, Augustus. 1827. *Commentar zu dem Evangelio Johannis.* Hamburg: Perthes.

[1857] 1860. *Commentary on the Gospel of St John.* Edinburgh: Clark. Translation of *Commentar zum Evangelium Johannis.* 7th ed. Gotha: Perthes, 1857.

Thomasius, Gottfried. [1853] 1857. *Christi Person und Werk: Darstellung der evangelisch-lutherischen Dogmatik vom Mittelpunkte der Christologie aus.* 2nd ed. Erlangen: Bläsing.

Thompson, G. H. P. 1960/61 "The Son of Man: The Evidence of the Dead Sea Scrolls." *ExpT* 72: 125.

1961. "The Son of Man – Some Further Considerations." *JTS* n.s. 12: 203–209.

Tideman. 1875. "De Apocalypse van Henoch en het Essenisme." *ThT* 9: 261–96. Summarized by.Charles [1893] 1912: xxxvi.

Tillmann, Fritz. 1907a. *Der Menschensohn: Jesu Selbstzeugnis für seine messianische Würde.* Freiburg i.B.: Herder.

1907b. "Hat die Selbstbezeichnung Jesus 'der Menschensohn' ihre Wurzeln in Dan., VII,13?" *BZ* 5: 35–47.

Tirinus, Jacobus. 1645. *Commentarius in sacram scripturam.* 2 vols. Antwerp.

Tödt, Heinz E. [1959] 1965. *The Son of Man in the Synoptic Tradition.* Philadelphia: Westminster. Translation of *Der Menschensohn in der synoptischen Überlieferung.* Gütersloh: Mohn, 1959.

Tödt, Ilse. 1978. "Der 'Menschensohn' und die Folgen." In *Schöpferische Nachfolge: Festschrift für Heinz Eduard Tödt,* ed. Christofer Frey and Wolfgang Huber, 541–61. Heidelberg.

Townsend, John T., trans. 1989. *Midrash Tanhuma. Vol. I: Genesis.* Hoboken, NJ: Ktav.

Trenkle, F. S. 1888. *Der Menschensohn: Eine exegetisch-kritische Untersuchung.* Freiburg.

Tuckett, Christopher. 1981. "Recent Work on the Son of Man." *Scripture Bulletin* 12: 14–18.

1982. "The Present Son of Man." *JSNT* 14: 58–81.

1993. "The Son of Man in Q." In *From Jesus to John: Essays on Jesus and New Testament Christology in Honour of Marinus de Jonge,* ed. Martinus C. De Boer, 196–215. JSNTSS 84. Sheffield: JSOT Press.

Uloth, C. B. E. 1862. "De beteekenis van de uitdrukking 'Zoon des menschen.'" *Godgeleerde Bijdragen* 36: 467–78. Summarized by Lietzmann 1896: 26 and M. Müller 1984a: 220.

Urbach, Ephraim E. 1979. *The Sages: Their Concepts and Beliefs.* Cambridge, MA: Harvard University Press.

Usteri, Johann Martin. 1886. "Die Selbstbezeichnung Jesu als des Menschen Sohn." *Theologische Zeitschrift aus der Schweiz* 3: 1–23.

Vaage, Leif E. 1991. "The Son of Man Sayings in Q: Stratigraphical Location and Significance." *Semeia* 55: 103–29.

Valentine, Cyril H. 1931. "The Son of Man Coming in the Clouds: Mark xiii.26; Matthew xxiv.30; Luke xxi.27." *Theology* 23: 14–21.

Vanderkam, J. C. 1992. "Righteous One, Messiah, Chosen One, and Son of Man in 1 Enoch 37–71." In *The Messiah: Developments in Earliest Judaism and Christianity*, ed. James H. Charlesworth, 169–91. Minneapolis: Fortress.

Vatablus, Franciscus (d. 1547). 1660. *Annotationes.* In *Critici sacri*, ed. John Pearson, vol. 6 at Matt. 16:13. London.

Vermes, Geza. 1967. "Appendix E: The Use of בר נשא/בר נש in Jewish Aramaic." In Matthew Black, *An Aramaic Approach to the Gospels and Acts*, 310–30. 3rd ed. Oxford: Clarendon Press. Reprinted in Vermes, *Post-biblical Jewish Studies*, 147–65. Leiden: Brill, 1975.

1973. *Jesus the Jew: A Historian's Reading of the Gospels.* London: Collins.

1978a. "The Present State of the 'Son of Man' Debate." *JJS* 29: 123–34. Reprinted in Geza Vermes, *Jesus and the World of Judaism*, 89–99. Philadelphia: Fortress, 1983.

1978b. "The 'Son of Man' Debate." *JSNT* 1: 19–32.

Vernes, Maurice. 1874. *Histoire des idées messianiques depuis Alexandre jusq'à l'empereur Hadrien.* Paris: Sandoz et Fischbacher.

Vielhauer, Philipp. 1957. "Gottesreich und Menschensohn in der Verkündigung Jesu." In *Festschrift für Günther Dehn*, ed. W. Schneemelcher, 51–79. Neukirchen: Erziehungsverein. Reprinted in Philipp Vielhauer, *Aufsätze zum Neuen Testament*, 55–91. ThBü 31. Munich: Kaiser, 1965.

1963. "Jesus und der Menschensohn: Zur Discussion mit Heinz Eduard Tödt und Eduard Schweizer." *ZTK* 60: 133–77. Reprinted in Philipp Vielhauer, *Aufsätze zum Neuen Testament*, 92–140. ThBü 31. Munich: Kaiser, 1965.

Vogt, Antonius. 1790. *Commentarius in libros novi testamenti.* Ed. Daniel Christoph Ries. Mogunt: Haeffner.

Vögtle, Anton. 1982. "Bezeugt die Logienquelle die authentische Redeweise Jesu vom 'Menschensohn'?" In *Logia: les paroles de Jésus – The Sayings of Jesus*, ed. Joël Delobel, 77–99. BETL 59. Leuven: Peeters; Leuven University Press.

1989. "Eine überholte 'Menschensohn'-Hypothese?" In *Wissenschaft und Kirche: Festschrift für Eduard Lohse*, ed. Kurt Aland and Siegfried Meurer, 70–95. Bielefeld: Luther-Verlag.

Volkmar, Gustav. 1860. "Beiträge zur Erklärung des Buches Henoch." *ZDMG* 14: 87–134, 296 (esp. 133).

1876. *Marcus und die Synopse der Evangelien.* Zurich: Schmidt. Second edition of *Die Evangelien; oder, Marcus und die Synopsis der kanonischen und ausserkanonischen Evangelien.* Leipzig: Fues, 1870.

1882. *Jesus Nazarenus und die erste christliche Zeit.* Zurich: Schmidt.

Völter, Daniel. 1907. *Das messianische Bewusstsein Jesu.* Strasburg: Heitz.

1914. *Jesus der Menschensohn; oder, Das Berufsbewusstsein Jesu.* Strasburg: Heitz.

1916. *Die Menschensohn-Frage neu untersucht.* Leiden: Brill.

Vorst, Johannes. 1665. *De Hebraismis novi testamenti commentarius.* Leipzig.

Vosté, James M. 1949. "The Title 'Son of Man' in the Synoptic Gospels." *American Ecclesiastical Review* 120: 310–26; 121: 18–33.

Wagner, Martin. 1924. "Der Menschensohn." *Neue Kirchliche Zeitschrift* 35: 245–78.

1932. "Der Menschensohn des 80. Psalms." *TSK* 104: 84–93.

Walaeus, Balduin. [1653] 1662. *Novi testamenti libri historici Graece et Latine perpetuo commentario . . . illustrati.* Lugduni-Batavorum: Wyngaerden.

Walker, William O., Jr. 1972. "The Origin of the Son of Man Concept as Applied to Jesus." *JBL* 91: 482–90.

1983. "The Son of Man: Some Recent Developments." *CBQ* 45: 584–607.

Walter, E. I. C. 1791. *Versuch eines schriftmässigen Beweis, dasz Joseph der wahre Vater Christi sey.* Berlin. Summarized by Scholten 1809: 158–60.

Wansbrough, Henry. 1975. "Jesus of Galilee: The Son of Man." *Clergy Review* 60: 760–66.

Weiss, Bernhard. 1862. *Der johanneische Lehrbegriff in seinen Grundzügen untersucht.* Berlin: Hertz.

[1868] 1893. *Biblical Theology of the New Testament.* Translated from the 3rd German ed. 2 vols. Edinburgh: Clark. Translation of *Lehrbuch der biblischen Theologie des Neuen Testaments.* Berlin: Hertz.

Weiss, Johannes. [1892] 1971. *Jesus' Proclamation of the Kingdom of God.* Philadelphia: Fortress. Translation of *Die Predigt Jesu vom Reiche Gottes.* Göttingen: Vandenhoeck & Ruprecht, 1892.

Weisse, Christian Hermann. 1856. *Die Evangelienfrage in ihrem gegenwärtigen Stadium.* Leipzig: Breitkopf und Härtel.

Weist, Ch. 1972. "Wer ist dieser Menschensohn? Die Geschichte der Exegese zum Menschensohn-Begriff." Dissertation, Vienna.

Weizsäcker, C. 1864. *Untersuchungen über die evangelische Geschichte.* Gotha: Besser.

Wellhausen, Julius. 1894. *Israelitische und jüdische Geschichte.* Berlin: Reimer.

1897. *Israelitische und jüdische Geschichte.* 3rd ed. Berlin: Reimer.

1899. "Des Menschen Sohn." In Julius Wellhausen, *Skizze und Vorarbeiten,* 6.187–215. Berlin: Reimer.

[1905] 1911. *Einleitung in die drei ersten Evangelien.* 2nd ed. Berlin: Reimer. Reprinted in Julius Wellhausen, *Evangelienkommentare.* Berlin: de Gruyter, 1987.

Wendt, Hans Hinrich. [1886–90] 1892. *The Teaching of Jesus.* 2 vols. New York: Scribner's. Translation of *Die Lehre Jesu.*

Westcott, Brooke Foss. 1908. *The Gospel According to St. John: The Greek Text with Introduction and Notes.* 2 vols. London: Murray.

Wette, Wilhelm Martin Leberecht de. [1836] 1845. *Kurzgefasstes exegetisches Handbuch zum Neuen Testament.* Vol. 1, Part 1: *Kurze Erklärung des Evangeliums Matthäi.* 3rd ed. Leipzig: Weidmann.

Whitby, Daniel. [1703] 1808. *A Paraphrase and Commentary on the New Testament.* 10th ed. 2 vols. London.

Wieseler, Karl Georg. 1882. "Zur Abfassungszeit des Buchs Henoch." *ZDMG* 36: 185–93. Summarized by Charles [1893] 1912: xxxix.

Wild, Johann. 1559. *Ennarationes in Matthaeum.* Mogunt.

Wilson, Frederick M. 1978. "The Son of Man in Jewish Apocalyptic Literature." *Studia biblica et theologica* 8: 28–52.

Wilson, William E. 1946. "The Coming of the Son of Man." *The Modern Churchman* 36: 44–66.

Winckler, Hugo. 1905. *Altorientalische Forschungen.* 3 vols. Leipzig: Pfeiffer.

Winter, Paul. 1968. Review of *Rediscovering the Teaching of Jesus,* by Norman Perrin. In *Deutsche Literaturzeitung* 89: 783–85.

Witherington, Ben, III. 1990. *The Christology of Jesus.* Minneapolis: Fortress.

Wittichen, Carl. 1868. *Beiträge zur biblischen Theologie.* Part 2: *Die Idee des Menschen: Zweiter Beitrag zur biblischen Theologie.* Göttingen: Dieterich.

1876. *Das Leben Jesu in urkundlicher Darstellung.* Jena: Dufft.

Wolf, Johann Christoph. [1725] 1739. *Curae philologicae et criticae in IV. ss. evangelia et actus apostolicos.* 3rd ed. 2 vols. Hamburg.

Wolfson, Harry A. 1956. *The Philosophy of the Church Fathers.* Vol. 1. Cambridge, MA: Harvard University Press.

Wolzogen, Johann Ludwig von. After 1656. *Commentaria in evangelium Matthaei.* In vol. 1 of his *Opera omnia, exegetica, didactica, et polemica.* Irenopolis.

Wörner, Ernst. 1882. *Die Lehre Jesu: Vorlesungen aus dem Nachlass.* Basle: Spittler.

Wrede, William. 1904. "Zum Thema 'Menschensohn.'" *ZNW* 5: 359–60.

Wünsche, August. [1892] 1967. *Midrash Tehillim oder Haggadische Erklärung der Psalmen.* Hildesheim: Georg Olms.

Youtsi, Y. 1940. "Der Menschensohn." *Theologia Fennica* 2: 45–52.

Zahn, Theodor. 1903. *Das Evangelium des Matthäus.* Leipzig: Deichert.

Zegers, Tacite Nicolas. 1553. *Scholion in omnes novi testamenti libros.* In *Critici sacri,* ed. John Pearson, vol. 6. London, 1660.

Zehrer, Franz. 1974. "Jesus, der Menschensohn." *BLit* 47: 165–76.

Zorn, R. O. 1980. "The Significance of Jesus' Self-Designation, 'The Son of Man.'" *Vox reformata* 34: 1–21.

Zwingli, Ulrich. 1531. *Annotationes in quatuor evangelia ac epistolas.* Tiguri.

INDEX OF PASSAGES

INDEX OF AUTHORS

Boers, Hendrikus 54, 56, 56 n. 22, 79
n. 24, 86 n. 12, 125
Bolten, Johann A. 88–89, 89 n. 19
Boman, Thorlief 45 n. 3
Borg, Marcus J. 72 n. 7, 72 n. 9, 76, 80
n. 26
Borgen, Peder 66
Boring, M. Eugene 2, 39 n. 11, 79 n. 23,
93 n. 30
Bornkamm, Günther 38 n. 9
Borsch, Frederick H. 6 n. 1, 6 n. 2, 62,
86 n. 12, 121, 125
Bousset, Wilhelm 28, 28 n. 14, 40,
43–44, 53
Bowker, John 19, 86 n. 12
Bowman, John W. 10, 47 n. 11
Brandt, Wilhelm 51 n. 18
Branscomb, B. Harvie 53, 123
Braun, F.-M. 66 n. 13
Braun, Herbert 38 n. 9
Brown, John P. 34
Brown, Raymond E. 97
Bruce, Alexander B. 25 n. 7, 43 n. 2, 69
n. 3
Bruce, F. F. 48 n. 12, 49 n. 15, 79 n. 22
Bruce, James 4, 27
Brückner, Wilhelm 26 n. 9
Bucer, Martin 14, 14 n. 4
Bühner, Jan-A. 66
Bulcock, H. 36 n. 5
Bullinger, Heinrich 15
Bultmann, Rudolf 34 n. 2, 37–39, 38
n. 8, 43, 45, 45–46 n. 5, 46, 49, 53,
66, 70, 74, 79, 90 n. 20, 94 n. 33, 123,
124
Burkett, Delbert 64 n. 8, 66–67, 82 n. 1,
87 n. 15, 125
Burkill, T. A. 46 n. 7
Bynaeus, Anthony 24 n. 5, 25 n. 8

Cadoux, A. T. 36 n. 4
Cadoux, Cecil J. 36 n. 5, 70 n. 5
Caird, G. B. 104 n. 16
Calixtus, Georg 16 n. 10
Calovius, Abraham 16 n. 8
Calvin, Jean 9, 23 n. 3
Cambe, Michel 47 n. 11
Camerarius, Joachim 83, 83 n. 3
Cameron, John 24 n. 5, 25
Campbell, George 16 n. 8
Campbell, J. Y. 31 n. 25, 85
Cangh, Jean-Marie Van 125
Cappel, Jacques 25 n. 8, 60
Caquot, A. 101 n. 11

Caragounis, Chrys C. 23 n. 1, 77, 77
n. 19, 82 n. 1, 98 n. 1, 117, 118, 125
Carpenter, J. Estlin 36
Cary, George L. 58, 58 n. 2
Case, Shirley Jackson 52–53
Casey, P. Maurice 23 n. 1, 76, 86 n. 12,
90, 90 n. 22, 92, 92 n. 28, 92 n. 29, 93,
94, 95, 101 n. 11, 103, 104 n. 18, 113
n. 33, 114, 116–17, 118, 118 n. 39, 119
n. 41, 125
Casey, R. P. 38 n. 9
Cavalier, H. O. 16 n. 10
Cellarius, Christoph 25 n. 8, 61 n. 5
Charles, R. H. 27, 28, 30, 31, 47, 68 n. 1,
69, 71
Charlesworth, James H. 72 n. 8, 72 n. 9,
72 n. 10, 73 n. 13, 73 n. 14, 77 n. 19,
98 n. 4
Châteillon, Sébastien 14 n. 2
Chemnitz, Martin 23–24, 24 n. 4, 25
n. 8, 57
Chilton, Bruce D. 79 n. 23, 86 n. 12, 90
n. 22, 92, 92 n. 27
Clarke, Adam 16 n. 10
Clarke, Samuel 88 n. 18
Clemen, Carl 28 n. 14
Cocceius, Johannes 83, 83n. 4
Cölln, Daniel G. C. von 25 n. 6
Colani, Timothée 30 n. 22, 60 n. 4, 69
n. 3, 84
Collins, Adela Yarbro 38–39 n. 10, 79,
86 n. 12, 104 n. 16
Collins, John J. 72 n. 10, 73 n. 14, 77, 77
n. 18, 78, 99 n. 5, 101 n. 10, 101 n. 11,
103, 103 n. 14, 105 n. 19, 105 n. 22,
106 n. 23, 110 n. 30, 111–13
Colpe, Carsten 6 n. 1, 29 n. 15, 46, 66
n. 12, 86 n. 12, 93 n. 30, 101 n. 10, 125
Cone, Orello 43 n. 1, 44
Conzelmann, Hans 38 n. 10, 56 n. 22, 79
n. 24
Coppens, Joseph 47 n. 10, 49 n. 14, 66
n. 13, 72 n. 10, 79 n. 22, 125
Cortés, Juan B. and Gatti, Florence M.
10
Cranfield, C. E. B. 48 n. 12
Creed, J. M. 28 n. 14
Cremer, Hermann 10 n. 14
Croskery, J. 125
Cross, Frank M. 72 n. 9, 72 n. 12
Crossan, John Dominic 90 n. 22, 92
Cruvellier, Jean 29 n. 17, 47 n. 10
Cullmann, Oscar 36 n. 5, 47 n. 8, 47
n. 11, 70

INDEX OF SUBJECTS